MOVE with English

A Workbook

Frances Bates–Treloar
Steve Thompson

Max Bill Sue May Pex Sam

Marshall Cavendish
Education

Let's Start!

The **Move With English A Workbook** correlates directly to the Pupil's Book so that learners consolidate new language items with focused practice. It builds on the vocabulary and language structures acquired in the Pupil's Book. Learners practise the skills of reading, listening, speaking and writing in meaningful and wider contexts.

The Workbook provides many opportunities for pratice of the main learning points. This ensures that learning outcomes are achieved. Cross-references in the Pupil's Book also guide learners to corresponding activities in the Workbook.

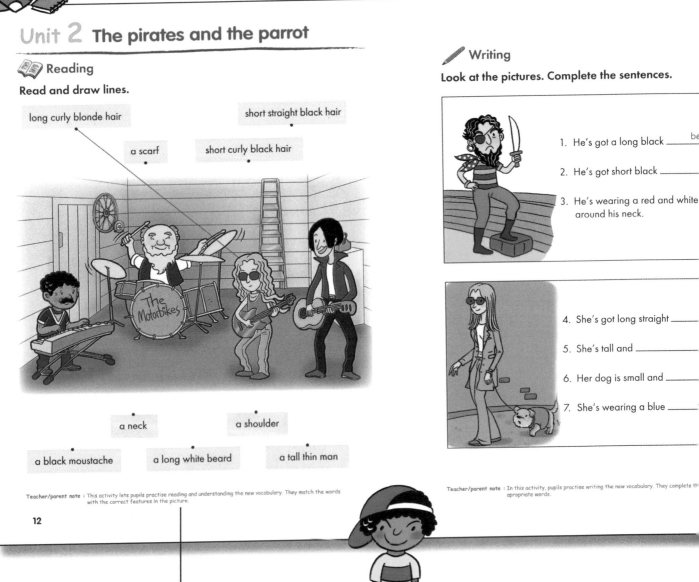

Unit 2 The pirates and the parrot

Reading

Read and draw lines.

long curly blonde hair

short straight black hair

a scarf

short curly black hair

a neck

a shoulder

a black moustache

a long white beard

a tall thin man

Teacher/parent note : This activity lets pupils practise reading and understanding the new vocabulary. They match the words with the correct features in the picture.

12

Writing

Look at the pictures. Complete the sentences.

1. He's got a long black _____ be

2. He's got short black _____

3. He's wearing a red and white _____ around his neck.

4. She's got long straight _____

5. She's tall and _____

6. Her dog is small and _____

7. She's wearing a blue _____

Teacher/parent note : In this activity, pupils practise writing the new vocabulary. They complete th apropriate words.

The teacher/parent note at the bottom of every page keeps parents involved in the learning process.

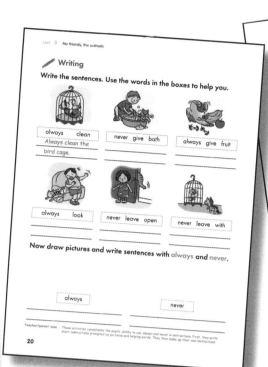

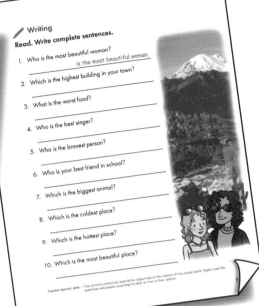

The writing activities focus on sentence-level activities that place language in meaningful contexts.

The revision units ensure that learners approach assessments with confidence. The activities correspond closely to the materials taught in the Pupil's Book, making it easy for learners to revise and consolidate what they have learnt.

Contents

Speaking	Reading	Writing
• Structure for asking and answering about others and themselves	• Vocabulary: countries, languages and nationalities • Conjunctions *but* and *and* • Verb *be*	• Vocabulary: countries, languages and nationalities • Times of the day
• Structures for asking and answering about physical appearances • Short *yes/no* answers	• Vocabulary: adjectives and nouns	• Vocabulary: adjectives and nouns • Preposition *with*
• Structures for asking and answering questions about routines • Adverbs of frequency *always*, *never*, *often* and *sometimes*	• Vocabulary: nouns • Adverbs of frequency *always*, *never*, *often* and *sometimes*	• Vocabulary: nouns • Adverbs of frequency *always*, *never*, *often* and *sometimes* • Spelling: nouns
• Modal verb phrase *have (got) to* • Adverbs of frequency *always*, *never*, *often* and *sometimes*	• Modal verb phrase *have (got) to/ haven't (got) to*	• Vocabulary: verbs • Modal verb phrase *have (got) to* • Adverbs of frequency *always* and *never*
• Vocabulary: adjectives and nouns • Verb *be*	• Vocabulary: adjectives and nouns	• Vocabulary: adjectives and nouns • Conjunctions *and* and *but* • Spelling: nouns and verbs
• Vocabulary: nouns • Ordinal numbers • Prepositions • Structures for asking and answering questions	• Vocabulary: nouns • Ordinal numbers • Prepositions	• Ordinal numbers • Prepositions • Conjunctions *and* and *but* • Structures for asking and answering questions
• Vocabulary: comparative adjectives • Nouns and numbers	• Vocabulary: comparative adjectives	• Vocabulary: comparative adjectives • Spelling: adjectives and nouns
• Vocabulary: superlative adjectives	• Vocabulary: comparative and superlative adjectives	• Vocabulary: comparative and superlative adjectives and nouns • Interrogative pronouns
• Vocabulary: days of the week and nouns • Adverbs of frequency • Structures for asking and answering questions • Interrogative pronoun *when*	• Structures for asking and answering questions • Modal verb *can* • Modal verb phrase *have (got) to*	• Vocabulary: days of the week and ordinal numbers • Spelling: days of the week
• Vocabulary: nouns • Conjunction *but*	• Vocabulary nouns • Structures for asking and answering questions • Modal verb *would like*	• Modal verb *would like* • Vocabulary: nouns
• Vocabulary: gerunds • Structures for asking and answering questions • Adverbs of degree	• Vocabulary: gerunds • Interrogative pronouns *who* and *why*	• Spelling: gerunds • Modal verb *have (got) to* • Verbs *enjoy* and *like* • Adverbs of degree
• Vocabulary: comparative adjectives • Conjunction *but*	• Modal verb *have (got) to* • Conjunction *but* • Verb *wants to*	• Vocabulary: adjectives • Conjunctions *because*, *but* and *so* • Modal verb *have (got) to*

Unit 1 Miss Sun is Australian

Which of these people are English? Listen and tick (✓).

1.  ☐

2.  ☐

3.  ☐

4.  ☐

5.  ☐

6.  ☐

Now listen again. Write the numbers.

1. Who is from Australia? _____

2. Who has got an English book? _____

3. Who learns English at school? _____

Teacher/parent note : In the first activity, pupils practise discriminating between the different meanings of *English*. They listen to discover which people in the pictures are English. In the second activity, pupils answer questions about the other people.

 # Writing

Where are they from? Write the words.

1. He is Chinese. He is from _____.

2. He is Indian. He is from _____.

3. He is Australian. He is from _____.

Where are you from? Write.

I am from _____.

Write the words.

1. g l i s h n e

   English _____

2. u s t a r l i n a a

   _____

3. d i n n i a

   _____

4. a i h t

   _____

5. n e h c i s e

   _____

6. l a y a i m s a n

   _____

Teacher/parent note : The first activity lets pupils practise writing the names of some countries. They then practise writing the name of their own country. In the third activity, they solve anagrams of nationalities.

✏ Writing

Write the sentences. Use the words in the boxes to help you.

eight years old	She's
She's is	Sunita
Indian	This

1. This is Sunita.

2. She's eight years old.

3. She's Indian.

This	ten years old
He's is	Lek
Thai	He's

1. _____

2. _____

3. _____

Malaysia	This	She's
from	is	Salina
She's	nine years old	

1. _____

2. _____

3. _____

Teacher/parent note : In this activity, pupils write short sentences about the children in the pictures. They use the words in the boxes to help them.

 **Speaking**

Look at page 8. Ask and answer.

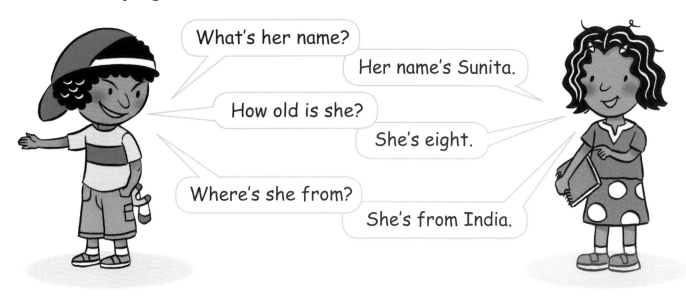

What's her name?

Her name's Sunita.

How old is she?

She's eight.

Where's she from?

She's from India.

Ask your friend.

Hello! What's your name?

I'm sorry. I didn't hear you. What did you say?

Where are you from?

What's your name?

How old are you?

Teacher/parent note : These activities give pupils practice in forming and answering questions about others and themselves. They ask and answer questions about the children illustrated on page 8 and then they ask and answer with their friends.

9

 **Writing**

Write the words.

Good morning!

Good morning, Max!

Good
_____morning____!

Good
_____!

Good
_____!

Good
_____!

When do you do these things?

1. Eat breakfast _____In the morning_____

2. Read and write _____

3. Talk _____

4. Play _____

5. Watch TV _____

6. Go to bed _____

Teacher/parent note : In the first activity, pupils write the times of the day in the context of greetings. The second activity lets them practise writing the times of the day in context of when they do certain activities.

 # Reading

Read and draw lines.

1. She isn't Malaysian. She goes to school but she isn't a teacher.

2. She speaks English. She isn't eight years old. She is a teacher.

3. It isn't a man and it isn't a pupil. It's from Australia but it doesn't speak English.

4. He isn't a man. He's eight years old. He's Indian.

5. She isn't a teacher and she isn't Chinese. She's Malaysian and she goes to school.

6. He's a pupil and he isn't Indian. He's Thai.

Teacher/parent note : This activity reinforces *but, and* and negative *be* structures. Pupils read short texts and deduce which characters they describe.

Unit 2 The pirates and the parrot

📖 Reading

Read and draw lines.

long curly blonde hair

short straight black hair

a scarf

short curly black hair

a neck

a shoulder

a black moustache

a long white beard

a tall thin man

Teacher/parent note : This activity lets pupils practise reading and understanding the new vocabulary. They match the words with the correct features in the picture.

 **Writing**

Look at the pictures. Complete the sentences.

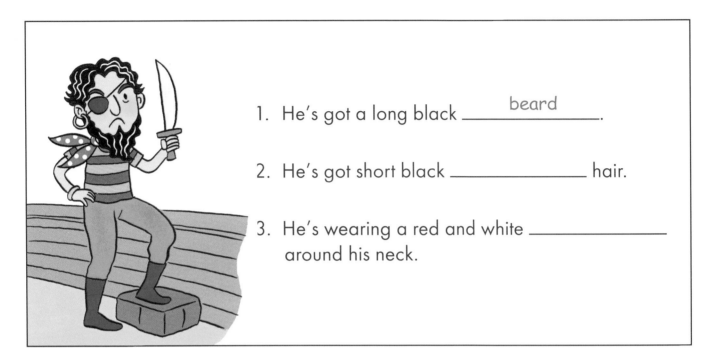

1. He's got a long black ___beard___.

2. He's got short black _____ hair.

3. He's wearing a red and white _____ around his neck.

4. She's got long straight _____ hair.

5. She's tall and _____.

6. Her dog is small and _____.

7. She's wearing a blue _____.

Speaking

Play the game. Who is your friend thinking about? Ask and answer.

Is it a girl ?

No, it isn't.

Is he wearing a green T-shirt?

No, he isn't.

Has he got blonde hair?

Yes, he has.

Is he wearing a scarf?

No, he isn't.

Is he "J"?

Yes, he is!

Teacher/parent note : This activity lets pupils practice asking and answering about physical appearances. In pairs, pupils ask each other yes/no questions. Through elimination, they deduce which person their partners have chosen.

 **Writing**

Look at page 14. Read and write the correct letter.

This person has got short curly blonde hair.
This person is wearing a red T-shirt.

Who is Max thinking about?

_____

Choose one person from page 14. Write about the person. Ask your friend who it is.

This person _____

_____

_____

_____

_____

Who is it ? _____

Listening

Listen and tick (✓).

1. Which man is the boy's father?

2. Which woman is the boy's mother?

3. Which girl is the boy's sister?

Teacher/parent note : This activity gives pupils practise listening to the new vocabulary and structures in short dialogues. Pupils tick the pictures that best illustrate the people described.

 Writing

Complete the sentences.

May

Sue

Sam

Bill

Who is Sam?	He's the boy with the black curly hair. He's wearing a yellow and red T-shirt.
Who is Bill?	He's the boy with the _____
Who is Sue?	She's the girl with the _____
Who is May?	She's the girl with the _____

Now talk about your friend.

Teacher/parent note : In this activity, pupils practise writing descriptions of people using *with*. They then use the same structures to talk about their friends.

✏️ **Writing**

Write the letters.

➡️ A c r o s s

4.

5.

7.

9.

11.

D
o
w
n

1.

2.

3.

4.

6.

8.

10.

Teacher/parent note : In this activity, pupils revise the names of animals through a crossword.

 Listening

Listen and tick (✓) the pictures of the animals you hear.

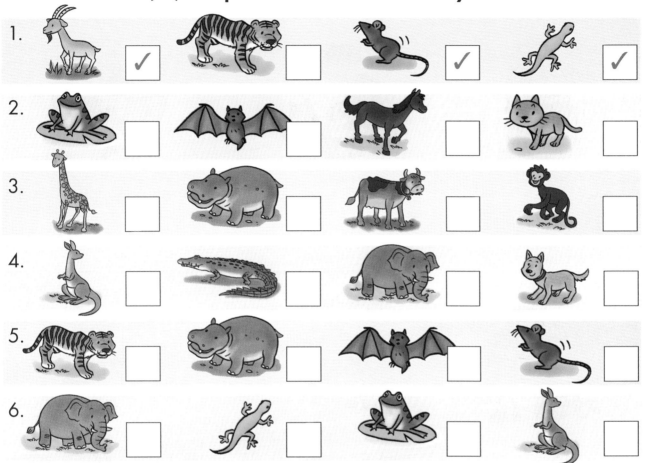

1. ✓ ☐ ✓ ✓
2. ☐ ☐ ☐ ☐
3. ☐ ☐ ☐ ☐
4. ☐ ☐ ☐ ☐
5. ☐ ☐ ☐ ☐
6. ☐ ☐ ☐ ☐

Listen and tick (✓) the correct word.

	always	never	often	sometimes
1. Max drinks lemonade.		✓		
2. Rex watches TV.				
3. Clover goes swimming.				
4. Pex plays with Rex.				
5. Dolly sleeps in the afternoon.				

Teacher/parent note : The first activity revises the names of animals. Pupils listen to the recording and tick the names of the animals they hear. In the second activity, pupils listen to statements and tick the correct adverb of frequency.

 Writing

Write the sentences. Use the words in the boxes to help you.

always	clean

Always clean the

bird cage.

never give bath

always give fruit

always	look

never leave open

never leave with

Now draw pictures and write sentences with always and never.

always

never

Teacher/parent note : These activities consolidate the pupils' ability to use *always* and *never* in instructions. First, they write short instructions prompted by pictures and helping words. They then make up their own instructions.

20

 # Reading

Read and write the numbers.

1. These animals sometimes eat meat. They often eat fish. They are sometimes orange, brown, white or black. They often live in houses.

2. These animals sometimes live on land and sometimes live in water. They have big teeth and they haven't got hair. They always eat grass and never eat meat.

3. These animals live only on land. They are sometimes black, sometimes brown and sometimes black and white. They eat grass and give us milk.

4. These animals live in water. They always have big teeth and long tails. They haven't got hair. They never eat fruit.

5. These animals often sleep in the day. They are orange, black and white and have got big teeth. They always eat meat.

6. These animals sometimes live in water and sometimes live in trees. They never walk or run.

21

Speaking

Ask and answer. Complete the table.

Do you read in the morning?

Yes, I do. I sometimes read in the morning.

Do you eat breakfast at school?

No, I don't. I never eat breakfast at school.

Write always, never, often or sometimes.

Me	Morning	My Friend
_____	Read	_____
_____	Eat breakfast at school	_____
_____	Play with friends	_____
_____	Watch television	_____
	Afternoon	
_____	Go fishing	_____
_____	Look after pets	_____
_____	Sleep	_____
_____	Play the piano	_____
	Evening	
_____	Learn English	_____
_____	Clean your room	_____
_____	Draw pictures	_____
_____	Write letters	_____

Now talk about your friend.

My friend sometimes reads in the morning.
She never eats breakfast at school.

Teacher/parent note : These activities let pupils practise asking and answering questions about routines using adverbs of frequency. They then record the information and use it to talk about their friends' routines.

 **Writing**

Write the sentences.

	Eats meat	Chases cats	Goes to the park	Sits in trees
Pex	✗	✗	✓	✓✓✓
Max	✗	✓✓	✓✓	✓✓
Rover	✓✓✓	✓✓	✓✓✓	✗
May	✓	✗	✓✓	✓

never: ✗
sometimes: ✓
often: ✓✓
always: ✓✓✓

1. Pex never eats meat. He never chases cats. He sometimes goes to the park. He always sits in trees.

2. _____

_____

3. _____

_____

4. _____

_____

Write sentences about yourself. Use always, often, sometimes and never.

_____

_____

_____

_____

_____

_____

Teacher/parent note : In these activities, pupils practise writing sentences in the first and third persons singular using adverbs of frequency.

23

Unit 4 Helping at school and at home

 Listening

Listen and repeat.

LET'S HELP!

There are a lot of things for us to do.
Can you help, Bill? Can you help, Sue?
We've got to tidy all the toys.
Can you help, girls? Can you help, boys?

We've got to close the cupboard door.
We've got to clean the classroom floor.
We've got to put brushes in the box.
We've got to tidy shoes and socks.

We've got to bring the footballs in.
We've got to empty the rubbish bin.
There are a lot of things for us to do.
Can you all help? May and Sam, too.

Listen and write the numbers.

Teacher/parent note : These activities consolidate the structure *have got* ... and classroom tasks. In the first activity, pupils listen to and repeat a rhyme. In the second activity, they listen to what the characters have to do and number the pictures.

 **Writing**

Write the words.

open

_____

_____

_____

_____

_____

_____

Write two things you do to help in class. Draw pictures.

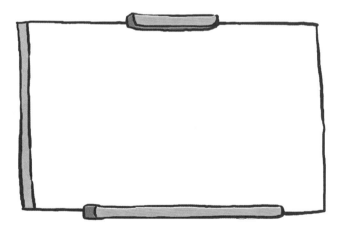

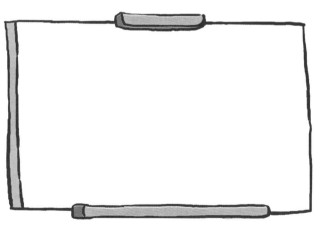

_____

_____

_____

_____

Teacher/parent note : In the first activity, pupils practise writing verbs prompted by the pictures. In the second activity, they write sentences and then draw pictures of things they do to help in class.

Speaking

Look at the pictures. Ask and answer. Use often, never, sometimes or always.

Have you got to sleep outside?

Yes, sometimes I've got to sleep outside.

Have you got to cook food?

No, I don't. I never have to cook food.

Now talk about your friend.

Max sometimes has to sleep outside. He always has to ...

Teacher/parent note : In pairs, pupils use the pictures to ask and answer questions using *have (got) to*. They then tell a new partner about the information they have gathered from the first activity.

 **Writing**

Write the sentences. Use the words in the boxes to help you.

| clean | bathroom |

The robot has to clean

the bathroom.

| make | breakfast |

_____

_____

| never | cook |

_____

_____

| does not | wash up |

_____

_____

| sometimes | take photos |

_____

_____

| sometimes | help |

_____

_____

Do you have to do these things at home? Tell your friend.

Teacher/parent note : In the first activity, pupils write sentences about what the robot has to do or doesn't have to do. In the second activity, they say sentences about whether they have to do these things at home.

Reading

Read. What have you got to do? Match the sentences with the correct pictures.

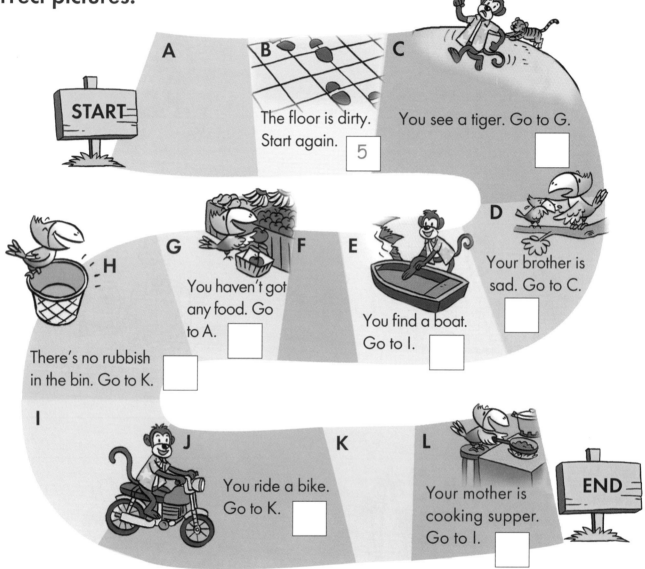

A

B The floor is dirty. Start again. 5

C You see a tiger. Go to G.

D Your brother is sad. Go to C.

E You find a boat. Go to I.

F

G You haven't got any food. Go to A.

H There's no rubbish in the bin. Go to K.

I

J You ride a bike. Go to K.

K

L Your mother is cooking supper. Go to I.

START

END

1. You don't have to walk.
2. You don't have to empty it.
3. You've got to talk to him.
4. You've got to run.
5. You've got to clean it.
6. You have to go to the market.
7. You have to help her.
8. You don't have to swim.

Now play the game. How quickly can you finish?

Teacher/parent note : In the first activity, pupils read sentences with (don't) have to and match them with the correct pictures. Pupils then play a game. They take turns to throw a die and move their counters accordingly. When they land on a square, they read and follow the instructions, if any. The pupil who finishes first wins.

 **Writing**

Look at the pictures. Write sentences.

Dear Jill,

I am sorry. I can't come to your

birthday party. I have to ___clean the___

___floor_____

and I have to _____

_____

from,
May

Dear Jill,

I am sorry. _____

_____

_____

_____

from,
Sam

Dear Jill,

I am sorry. _____

_____

_____

_____

_____

from,
Robot

Teacher/parent note : In this activity, pupils pretend to be different characters and write letters to explain why they are unable to attend a birthday party.

Unit  The weather's very nice

Reading

Look at the picture. Read and tick (✓) or cross (✗).

1. There are four hippos in the picture.   ✗

2. The big hippos are drinking.   ____

3. The small hippos want to play.   ____

4. The weather is cold and wet.   ____

5. There are oranges on the table.   ____

6. It isn't windy.   ____

7. It is very cloudy today.   ____

8. There is a plane in the sky.   ____

9. The sky is blue.   ____

10. The hippos are swimming in the water.   ____

Teacher/parent note : This activity consolidates weather vocabulary. Pupils read statements about the picture and determine if they are true or false.

 # Writing

Look at page 30 again. Correct the wrong sentences.

1. There aren't four hippos in the picture.

    There are five hippos.

2. _____

    _____

3. _____

    _____

4. _____

    _____

5. _____

    _____

6. _____

    _____

Answer the questions. Write complete sentences.

1. Are you hot or cold?

    _____

2. Is the weather hot or cold today?

    _____

3. Is the weather wet?

    _____

4. What colour is the sky?

    _____

5. Is the wind blowing?

    _____

Teacher/parent note : In the first activity, pupils correct the wrong statements from page 30. In the second activity, pupils answer questions in full, according to actual weather conditions.

🎧 Listening

Listen and circle the correct pictures and words.

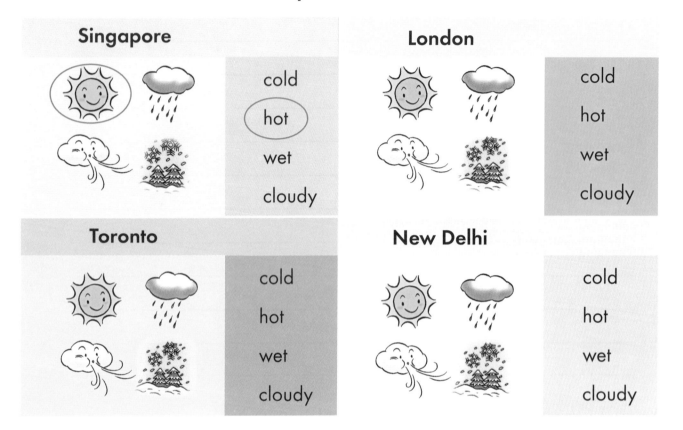

Listen and write the numbers.

 Writing

Write the letters.

A c r o s s

Teacher/parent note : This activity gives pupils practice in labeling and spelling vocabulary relating to weather and geographical features.

33

Speaking

Look at Sue's pictures.

A

B

Find ten differences. Say the differences.

In picture A, there are two people.

In picture B, there are three people.

Teacher/parent note : This activity consolidates the vocabulary and structures taught in the unit. Pupils find and say the differences between the two pictures.

34

 # Writing

Complete the sentences. Use and or but.

1. It's raining ___but___ it isn't cold.

2. It's hot _____ the sun is shining.

3. I can see a cat _____ a dog.

4. Sam is cold _____ he isn't wearing his sweater.

5. There's a mountain _____ a river.

6. The weather is cold _____ it isn't snowing.

7. The sky is grey _____ cloudy _____ it isn't raining today.

8. There are two birds _____ a boat _____ there aren't any whales.

Write about Sue's and May's clothes.

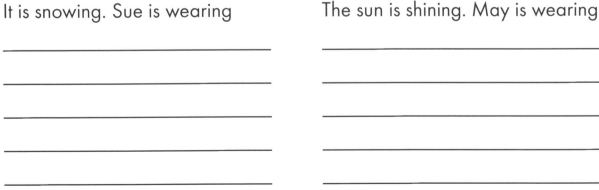

It is snowing. Sue is wearing

_____

_____

_____

_____

The sun is shining. May is wearing

_____

_____

_____

_____

Teacher/parent note : In the first activity, pupils consolidate their understanding of the conjunctions *and* and *but*. The second activity gives them practice in writing descriptions of clothing.

Unit 6 New places to live

 **Listening**

Listen. Colour the correct pictures.

1.
2.
3.
4.
5.
6.

✏️ **Writing**

Look at the pictures. Write the words.

first	second	third	fourth	fifth	sixth	seventh	eighth

1. the ___fourth___ fish

2. the _____ box

3. the _____ pencil

4. the _____ tree

5. the _____ shoe

6. the _____ toy

7. the _____ hat

8. the _____ dog

Teacher/parent note : These activities consolidate ordinal numbers. In the first activity, pupils listen to short instructions and colour the appropriate picture. In the second activity, pupils label pictures with ordinal numbers.

36

Speaking

Look at the picture. Say where the things are.

The ball is under the cupboard.

Mary is helping Sue. Tell her where to put the things.

Put the ball in the box, Mary.

🎧 Listening

Listen and write the numbers.

✏️ Writing

Look at the map. Where are these places? Write.

1. The school is _____next to_____ the library.

2. The hospital is _____ the river and the forest.

3. The bus station is _____ the cinema.

4. The supermarket is _____ the park.

5. The bank is _____ the flats.

6. The market is _____ the café.

7. The park is _____ the bus station.

Teacher/parent note : These activities consolidate prepositions and vocabulary related to local places. Pupils listen and identify places on a map. They then write words to describe the location of the places.

 **Reading**

Read Molly's email. Write the numbers.

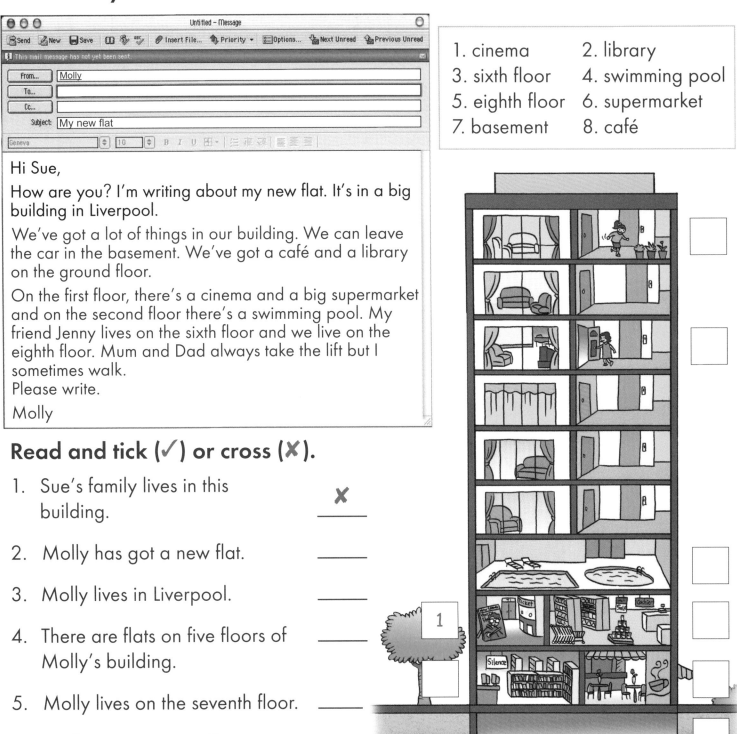

Untitled – Message

Send | New | Save | | Insert File... | Priority ▾ | Options... | Next Unread | Previous Unread

This mail message has not yet been sent.

From... Molly
To...
Cc...
Subject: My new flat

Geneva | 10 | B I U ▦▾

Hi Sue,

How are you? I'm writing about my new flat. It's in a big building in Liverpool.

We've got a lot of things in our building. We can leave the car in the basement. We've got a café and a library on the ground floor.

On the first floor, there's a cinema and a big supermarket and on the second floor there's a swimming pool. My friend Jenny lives on the sixth floor and we live on the eighth floor. Mum and Dad always take the lift but I sometimes walk.
Please write.
Molly

1. cinema	2. library
3. sixth floor	4. swimming pool
5. eighth floor	6. supermarket
7. basement	8. café

Read and tick (✓) or cross (✗).

1. Sue's family lives in this building.   ✗ _____

2. Molly has got a new flat. _____

3. Molly lives in Liverpool. _____

4. There are flats on five floors of Molly's building. _____

5. Molly lives on the seventh floor. _____

6. Molly sometimes walks up to her flat. _____

Teacher/parent note : This activity reinforces the vocabulary to describe parts of a building and revises the ordinal numbers *first* to *eighth*. Pupils read Molly's e-mail and decide if statements describing it are true or false.

 Speaking

**Look at the picture.
Talk about the building.**

There is a toy shop.

It's on the third floor.

Now ask and answer.

Where's the swimming pool?

It's on the fourth floor,
above the shops.

Teacher/parent note :   The first activity allows pupils to practise talking about the different places in a building. Pupils then ask
about and give the locations of these places.

 **Writing**

Look at page 40 again. Write complete sentences.

1. Where is the swimming pool?

   _____

2. Where is the library?

   _____

3. Where is the toy shop?

   _____

4. Where is the café?

   _____

Complete the sentences. Use and or but.

1. There is a toy shop ___but___ there isn't a shoe shop.

2. There is a swimming pool ___and___ there are some shops.

3. The library _____ the cafe are on the ground floor _____ the cinema is on the second floor.

4. There is a library _____ there isn't a bank.

5. There is a supermarket _____ there is a cinema.

Answer the questions. Write complete sentences.

1. Do you live in a house or a flat?

   I live _____

2. Which road do you live in?

   I live in _____

3. How many rooms are there in your home?

   There are _____

4. How many bedrooms are there in your home?

   There are _____

Teacher/parent note : In the first activity, pupils give locations in a building using vocabulary introduced in this unit. In the second activity, pupils practise the use of *and* and *but* to join sentences. In the third activity, pupils answer questions about their own homes.

Revision Unit 1

 **Listening**

Listen and strike out the wrong words.

Name: ~~Tom~~ / Joe / ~~Ben~~

Age: 8 / 9 / 10

Class: 6A / 6B / 6C

From: Thailand / Australia / Hong Kong

Lives in: New Street / Market Street / Park Street

Likes: football / tennis / swimming

chicken / burgers / sausages

Music: plays the guitar / sings / plays the piano

a b c
d e f
g h i

Now talk to your friend. Write and draw.

Name: _____

Age: _____

Class: _____

From: _____

Lives in: _____

Likes: _____

Music: _____

a b c
d e f
g h i

 # Reading

Look at the picture. Read and write yes or no.

1. Bill and Max are at a bus station.   _yes_

2. The man with the black moustache is riding a bike.   _____

3. There is a monkey on the bus.   _____

4. Max has got a scarf around his neck.   _____

5. The man behind Bill hasn't got a moustache.   _____

6. On the bus, there is a picture of a forest.   _____

7. The woman's hair is short and curly.   _____

8. The girl with the long brown hair is looking at the monkey.   _____

Teacher/parent note : This activity gives pupils practice in reading the structures and vocabulary introduced. Pupils read statements about the picture and determine if they are true or false.

Writing

Read. Write the words. Use the words in the box to help you.

Bill: Good morning, Pex.

Pex: Good morning!
          The weather (1) _____is_____ nice today, isn't it?

Bill: Yes, it is. Can you (2) _____ to the park with me?

Pex: No, sorry, I can't. I (3) _____ to visit my friend.

Bill: Where (4) _____ your friend live?

Pex: He (5) _____ in the forest. What (6) _____ you got in your bag?

Bill: My kite (7) _____ some bread and cheese. I've got some fruit for you. But you can't come to the park, so Max can have it.

Pex: No, no, no! I can visit my friend tomorrow. (8) _____ I have some fruit now?

Bill: Sure!

(1)	am	is	are
(2)	go	going	goes
(3)	got	has got	have got
(4)	is	has	does
(5)	live	lives	living
(6)	have	do	are
(7)	but	or	and
(8)	Am	Got	Can

Teacher/parent note : This activity gives pupils practice on the structures and vocabulary introduced, with a focus on simple present tense and *have got to*. Pupils select the answers from the box and fill in the gaps in the text.

 Speaking

Look at the pictures. Tell the story. Use the words in the box to help you.

> It's a nice day. There is a lorry in the street. It is in front of a bank. The lorry driver is giving a box to a woman.

lorry	lorry driver	box
flat	ground floor	library
bank	market	

> Thank you, Daddy!

✏️ **Writing**

Write the letters.

➡️ A c r o s s

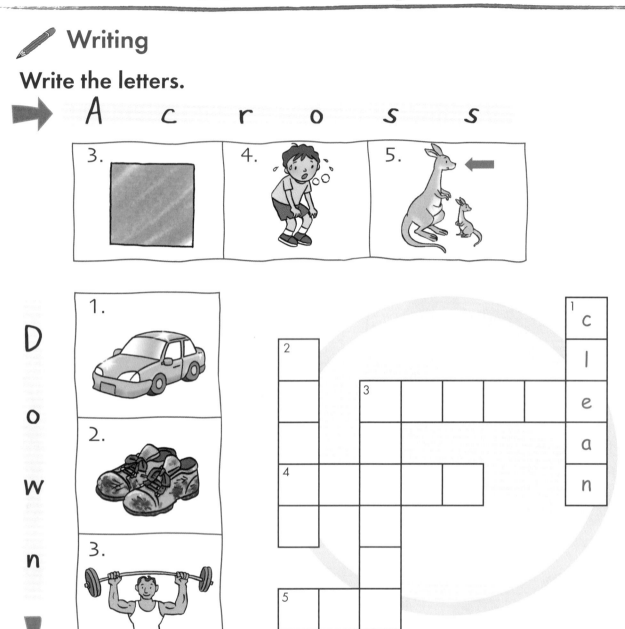

Look at the pictures. Write complete sentences.

Down

1. The car is clean.

2. _____

3. _____

Across

3. _____

4. _____

5. _____

Teacher/parent note : This activity allows pupils to revise the new vocabulary introduced through a crossword. They then write sentences using these words.

 **Listening**

Listen and write the words.

This is a _____ new _____ house. It's got three _____

bedrooms and a bathroom. The bathroom is _____. The

house has got a lot of _____ windows and one round window.

There is an _____ tree in the garden. There is a

_____ car in front of the house. A man lives in the house. He is

very _____.

Read the text again. Look at the picture. Write first, second, third or fourth.

Which house is it? The _____ house.

Teacher/parent note : This activity consolidates new and previously taught adjectives. Pupils listen to a description of a house
and fill in the blanks. They then read the completed text again to find out which house it describes.

Speaking

Say and point.

The woman is taller than the man.

1.
fatter
thinner
taller
shorter

2.
bigger
smaller
louder
quieter

3.
happier
sadder
quicker
slower

Teacher/parent note : This activity consolidates comparative adjectives. Pupils say the adjectives, look at the pictures and point to the character that each word describes.

 # Writing

Look at the pictures on page 48. Complete the sentences.

a. The woman is _taller than the man._

b. The man is _shorter than the woman._

c. The woman is _____

d. The man is _____

a. The elephant is _____

b. The bird is _____

c. The elephant is _____

d. The bird is _____

a. The motorbike _____

b. The car _____

c. Mr Lee _____

d. Bill _____

Teacher/parent note : This activity gives pupils practice on writing sentences using comparative adjectives. Pupils write sentences comparing the characters in each picture on page 48.

Speaking

Look at the pictures on page 51. Say the differences.

In picture A, the monster is shorter than the robot. In picture B, the monster is taller than the robot.

Reading

Read the sentences. Look at page 51. Which is the right picture? Write A or B.

1. The robot is shorter than the monster.   _____B_____

2. The girl is more afraid than the boy.   _____

3. The boy's bag is bigger than the girl's bag.   _____

4. The robot is thinner than the monster.   _____

5. The red bus is dirtier than the blue bus.   _____

What is the best title for the pictures? Tick (✓).

☐   The Animals in the Street

☐   A Girl and Her Pets

☐   A Monster, a Robot and Two Children Meet

Teacher/parent note : The first activity gives pupils further practice making sentences using comparative adjectives. Pupils look at the pictures and talk about the differences between them. In the second activity, pupils decide which picture accurately illustrates each sentence. In the third activity, pupils choose an appropriate title for the pictures.

A

B

Unit 8 Welcome to Coco Island!

 Writing

Look at Pupil's Book pages 52 — 53. Complete the sentences.

1. The smallest mountain on Coco Island is _____.

2. The longest river is _____.

3. The best café is _____.

Now read and write.

Mount Everest: 8 850m
K2: 8 611m
Kangchenjunga: 8 586m

Lake Victoria: 69 500 square km
Lake Huron: 59 600 square km
Lake Superior: 82 000 square km

Amazon River: 6 500km
River Nile: 6 695km
Yangtze River: 6 378km

1. The highest mountain is _____

2. The longest river is _____

3. The biggest lake is _____

Now write sentences about your own country.

1. _____

2. _____

3. _____

Teacher/parent note : In these activities, pupils become familiar with and understand the use of superlative adjectives to describe geographical features.

 **Reading**

Who are they? Read. Then write the names.

1. Jo is the shortest. Kim is shorter than Mo.

Mo   Kim   Jo

_____   _____   _____

2. Nick's house is smaller than Pat's house. Tom's house is the smallest.

_____   _____   _____

3. Tib's tail is longer than Tab's tail. Tub's tail is the longest.

_____   _____   _____

4. Jack is the oldest. Jim is older than John.

_____   _____   _____

Teacher/parent note : In this activity, pupils practise reading sentences with comparative and superlative adjectives. Pupils read the sentences and label the pictures with the correct names.

Listening

Listen and tick (✓).

1. ☐ short	✓ shorter than	☐ the shortest
2. ☐ high	☐ higher than	☐ the highest
3. ☐ hungry	☐ hungrier than	☐ the hungriest
4. ☐ angry	☐ angrier than	☐ the angriest
5. ☐ brave	☐ braver than	☐ the bravest
6. ☐ beautiful	☐ more beautiful than	☐ the most beautiful
7. ☐ small	☐ smaller than	☐ the smallest
8. ☐ big	☐ bigger than	☐ the biggest
9. ☐ good	☐ better than	☐ the best

Listen and colour.

Teacher/parent note : In the first activity, pupils practise recognising different forms of adjectives. The second activity provides further practice on superlative adjectives. Pupils listen and colour the appropriate objects.

 Writing

Read. Write complete sentences.

1. Who is the most beautiful woman?

_____ is the most beautiful woman.

2. Which is the highest building in your town?

_____

3. What is the worst food?

_____

4. Who is the best singer?

_____

5. Who is the bravest person?

_____

6. Who is your best friend in school?

_____

7. Which is the biggest animal?

_____

8. Which is the coldest place?

_____

9. Which is the hottest place?

_____

10. Which is the most beautiful place?

_____

Teacher/parent note : This activity reinforces superlative adjectives in the context of the actual world. Pupils read the questions and answer according to what is true in their opinion.

Speaking

Look and say. Use the words in the boxes to help you.

The plane is the biggest.

big   small   fast   slow   noisy   quiet

long   thin   round

tall   short   beautiful   old

Teacher/parent note : In this activity, pupils say the superlative adjectives from the given adjectives and use these to say sentences about the pictures.

 Writing

Write about yourself and your friends. Then answer the questions.

Name			
How old?			
How many sisters?			
How many brothers?			
Hands	big / small	big / small	big / small
Hair	short / long	short / long	short / long

Who is the oldest? _____

Who is the youngest? _____

Who has got the longest hair? _____

Who has got the shortest hair? _____

Who has got the smallest hands? _____

Who has got the biggest hands? _____

Who has got the biggest family? _____

Teacher/parent note : These activities give pupils practice in using superlative adjectives in the context of comparing their physical attributes with their friends. Pupils work in groups to gather information about each other.

Unit 9 Can you come to the party?

✏ Writing

Write the days.

1. u n d y s a   _____Sunday_____

2. d w n e s y a d e   _____

3. u y a e s t d   _____

4. i f r y a d   _____

5. h u r t y s d a   _____

6. d s y a t u r a   _____

7. n a y m d o   _____

Read and write. Then listen and say.

Monday's first, first, first

And _____Tuesday_____'s next.

Wednesday's third, third, third

And _____'s next.

_____'s fifth, fifth, fifth.

What's next? What's next?

Saturday, Saturday, Saturday.

What's next? What's next?

_____! It's time to play, hooray!

Teacher/parent note : The first activity lets pupils practise spelling the days of the week. The second activity consolidates pupils' understanding of the order of the days in a week. Pupils fill in the blanks in the rhyme.

 # Listening

Listen. Write the days.

| Mondays | Tuesdays | Wednesdays | Thursdays |
| Fridays | Saturdays | Sundays |

Mondays

_____

_____

_____

_____

_____

_____

Teacher/parent note : In this activity, pupils practise listening for specific information relating to activities and days of the week.

 **Reading**

Read.

Can you play tennis with me after school today, Sue?

No, sorry. I've got to do my homework.

Can you play tennis with me after school today, Sam?

No, sorry. I've got to go to my uncle's house.

Now tick (✓) or cross (✗).

1. Sue's got to play tennis after school today.   ___✗___

2. May has to do her homework.   _____

3. Sam's got to visit his uncle after school today.   _____

4. Bill can play tennis after school today.   _____

5. Max is playing tennis with May.   _____

Teacher/parent note : These activities revise the structures for asking and answering questions as to whether someone can attend an event. Pupils read a story strip. They then read statements about the story strip and decide if the statements are true or false.

Speaking

Ask and answer.

Can you play tennis with me after school today?

No, sorry. I've got to do my homework.

Can you play tennis with me after school on Tuesday?

Yes, I can.

Teacher/parent note : This activity provides practice on the structure *Can you ...?* Pupils ask each other if they can play tennis on a certain day and respond with answers that are true for them.

61

 Writing

Look at the pictures. Write complete sentences. Use the words in the box to help you.

play football	read to the teacher	have music lessons
paint pictures	have English lessons	

1.  on Mondays

   On Mondays, they have English lessons.
   _____

2. on Tuesdays

   _____

3.  on Wednesdays

   _____

4. on Thursdays

   _____

5.  on Fridays

   _____

Teacher/parent note : In this activity, pupils look at the pictures and write sentences about what the characters do each weekday.

 Speaking

Look at the pictures on page 62. Ask and answer.

When do they have English lessons?

They have English lessons on Mondays.

Now ask and answer. Use the words in the boxes to help you.

What?

play football	have music lessons	tidy your bedroom
go to the park	go to the supermarket	go to the library
watch TV	have fish for dinner	play hockey

How often?

never
every day
once a week
twice a week

When?

on Mondays
on Tuesdays
on Wednesdays
on Thursdays
on Fridays
on Saturdays
on Sundays

How often do you play football?

I play football once a week.

When do you play football?

I play football on Saturdays.

Teacher/parent note : In the first activity, pupils ask and answer questions about the pictures on page 62. In the second activity, they ask questions using *When ...?* and *How often ...?* as prompted by the words in the boxes and respond with answers that are true for them.

Unit 10　The picnic by the waterfall

🎧 Listening

Listen, point and write.

What is in the kitchen?

cups

Listen and circle.

1. A ⬭ / ⬭ of soup

2. A ⬭ / ⬭ of toys

3. A ⬭ / ⬭ of sandwiches

4. A ⬭ / ⬭ of orange juice

5. A ⬭ / ⬭ of lemonade

Teacher/parent note : In the first activity, pupils revise the new vocabulary. They listen, point to and label the containers in the picture. In the second activity, they circle the containers according to what they hear.

 **Writing**

Write complete sentences. Use the words in the boxes to help you.

a bowl	a bottle			
a cup	a plate			
a glass	a box	of		
a bag				

sausages	ice-cream	fruit
toys	eggs	tea
chips	cakes	
sandwiches	water	
lemonade	orange juice	

1. There is a cup of lemonade. _____

2. _____

3. _____

4. _____

5. _____

6. _____

7. _____

8. _____

Teacher/parent note : In this activity, pupils write sentences about the picture using phrases related to containers.
They read the words in the boxes and use the appropriate words to describe the picture.

Speaking

Look at the pictures on pages 66 — 67. Say the differences.

A

In Picture A, there is a plate of cakes, but in Picture B, there is a plate of sandwiches.

In Picture A, there is a bottle of orange juice, but ...

Teacher/parent note : This activity gives pupils practice describing things in containers. Pupils look at the pictures on pages 66 — 67 and talk about the differences between them.

B

✏ Writing

Choose one picture. Write about it.

1.   On the table in Picture _____, there is _____

_____

2.   _____

_____

3.   _____

_____

4.   _____

_____

Teacher/parent note : In this activity, pupils form sentences using phrases related to containers. They choose a picture and
                        write four sentences to describe it.

✏ Writing

Look at the pictures. Write complete sentences.

What would you like, everyone?

I'd like a burger _____

_____, please.

Teacher/parent note : This activity lets pupils practise using *would like* as a polite request. They look at the pictures and write polite requests for the characters.

68

 **Reading**

Read and complete the sentences. Use the words in the box to help you.

| like | I'd | would | would | thanks |

What ___would___ you like for lunch, Sue?

_____ like a chicken sandwich, please.

Ok. _____ you _____ some salad, too?

No, _____.

Read the menu. Write sentences.

Menu ✛ **Meat**
Sausages
Burger
Chicken

✛ **Ice-cream**
Coffee
Mango
Coconut

✛ **Drinks**
Lemonade
Water
Apple juice
Tea
Coffee

What meat would you like?

I'd like _____

What ice-cream would you like?

_____

What drink would you like?

_____

Teacher/parent note : These activities give pupils further practise on *would like* structures. In the first activity, pupils complete the gaps in a dialogue. In the second activity, they look at the menu and answer questions about what they would like.

✏️ Writing

Write the letters.

1. <u>s k a t</u> ing

2. _ _ _ _ _ ing _ _

3. _ _ _ _ _ ing

4. _ _ ing _ _ _ _ _ _ _ _ _

5. _ _ _ _ _ ing _ _ _ _ _ _

6. _ _ _ _ _ ing

7. _ _ _ _ _ _ ing

8. _ _ _ _ _ ing

9. _ _ _ _ _ ing _ _ _ _ _ _ pets

10. _ _ _ _ _ _ ing the bin

Teacher/parent note : This activity consolidates the verb + -*ing* form. Pupils look at the pictures and write the letters.

 **Reading**

Read. Answer the questions.

Mr Lee isn't happy. He likes swimming but it is too cold today.

The robot isn't having fun. He doesn't like finding spiders.

Bill isn't enjoying his day by the river. Mary is looking after him!

May is smiling. She likes playing badminton with me.

Sam likes sleeping by the river. He always enjoys sleeping!

Rover and Clover are happy. They like playing in the water.

1. Why is May smiling?
   She likes playing badminton with Sue.

2. Why doesn't Mr Lee like swimming today?
   _____

3. Who likes sleeping by the river?
   _____

4. Why isn't the robot having fun?
   _____

5. Why isn't Bill enjoying his day?
   _____

6. Why are Rover and Clover happy?
   _____

Teacher/parent note : This activity reinforces the verb + *-ing* form. Pupils read a text and answer questions about it.

🎧 Listening

Listen. Then ask and answer.

How many hobbies has Ogg got?
What are his hobbies?
Which hobby does Ogg like the best?

Read. Strike out the wrong words. Then listen and draw lines.

Ogg likes chasing / chase cars.	He says they is / are beautiful.
Ogg likes looks / looking after his bat.	He can see / seeing a lot of buildings.
Ogg likes flying / flies on mats.	It is / are very clever.
Ogg enjoys paints / painting pictures of boxes.	It is / are very hot in there.
Ogg likes having / has picnics in the library.	He wants / wanting to be strong and fast.

Teacher/parent note : In the first activity, pupils listen to a short dialogue then ask and answer questions about it. The second
activity reinforces the verb + -ing form. Pupils strike out the wrong words. They then listen to another
dialogue and match the sentences.

 **Speaking**

Read. What do you like doing? Tick (✓).

	You	Your friend		You	Your friend
At home			**At school**		
Washing up			Answering questions		
Cleaning the bedroom			Asking questions		
Cooking lunch			Cleaning the board		
Doing homework			Emptying the bin		
Washing the car			Tidying the books		
Sports			**Hobbies**		
Football			Shopping		
Skating			Phoning friends		
Hockey			Having picnics		
Swimming			Listening to music		
Running			Singing		

Ask and answer.

 Do you like washing up?

 No, I don't.

 Do you enjoy cleaning your room?

 Yes, I do.

Now say how much you like these things.

 I hate shopping. I don't like cooking lunch.

I quite like asking questions. I like having picnics a lot.

Teacher/parent note : These activities let pupils practise making sentences with the verb + *-ing* form. In pairs, they talk about what they like or don't like doing. They then practise using adverbs of degree to say how much they like doing something.

✏️ Writing

Complete the sentences. Use the words to help you.

1. Agg ____has to empty____ (have, empty) the rubbish bins on Fridays.

2. Egg ____enjoys taking____ (enjoy, take) the dog for a walk.

3. Agg and Egg _____ (like, play) football in the park.

4. Agg _____ (have, do) homework on Saturday nights.

5. Ogg _____ (like, study) English a lot.

6. Agg _____ (not have, wash up) on Sundays.

7. Egg and Ogg _____ (have, walk) to school.

8. Ogg _____ (enjoy, go) to the library.

Write sentences. Use the words in the boxes to help you.

hates

Mary hates going shopping.

_____

likes   a lot

_____

doesn't like

_____

_____

quite likes

_____

_____

Teacher/parent note : The first activity contrasts the forms of verbs which follow *have to*, *enjoy* and *like*. Pupils complete the blanks with the help of the main verbs provided. In the second activity, pupils practise making sentences using adverbs of degree.

What does Cindy like? What doesn't she like? Write sentences.

Skating 😟   Playing table tennis 😠

Running 😊   Playing football 😟

Painting 😞   Looking after pets 🙂

Reading 😊   Playing the guitar 😄

Shopping 😊   Watching TV 🙂

Swimming 🙂   Talking to friends 😄

likes ... the best 😄
likes ... a lot 😊 
enjoys 🙂 
doesn't like 😟 
hates 😞 

Cindy enjoys swimming.

_____

_____

_____

_____

_____

What do you like doing? What don't you like doing? Write sentences.

_____

_____

_____

_____

_____

_____

_____

Teacher/parent note : In the first activity, pupils revise the verb + -ing form and adverbs of degree. They look at the key and write about what a character likes and doesn't like doing. In the second activity, pupils write about what they like and don't like doing.

Unit 12 In the holidays

 Listening

Listen, draw and colour.

Mary is drawing monsters.
Let's help her!

Teacher/parent note : This activity revises vocabulary and structures to describe physical appearances. Pupils listen to Mary talk about her monsters they then draw and colour the drawings accordingly.

 **Writing**

Write complete sentences. Use the words in the box to help you.

big	blonde	curly	fat	long	round
short	red	small	square	strong	thin

That's a nice clown, Mary!

1. The clown's got a big head.

2. _____

3. _____

4. _____

5. _____

6. _____

7. _____

Draw a monster. Talk about it.

My monster's got a long blue tail!

My monster's got curly red hair.

Teacher/parent note : This activity revises vocabulary and structures to describe physical appearances. Pupils look at the pictures of the clown and write sentences about it.

77

Reading

Read. Then tick (✓) or cross (✗).

Dear Mum,

I'm on holiday now with my class. I'm not very happy.

I want to get up late but we always have to get up early. I always eat frogs and spiders for breakfast at home but here we only have bread and milk. After breakfast, we have classes. We have to look at the birds in the forest. I want to run after the birds but my teacher won't let me.

We always have classes in the morning but I want to play with my bat. We often paint and draw after lunch. That's nice. I always paint boxes because I think they're beautiful. My teacher says they are nice but I have to paint flowers. In the evening, we sing and play music. The other children are afraid when I sing so I have to be quiet.

Mum, I don't like my holiday here. Can I come home on Friday, please?

Love,
Agg

1. Agg is writing to his mother.   ✓ _____

2. Agg is enjoying his holiday.   _____

3. Agg can't chase the birds after breakfast.   _____

4. The teacher likes Agg's pictures of boxes.   _____

5. The other children don't want Agg to sing.   _____

Say what Agg has to do. Say what he wants to do.

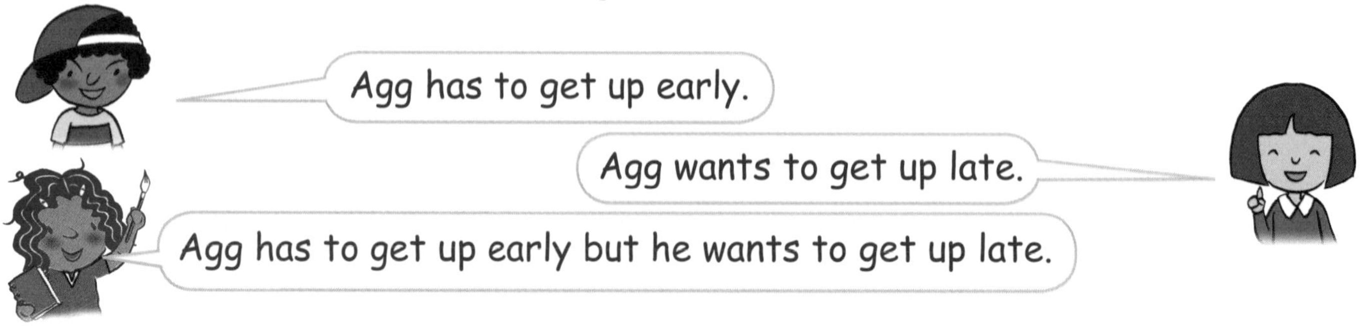

Agg has to get up early.

Agg wants to get up late.

Agg has to get up early but he wants to get up late.

Teacher/parent note : These activities reinforce the conjunction *but* and the structures *has to* and *wants to*. Pupils read Agg's letter and decide if statements about it are true or false. They then talk about what Ogg has to do and what he wants to do.

78

Speaking

Look at the pictures. Say the differences.

Ogg's room is bigger than Egg's room.

Egg's room is smaller than Ogg's room.

Ogg's room

Egg's room

Now use but to compare the rooms.

Ogg's room is bigger but Egg's bed is bigger.

Teacher/parent note : This activity revises comparative adjectives and the conjunction *but*. Pupils look at the pictures and compare the details in both rooms.

✏ Writing

Complete the sentences. Use so or because.

1. Agg is happy __because the__ __water is cold.__

2. Egg is sad _____ _____

3. It is raining _____ _____ (Ogg)

4. Agg is hungry _____ _____

5. The room is dirty _____ _____ (Egg)

6. Ogg is angry _____ _____

Teacher/parent note : This activity gives pupils practice using *so* and *because* to express reason. They look at the pictures and complete the sentences.

What do they do in the holidays? Write sentences using but.

	Sue and Mary	Bill
Morning	Get up late Read	Gets up early Cleans his bedroom
Afternoon	Go to the beach Go shopping Use the computer	Plays football Plays games on the computer Plays tennis
Evening	Wash up	Takes his dogs for a walk

Sue and Mary get up late but Bill gets up early.

_____

_____

_____

_____

_____

Now write sentences using so or because. Use the words in the box to help you.

has to   wants to

Bill doesn't get up late because he has to give water to his pets.

_____

_____

_____

What do you do in the holidays? Write complete sentences.

_____

_____

_____

Teacher/parent note : These activities reinforce the use of *but, so, because, has to* and *wants to*. Pupils contrast the different holiday routines of the characters. They then give reasons why the characters have these routines. Finally, they write sentences about their own routines.

Revision Unit 2

 Listening

Listen and tick (✓).

Lunch

Sue	✓						
Mary							

Mary and Sue are going to the beach. What are they going to eat?

Dinner

Sue									
Mary									

In the afternoon

Sue				
Mary				

What are they going to do?

Teacher/parent note : In this activity, pupils revise vocabulary relating to containers, food and activities. They listen to the conversation and tick the correct items and activities.

 **Reading**

Read. Look at the pictures and write the words.

plates   tired   sandwiches   picnic   sailing

waterfall   lake   hungry   fishing

It's a nice day today. Sue, Bill and I are sitting by the (1) _____lake_____.

We can hear the (2) _____. We're having a (3) _____.

We've got cups, bowls and (4) _____. We've also got lots of food like

salad, soup, burgers, fruit and (5) _____. Bill is very (6) _____.

He's eating two burgers! Sue is (7) _____ so she's sleeping under a tree.

I am (8) _____ a boat on the lake. I like (9) _____ too

but I'm not catching any fish!

What is the best title for this story? Tick (✓).

☐ Bill's Animals   ☐ Our Day Out   ☐ A Day at the Shops

Teacher/parent note : In this activity, pupils read a story and revise vocabulary from Units 7 — 12. They then choose a suitable title for the story.

✏️ Writing

Read. Write the words. Use the words in the box to help you.

Pex: Hello Max! What (1) _____is_____ in

that bowl? What (2) _____ you eating?

Max: Fruit and ice-cream. (3) _____ you

like some?

Pex: Yes, please. (4) _____ you got any more?

Max: Yes, I have. Here you are.

Pex: Thank you, Max. Oh, this is very good. I like fruit and ice-cream (5) _____.

Max: Me too. I like (6) _____ fruit and ice-cream for lunch.

Pex: How often (7) _____ you eat it?

Max: I eat fruit and ice-cream once (8) _____ week.

Bill always gives me some (9) _____ Fridays. He's very nice!

(1)	am	is	are
(2)	am	is	are
(3)	Have	Would	Can
(4)	Haven't	Have	Have to
(5)	quite	very	a lot
(6)	eating	eats	eat
(7)	are	do	does
(8)	a	an	the
(9)	at	in	on

Teacher/parent note : In this activity, pupils practise structures and vocabulary from Units 7 — 12. They select answers from the box and fill in the gaps in the text.

Speaking

Look at the pictures. Talk about Ogg's and Egg's day. Use the words in the box to help you.

What are Ogg and Egg doing?
What have they got?
Where are they?
Are they happy? Why?

wash up
do homework
play the piano
take the dog for a walk

Teacher/parent note : In this activity, pupils consolidate the structures and vocabulary introduced from Units 7 — 12. Pupils tell the story depicted in the pictures.

Let's play!

Play the game and get to the top!

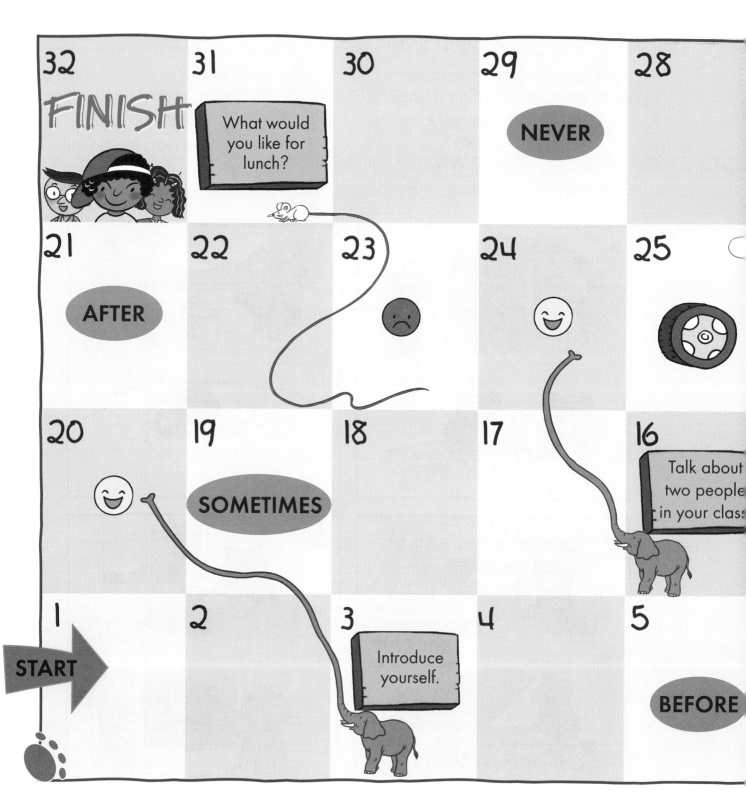

Teacher/parent note : Pupils throw a die and move their counters accordingly. When they land on a picture, they say and spell the word it illustrates. When they land on an adverb, they make a sentence with it. If they do these activities incorrectly, they miss a turn. When pupils land on an elephant and do the task correctly, they move up the elephant's trunk. If they land on a mouse and do the task incorrectly, they slide down the mouse's tail.

When you land on ...	You've got to ...
	Say and spell the name of the thing.
BEFORE	Make a sentence using the word on the card.
	Do the task correctly and you can move up the elephant's nose.
	Do the task correctly or you've got to slide down the mouse's tail.

7

6

Talk about things you've got to do.

15	14	13	12	11
		ALWAYS		

	7	8	9	10
			OFTEN	

Write the words.

My name is _____.

I have finished **MOVE** with **English** **A** !

Now I can:

☆ talk about people and things

☆ compare things

☆ say what I would like to have

☆ talk about what I like and don't like

... and much more!

Please ask your teacher, parent or guardian to fill this in.

Well done, _____ !

You are now ready for **MOVE** with **English** **B** !

_____
(Teacher / Parent / Guardian)

great *sporting* moments

With grateful thanks to Frances Banfield, Andrea P. A. Belloli, Helen Courtney, Lucinda Hawksley, Helen Johnson, Lee Matthews, Morse Modaberi, Sonya Newland, Marion Paull, Ian Powling, Phil Shaw, Nick Wells and Rana K. Williamson.

ISBN 1 85833 936 7

First published in 1998 by
DEMPSEY PARR
13 Whiteladies Road
Clifton
Bristol
BS8 1PB

CLD 21135
This edition published in 1999 for
COLOUR LIBRARY DIRECT
Godalming Business Centre
Woolsack Way
Godalming
Surrey
GU7 1XW

Produced for Dempsey Parr by
FOUNDRY DESIGN & PRODUCTION
a part of The Foundry Creative Media Company Ltd
Crabtree Hall
Crabtree Lane
Fulham, London
SW6 6TY

Years of Change

great
sporting
moments

**Chris Ewers, David Harding, Nigel Gross, Karen Hurrell,
Dylan Lobo, and Jason Tomas**

Introduction by
Ian Cole
Chairman, Sports Writers' Association of Great Britain

Colour
Library
Direct

Contents

Introduction

Whether you are nine or ninety you will probably have a favourite sporting moment. It might be Bobby Moore's euphoria at lifting the World Cup at Wembley, the drama of Muhammad Ali reclaiming the world boxing crown in the 'Rumble in the Jungle', or the emotion of Nelson Mandela presenting rugby's World Cup to the post-Apartheid Springboks. Maybe your moment is more personal: the day you successfully completed a charity fun-run, or when the horse you drew in the office sweepstake won by a mile at 66–1.

As media technologies have developed during the twentieth century, so have the ways in which we experience sport. Some of the century's great sporting moments – the Stanley Matthews FA Cup Final of 1953 and Roger Bannister's first sub-four-minute mile the following year, for example – were recorded on flickering black-and-white newsreel film. In Britain you had to take a transistor radio to bed if you wanted live commentary of Cassius Clay (now known as Muhammad Ali) battling it out with Sonny Liston in 1963 or Ray Illingworth winning back the Ashes in Australia in 1971. During the second half of the century, television arrived in virtually every home, followed more recently by specialist cable and satellite sports channels. As the century draws to a close the great sporting moment now arrives at the flick of a switch. Whether it is the Olympics from Atlanta, a Lions tour of New Zealand or a World Cup qualifier from Moldova, we share the experience with millions around the world.

Inevitably, each one of us has an opinion on what we are watching. That is another great characteristic of the sporting moment. When you sit in your local café or club and challenge your friends to name their five all-time great football matches, tennis finals, or athletics achievements, there is only one thing you can be sure of. The proprietor will be closing up before you come halfway to agreement.

The stories in this collection of great sporting moments will provide marvellous material for such debates. Not only that, a flip through its pages will fuel the mind for a mouth-watering catalogue of hypothetical showdowns. How, for instance, would Seb Coe have fared against Wilson Kipketer if both had been born in the same generation? Coe, Britain's greatest middle distance runner, held the world 800 m record for 16 years until Kenyan-born Kipketer broke it in 1997. What a contest there would have been between Jesse Owens, the American hero of the 1936 Berlin Olympics (gold medals in the 100 m, 200 m, long jump and 4-x-100 m relay) and Britain's Carl Lewis, who emulated that feat 48 years later.

Records have continued to fall throughout the century as men and women have used science and legitimate forms of medicine, coupled with diet, to push their bodies to performance levels their ancestors could never have contemplated. Team games, too, have followed a similar pattern of evolution as fitness levels and training regimes have improved over the years. My father thought Tom Finney was the ultimate footballer because he could play left wing, right wing or centre forward in successive games. Try telling that now to Alan Shearer, who fills all those three positions in successive minutes.

In the film of that magical 1953 Matthews Cup Final the thing that always strikes me is the lack of a tackle coming in while the maestro weighs up which way to run. These days three opponents would clatter him from all sides. That is not to say that Matthews, who was supremely fit by 1950s standards, would not have been able to adapt to modern demands.

Similarly, in the world of cricket, how do you compare Len Hutton's 364 in 1938 with Garfield Sobers' 365 in 1958 and Brian Lara's 375 in 1994? You could argue that Lara had to pierce a ring of fielders who would throw themselves at the ball as if their lives depended on stopping it. In Hutton's day, once he had beaten the field it seemed as though the opposition simply clapped the ball to the boundary.

I recently asked Rory Underwood, England's most-capped rugby international and top try scorer – 85 caps, 19 tries – how long he thought his records would stand, bearing in mind there were 14 internationals planned for 1997–98, compared with the four or five which had previously been the norm. Underwood argued there was a good case for believing his record statistics would remain for some time. He reminded me that his international career had spanned 13 years, and doubted that any player's body could withstand the pressures of today's intense schedules for more that just a few seasons before burning out.

In compiling this journey through the sporting century, the authors have given us more than enough food for thought to sustain us to the millennium and beyond. The fascinating thing is that, when the votes are counted and the result declared, we are all winners. Sport is that sort of game.

Ian Cole
Chairman, Sports Writers' Association of Great Britain

American Football, Baseball & Basketball

1

... *at that rate they'll last a thousand years*. Multi-millionaire oil tycoon **Clint Murchison Jnr**, on being told his team, The Dallas Cowboys, had lost a million dollars in their first season in 1960.

1920
Bob Nash, football's first transfer

HISTORIES OF AMERICAN FOOTBALL generally agree that a recognizable form of the game was played from 1867. In that year, a set of rules – the Princeton Rules – was formulated. From those first rules, the game developed into the version played today.

By the turn of the century, football was played at its highest level in various universities, with Stanford and California producing the strongest teams. The need for a national governing body was becoming apparent when no less a person than Teddy Roosevelt threatened to ban the game because it was so dangerous. A governing body was set up for the amateur game in 1906, but the professional side remained in a state of chaos. The need for a single set of rules and a unified league was desperate, though neither was organized until 1920 due to the fragmented nature of the sport.

Before that time, there were no set standards or systems for either recruiting players or transferring them from other teams. There were numerous instances of clubs purchasing rivals' key players, and in some instances whole teams! After years of trying, a meeting of all interested parties was held in August 1920 in Canton, Ohio. A second followed in September. At long last, the American Professional Football Association was formed. This forerunner of the National Football League included teams from four states, descendants of which still play today. Jim Thorpe, one of the pro game's biggest names, was chosen to be president of the new league. Each member team was charged a nominal annual fee of $100, although records show that not a single team ever paid it!

New teams continued to join the fledgling organization, but despite Thorpe's best efforts things remained a shambles. Member teams played outsiders as often as other league members. No official rankings or standings were maintained. Despite his reputation within the game, Thorpe proved to be a bureaucratic disaster and was replaced after a single season.

The new league nonetheless managed to codify the basic principles of the game as regards transfers and recruitment. The concept of the draft was introduced, and rules were laid down to govern fees and contracts for transferring players. This largely put a stop to the practices of less scrupulous team owners that had made such a farce of the earlier professional game. The first player to be transferred under the new rules was Bob Nash, the tackle and tight end for Akron. The fee was $300, which even then was not a lot of money. Neither of the two teams or Nash himself went on to great things, but at least they did what they did in an orderly fashion.

Overleaf: two of the biggest names in American football – Jerry Rice of the 49ers and Deion Sanders of the Dallas Cowboys (see page 20).

Right: the San Francisco 49ers' number 80 shirt, worn by Jerry Rice.

1920
Babe Ruth joins the Yankees for a record transfer fee

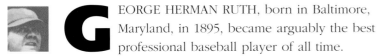

GEORGE HERMAN RUTH, born in Baltimore, Maryland, in 1895, became arguably the best professional baseball player of all time.

Ruth, universally referred to by his nickname 'Babe', started his pro career in 1915 with the Boston Red Sox, a team which had been founded in 1901 under another name as part of the new American League. The Sox quickly stamped their authority on the league and came to dominate the game in the years leading up to 1910. Things went off the rails a bit when the Sox were bought by John I. Taylor, owner of the *Boston Globe.* Fortunately, Taylor soon departed, and success returned to the Sox at more or less the moment when Babe Ruth joined the team. Although he had started out as a left-handed

pitcher, by 1919 Ruth had been moved to the outfield because of his awesome talent with the bat. Throughout his tenure, the Red Sox enjoyed enormous success, winning both the league title and the World Series in 1915, 1916 and 1918.

The American entry into the First World War led to a great deal of disruption to the major teams. In 1916, the Red Sox had been bought by Hugh Ward and Harry Frazee, two theatrical entrepreneurs. By 1919, Ward and Frazee were in serious financial difficulty. Despite the fact that he scored a record 29 home runs that year, Babe Ruth was sold at the end of the season to the New York Yankees for $100,000 and a $300,000 loan, a record sum for its day. His departure marked the end of the Red Sox's winning streak and the start of their descent into the second division.

For the Yankees, however, things were only just starting to look up. Founded in 1901, the team had won absolutely nothing in their first 20 seasons, yet for the next 44 years they totally dominated pro baseball, winning two out of every three pennants and claiming no fewer than 20 World Series titles. Ruth was not the only Red Sox player to move over to the Yankees, and these transfers transformed the team's ability to win. The first pennant came in 1921, helped along considerably by Ruth's 59 home runs and record 171 runs batted in (RBIs). The year 1922 bought another pennant, and 1923 the Yankees' first World Series victory.

As the years passed and the titles and accolades rolled in, one can only wonder at what Ward and Frazee must have been thinking. How different things might have been if they had not sold the Babe!

Left: Babe Ruth playing for the New York Yankees in 1926; photographed at the Yankees' Stadium.

Right: Babe Ruth is arguably the best baseball player of all time. He is seen here playing for the New York Yankees.

1932
Babe Ruth and the World Series final

SUCH WAS BABE RUTH'S success with the New York Yankees, at both batting and pitching, that he became a national institution, with the 1920s often being referred to in sporting circles as the Babe Ruth Era. The 'Sultan of Swat', as Ruth was often called, established close to 200 pitching and batting records during his career, a fair few of which still stand today! Even to attempt to list them would be impossible here, although the fact that he compiled a massive 714 home runs must be mentioned.

To pick the greatest moment of such a sportsman's career is not an easy task, but it is perhaps the World Series final of 1932 that people remember the most. In that year, the Yankees faced the Chicago Cubs to decide the contest. The first two games in the series had been won by the Yankees in their home stadium in New York, a stadium which the fans called 'The House that Ruth Built'. The series now moved to Wrigley Field, home stadium of the Cubs, a place where Ruth was a none-too-popular figure.

Ruth came out to the plate with the game tied at 4–4 and to a crescendo of boos and whistles from the Cubs' fans. Charlie Root, the Cubs pitcher, put his first ball straight past Ruth. Strike one. In reply, Ruth lifted a single finger to the crowd. Root missed with his next two pitches; one more and Ruth would be able to take a free walk. Root's next pitch whistled past him, and Ruth raised two fingers to the crowd. The noise level was deafening. Seemingly not content with keeping track of the strikes for the crowd, Ruth theatrically pointed to the centre field. Root made his pitch, and the Babe blasted the ball straight where he had just pointed, high into the sky and over the wall. It was a home run!

Babe Ruth would never say whether his gestures had been meant as instructions to his team-mates or elements in his psychological war against the hapless Root. In any event, the Yankees went on to win the game and the Series with an unbeaten clean sweep. Ruth left the Yankees in 1934, ending his playing career at the Boston Braves. Sadly, like many legends he did not live into old age, dying from cancer aged 53.

Babe Ruth in action against the White Sox – demonstrating the worth of his record transfer fee.

Babe Ruth was so popular that the 1920s are often referred to in sporting circles as 'the Babe Ruth era'.

 *Joltin' Joe*

1949
Joltin' Joe becomes baseball's top earner

TO NON-BASEBALL AFICIONADOS, Joe DiMaggio is probably best remembered for his turbulent and short-lived marriage to one Norma Jean Baker, better known as Marilyn Monroe, and for his appearance in the lyrics of Simon and Garfunkel's hit song 'Mrs Robinson'. To fans of the game, he is remembered as one of its all-time great proponents, second only to the great Babe Ruth himself in many people's eyes.

DiMaggio was born in Martinez, California, in 1914, just about the time that Babe Ruth joined the Boston Red Sox. Fascinated with the game from an early age, DiMaggio started his career in the Pacific Coast League in 1932 before moving to the New York Yankees in 1936, just two years after Ruth retired from the same team. Joe's two brothers, Dominic and Vincent, also went into the professional game, and whilst not reaching the same heights as their brother, they had creditable careers.

DiMaggio served the Yankees well, becoming one of the best outfielders of all time and rapidly earning the nickname 'The Yankee Clipper'. Not content with this, he also set about building a reputation for thunderous offensive play, setting a major-league record in 1941 when he scored in 56 consecutive games. This aspect of his play lent him a further nickname, 'Joltin' Joe'. As well as bringing DiMaggio his second Most Valuable Player award, 1941 also brought America into the Second World War, thus robbing him of four years of play when he was at the peak of his ability. He later returned to the game, and after a mediocre 1946 performance won his third MVP award in 1947 by blasting two home runs in that year's World Series.

In view of such a glittering career, it is hardly surprising that DiMaggio was a top earner. In 1949, he became the first player to sign a $100,000 contract. He managed to remain the world's highest-paid player for three years running before retiring in 1951 with an all-time batting average of 325. He had amassed 361 home runs, 1537 runs, and no fewer than 2214 hits in a total of 1736 games – a staggering all-round achievement.

The essence of the All-American Hero, DiMaggio remained very much in the limelight and in 1954 married another American legend, Marilyn Monroe. The ceremony took place in San Francisco amidst a storm of media interest. Sadly, the marriage lasted just nine months. DiMaggio's hero status remains untarnished to this day. A member of the All Time Baseball Hall of Fame, he received the Ellis Medal of Honor for his sporting achievements.

Opposite: a portrait of Joe DiMaggio, taken in May 1951, when he was with the New York Yankees.

Left: New York adulation: Joe DiMaggio signing autographs after a match, August 1960.

1960

The Dallas Cowboys come out fighting

THE FOUNDING OF THE DALLAS COWBOYS in 1960 might well have inspired some of the antics in the internationally popular 1970s soap opera set in the same Texas city.

Acting behind the scenes were two fabulously wealthy oil tycoons, Lamar Hunt and Clint Murchison Jnr. Hunt, who had a lifelong interest in the game, and who had for some time been trying to persuade the National Football League to grant a team franchise for Dallas. The NFL dragged its heels to such a degree that Hunt, a man well used to getting his own way, decided that he had had enough. In 1959, he organized a meeting in Chicago, Illinois, at which he and the representatives of five other cities formed the breakaway American Football League with Joe Foss as its first commissioner. Hunt formed his own team to represent Dallas, which he christened the Dallas Texans.

Despite initial scorn from the NFL, another two clubs soon joined the AFL. Then, as if to complicate things even further, long-serving NFL Commissioner Bell died of a heart attack. Galvanized by the threat from the newly formed AFL, the NFL re-entered negotiations for its own team franchise in Dallas, with Hunt's arch-rival Murchison as the new club's founder.

Murchison closed the deal in double-quick time, and Dallas's new NFL team, the Dallas Cowboys (they dropped their original name of Dallas Rangers after a couple of months), were ready to play in time for the 1960 season. With no infrastructure to speak of, all Murchison could do was to import 36 players from other teams and hope for the best. With over a billion dollars to spend, money was no problem. When told that the Cowboys had lost a million dollars in their first season, Murchison remarked dryly, 'at that rate they'll last a thousand years'.

Despite having bought a considerable amount of talent and been lucky enough to acquire Tom Landry as coach, the Cowboys could not achieve miracles. Their first season was a resounding failure. Attendance was low, being split with Hunt's Texans, and performances were poor. Out of 12 games played, the Cowboys could only manage one draw against 11 losses.

However, in the end it was the Cowboys who won the battle of Dallas. Hunt moved his team to Kansas, where they became the Kansas City Chiefs. The Cowboys set about building a team system which was to lead to seven Super Bowl appearances (more than any other team), four Super Bowl victories, and a host of other honours. In light of their achievements, the Cowboys' first season was not quite so bad, it being a miracle that they managed to field a team at all.

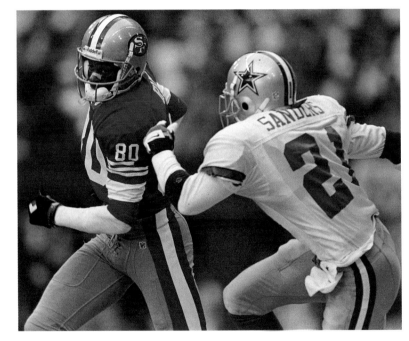

Top: one of the Cowboys' strongest adversaries – Jerry Rice of the San Francisco 49ers.

Bottom: a winning player – Deion Sanders of the Dallas Cowboys.

1967
The birth of Super Bowl

ALTHOUGH SUPER BOWL is now a well-established American sporting institution, it is still a relatively young event.

The concept of Super Bowl was devised by Lamar Hunt, owner of the Kansas City Chiefs and main instigator of the American Football League. Hunt, whose team had been enjoying great success, came up with the idea of a competition between the winners of the AFL and NFL. An ever-suspicious NFL finally agreed to his proposal just in time for the 1966 season winners to play.

The venue chosen was the Memorial Coliseum in Los Angeles, home of the Los Angeles Raiders. A well-orchestrated media campaign ensured that there was a great deal of interest in the game, though somewhat surprisingly only 61,946 fans watched the match, leaving 30,000 seats empty on the night. The Chiefs' opponents were the Green Bay Packers from Wisconsin, who had beaten Hunt's arch-rivals, the Dallas Cowboys, to win the 1966 NFL championship. Both teams were enjoying very successful periods in their histories, so the game promised to be an interesting one.

As is so often the way with one-off, high-pressure matches, the result was a surprise. The Chiefs were entirely overwhelmed by the Packers, who stormed home to a memorable 35–10 victory. Hero of the match, and winner of the Super Bowl's first Most Valuable Player (MVP) award, was Bart Starr. Starr had joined the Packers as a 17th-round draftee and inspired quarterback. It is rare for players picked so late to amount to much, but Starr was a shining exception. He provided the strategy and tactics for the Packers as well as the superb individual tally of 16 completed passes out of 23 for a total of 250 yds. Strangely, it was Len Dawson of the Chiefs who had the most consecutive competitions in the game (eight), a record which stood until Super Bowl XVIII.

Super Bowl victors are awarded the Vince Lombardi Trophy, named after the legendary coach of the Green Bay Packers. Made of solid silver, it is 50 cm (20 in) high and weighs just over 3 kg (7 lb). A new trophy is cast each year as the winning club keeps theirs permanently. In addition to the cup, each team member is given a ring to commemorate their success. These are a different design each year and are often very complex.

Super Bowl is now a multi-million dollar event watched via satellite all over the world. Few moments in the sporting calendar produce quite so much good ol' American razzmatazz!

1972
USA feels cheated out of gold

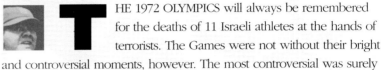**T**HE 1972 OLYMPICS will always be remembered for the deaths of 11 Israeli athletes at the hands of terrorists. The Games were not without their bright and controversial moments, however. The most controversial was surely the men's basketball final, played between the USA and the USSR.

Both teams were hotly fancied for the title, and both had come through the earlier rounds unbeaten. Everything suggested a great final. The Soviets took an early lead and maintained it, being 26–21 up at half-time. With the clock at 1:18 remaining, they were still clinging to the lead at 38–34 when a scuffle occurred between the USA's top scorer, Dwight Jones, and the Soviet player Dvorn Edeshko. This resulted in both players being ejected from the game. The loss of their top scorer was a major blow to the USA, but worse awaited them when, on the very next play, Jim Brewer suffered concussion after being knocked to the floor.

Despite these major setbacks, the USA managed to reduce the margin to just one point at the 40-second mark, when the scores stood at 49–48. By this time, the atmosphere in the stadium had become electric. For 30 seconds, the Soviets maintained possession, but with barely 10 seconds remaining, Doug Collins intercepted the ball and made for the Soviet basket, only to be fouled on the way. The Americans were awarded two free throws, which Collins promptly put away, despite the end-of-game horn going off between shots. The score now stood at 49–50 in favour of the USA.

The Soviets made a frantic attempt at a long basket and failed, but an official had already whistled to stop play with just one second on the clock. After some arguing with the Soviets, the referee agreed to reset the clock to three seconds. He put the ball into play, and the Soviets made another desperate and unsuccessful long-ball play, the end-of-game horn sounded, and the USA went mad thinking that they had won. However, R. William Jones, the secretary-general of basketball's international governing body, stepped in and ordered that the last three seconds of the game be replayed yet again. This time, the Soviets' Aleksander Belov neatly collected a long pass from Ivan Edeshenko and scored, making the final result 51–50. Despite protests from the USA, the score now stood and the Soviets were awarded the gold medal. The Americans, utterly aghast, voted unanimously to refuse their medals, a dramatic end to what is probably the most controversial basketball match ever played.

Left: April 1994. Jerry Rice playing for the 49ers against the Atlanta Falcons. Final score: Falcons 14; 49ers 50.

1994
Jerry Rice's record-breaking 127th touchdown

BORN IN 1962, JERRY RICE has become a legend in his 11 years as a professional footballer, having achieved no fewer than five Super Bowl records and eight other National Football League records. These include the highest number of touchdowns, at 165; 1000-yd seasons, at 10; and 100-yd receiving games, at 59.

Rice began his professional career in 1985 as the first draft out of Mississippi Valley State. The San Francisco 49ers were the team lucky enough to pick him up. Rice was the third wide receiver to be chosen that year, coming out behind Al Toon of the New York Jets and Eddie Brown of the Cincinnati Bengals.

The wide-receiver position is not usually associated with record-breaking, and the present fame of this position in the game is totally down to Jerry Rice. In his first year with the 49ers, he set a record for a rookie when he managed 927 received yards in his first season. Rice's first-ever professional touchdown came, interestingly enough, from a 25-yd pass made by another footballing legend, Joe Montana. By his third season, Rice had already set two NFL season records with 138 scored points and 22 receiving touchdowns. The very next year, he not only established a team record with a staggering 96-yard touchdown but also was named Most Valuable Player in his first Super Bowl appearance. By 1989, Rice had been elected to the Pro Football Hall of Fame; in Super Bowl XXIV, he again set a record with three touchdowns against Denver.

Rice went from triumph to triumph. His finest moment, however, occurred in the first game of the 1994 season, when the 49ers faced the Los Angeles Raiders in an NFL game. This match saw Rice score yet another touchdown: the 127th of his professional career, a new all-time record which broke that held by Jim Brown since the 1960s. Not content with this, Rice went on to appear in his third Super Bowl, again scoring three touchdowns. The first took him all of 84 seconds to achieve!

Although at the time of writing he is sadly out of the game due to injury, Jerry Rice continues to break records to this day. He has proclaimed his intention to play on and own 'every major offensive record' by the end of his career. If past performances are anything to go on, he looks almost certain to accomplish his goal.

Left: December 1995, Jerry Rice in the process of beating the Dallas Cowboys 38–20.

Right: Jerry Rice has broken many of American Football's most prestigious records. In 1994, he scored the 127th touchdown of his professional career.

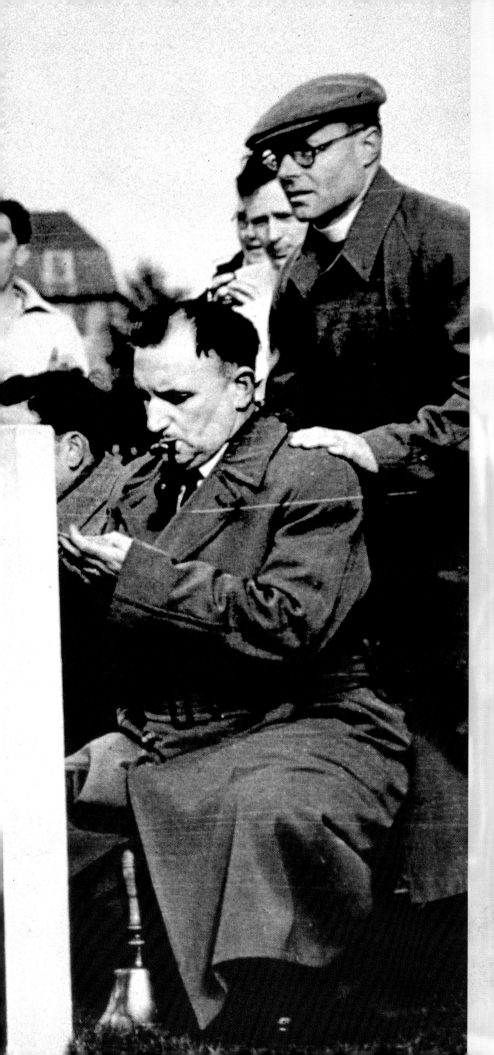

Athletics, Gymnastics & Swimming

Swimming isn't everything, winning is.
Arnold Spitz, to young son Mark in 1960. Mark went on to win seven gold medals at the Munich Olympics in 1972.

1913
Jim Thorpe stripped of his medals

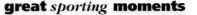

JIM THORPE, undoubtedly one of the greatest athletes of the twentieth century, was probably its most natural sportsman. He excelled at so many sports that almost a century later it is nearly impossible to believe the extent of his achievements. As well as being an Olympic gold medal winner in both the pentathlon and the decathlon at the 1912 Olympics in Stockholm – an almost unimaginable feat on its own – Thorpe was also a fantastic gridiron specialist and solid baseball player, as well as excelling in basketball, boxing, lacrosse, swimming and hockey. Just for good measure, he also won the 1912 intercollegiate ballroom-dancing championship. It is surely only because his achievements came before the days of mass media, particularly television, that Thorpe is not as famous as, say, Jesse Owens or Muhammad Ali.

Overleaf: Roger Bannister breaking the four-minute mile – he ran it in 3 minutes, 59.4 seconds (see page 31).

*Jim Thorpe of the USA at the Stockholm Olympics in June 1912: **top**: throwing the discus; **bottom**: winning the pentathlon.*

Born James Francis Thorpe in 1886 in what was then Oklahoma, Thorpe was of Irish and Indian parentage. His mother gave him the name Wa-Tho-Huck, which means 'Bright Path'. Thorpe first made headlines playing American football and was so good at athletics that he was selected for the 1912 Olympics. He won the pentathlon and came fourth in the high jump and seventh in the long jump. Then, over the course of three days, he won the decathlon by setting a new world record of 8412 points, almost 800 clear of his nearest competitor. The same performance would have won him a silver at the 1948 Olympics! Thorpe went on to play major-league baseball and professional football from 1915 to 1928.

In 1950, Thorpe was voted the greatest American athlete and the greatest football player of the first half of the century by American writers and broadcasters. Despite his unparalleled expertise, his place in the history books is largely due to controversy, however. The gold medals he won in 1912 were stripped from him in 1913 after it was found that he had received $15 a week for playing minor-league baseball in North Carolina a few years earlier. Under the rules of the day, this made him a professional, and he should not have competed at Stockholm. In later life, he was reduced to poverty and received a mere $1500 for the rights to a film about his life which starred Burt Lancaster.

Thorpe died of a heart attack in 1953 and was buried in a town called Mauch Chunk which changed its name to Jim Thorpe for the right to have his body buried there. In 1982, after a 40-year struggle, his medals were returned to his family and his name to the record books. It was the least the world of sport owed him.

1936
Jesse Owens' Olympics

JESSE OWENS is easily one of the most famous sportsmen of the century, a symbol of both supreme athleticism and the struggle against racism and bigotry everywhere. His finest hour was at the 1936 Berlin Olympics, where he won four gold medals, triumphing in the 100 and 200 m, the 4x100-m relay, and the long jump. Nazi leader Adolf Hitler, however, refused to shake Owens' hand or present him with his medals. Hitler's handshake would have been superfluous in any case. His disdain of Owens' achievements makes them stand as one of the greatest sporting stories of the century.

Owens' well-documented success at Berlin is only half the story. Born in Alabama in 1913, James 'Jesse' Cleveland Owens dominated the sprint distances in the 1930s. His stature as a world-class athlete was confirmed in 1935, when he broke five world records and equalled a sixth in the space of 45 minutes while competing at the Big Ten Championships in Michigan. Starting at 3.15 p.m., Owens equalled the 100-yd-dash world record and beat the long jump, 220-yd dash, 200-m dash, and 220-yd low hurdles. En route, he smashed the 200-m-hurdles record. His long-jump record was to stand until 1960. Not bad for someone who smoked 35 cigarettes a day.

Despite Owens' eventual success at Berlin, it is not so well known that he almost came home with 'only' two gold medals. Trying to qualify for the long-jump final, he had trouble with his run-up and fouled his first two attempts. In a supreme act of sportsmanship, his main rival, the German Carl Ludwig 'Luz' Long, placed his towel in front of the foul line for Owens to use as a marker for his final attempt. Owens qualified for the final, and went on to win the event with Long taking the silver.

Afterwards, in an act of bravery considering that Hitler was looking on, Long walked past the Nazi leader's box arm-in-arm with the man portrayed as a 'black auxiliary' by German propaganda.

More sinister was the second medal Owens almost missed out on. He was selected for the relay team at the expense of a Jewish athlete, the rumour being that pressure from the Nazis had led to Jewish sprinters being dropped from the team. The American team won, and Owens picked up his fourth gold to go alongside those for the 100-m and 200-m sprint events. In the process, he tied the Olympic 100-m record and broke the Olympic and world records for the 200 m. The relay team also broke the world record. Owens' record of four track-and-field medals in the men's events would not be emulated until 1984.

Top: *US athlete Jesse Owens, star of the 1936 Olympics.*

Bottom: *Jesse Owens at the 1936 Olympics in Berlin – on his way to winning one of his four gold medals.*

1948

Fanny Blankers-Koen takes London by storm

R ARELY CAN VICTORIES IN THE OLYMPICS have proved as emotional as Fanny Blankers-Koen's quadruple success in the London Olympics in 1948. To win her four gold medals, she overcame press derision in her native Holland, sexism and homesickness for the Netherlands and her two small children. In fact, so painful was the last that Blankers-Koen threatened to quit the Olympics after having won her first two golds. But she was persuaded to stay and became the first-ever woman to win four gold medals at one Olympics, emulating her hero Jesse Owens. Blankers-Koen won gold in the 100 m, 200 m, 80-m hurdles, and 4x100-m relay. Incredibly, she opted not to take part in two other events, the long jump and the high jump, in which she held the world records.

Left: Fanny Blankers-Koen wins the Olympic gold for Holland, narrowly beating Britain's Maureen Gardener. London, 1948.

Right top and bottom: Fanny Blankers-Koen's Dutch team takes the gold in the 400 m relay. London, 1948.

Blankers-Koen's decision to opt for the running events shocked the Dutch, who considered her, at 30, too old for the sprints. A British Olympic official, Jack Crump, was even ruder. He asked why 'a 30-year-old mother of two was running in short pants at the expense of leaving her family'. Such remarks provided Blankers-Koen with all the incentive she needed. Her first victory was in the 100 m, which she won comfortably by 3 yards in muddy conditions. In the 80-m hurdles, her second gold medal event, Blankers-Koen set an Olympic record to win in a time of 11.2 seconds. In a close finish, she just beat Britain's Maureen Gardner for the gold. The finish was so close that no one immediately afterwards knew who had won. Suddenly, the band started playing 'God Save the King', and Blankers-Koen assumed she had lost. But the band was marking the entry of the British Royal Family, who had just come into the stadium. Moments later, the Dutchwoman was declared the winner.

These victories seemed to do little for Blankers-Koen. Reports that she was close to a mental breakdown do not seem exaggerated. The press continued to berate her, and after talking to her children her urge to go home was even greater. Her husband and coach Jan's attempts to persuade her to run seemed to no avail until he evoked Jesse Owens. Blankers-Koen decided to run and ended up winning the final by 7 yards, the largest-ever victory in the women's 200 m. She gained her fourth gold when she ran the anchor leg in the 4x100-m relay despite the fact that when she took the baton, the Dutch team were in fourth place. It should also be noted that the winning jump in the long jump was some 20 inches shorter than her world record. After the Olympics, she received another prize – an apology from Jack Crump.

1953
Marathon Man

ON 13 JUNE 1953, JIM PETERS, one of the world's supreme marathon runners, put bitter disappointment behind him to shatter the world record for running's most gruelling event. Running the 26-mile 385-yd course between Windsor Castle and Chiswick, Peters came home in an astonishing time of 2 hours 18 minutes 40.2 seconds, two minutes faster than he had run the previous year and 10 seconds faster than the existing world record held by Japan's Yamada.

For Peters, a 34-year-old optician from Mitcham who ran with the Essex Beagles club, this achievement completed an astonishing come-back from huge disappointment at the 1952 Helsinki Olympics, where he had entered the race as the favourite to win the gold. Here he was upstaged by one of the century's greatest long-distance runners, Emil Zatopek of Czechoslovakia. At Helsinki, Zatopek was in incredible form. He took the gold in the 5000 m and 10,000 m, but still it was not enough. After hundreds of interviews, he told one reporter he was bored and would run the marathon, even though he had never run one in his life before.

At the line-up for the race, Zatopek introduced himself to Peters and asked if he could run alongside the Essex man as he considered him to be the favourite to win. A surprised Peters agreed and set off at his usual blistering pace over the first few miles. Incredibly, Zatopek kept shoulder-to-shoulder with the more experienced marathon runner. After about 10 miles, he asked the Briton about the pace. 'The pace in the beginning was very fast,' said Zatopek. 'I was so tired and Jim was running like he could do this forever. I couldn't believe what was happening, so I said to him, "Isn't this pace too fast?"'

Depending on which story you believe, Peters, either in jest or in an attempt to put on a brave face, replied that they should be running faster. Zatopek took him at his word and took up the pace, destroying Peters in the process and, incredibly, taking the gold. Peters pulled out because of exhaustion and was taken to hospital.

Although to lose to Zatopek was no disgrace, the Helsinki Olympics were a chastening experience for Peters. Between then and his world-record success, he ran about 3200 miles in training,

about 100 miles a week. And he changed his tactics. During the Windsor-to-Chiswick run, he modified his usual blistering start, taking a more relaxed pace over the initial 5 miles. He completed the first 10.5 miles in 55 minutes 42 seconds, slower than his 1952 run, but broke the record with plenty to spare. *The Times* reported that 'it should be added that Peters finished not only completely alone but fresher than any of the runners who arrived in due course'.

Left: *13 June 1953, Jim Peters about to break the marathon winning line – he ran from Windsor to Chiswick in 2 hours, 18 minutes, 40.2 seconds.*

Right: *a portrait of Jim Peters taken in July 1952, the same year he suffered such disappointment at the Helsinki Olympics.*

Roger Bannister gasping for breath after completing his amazing sub-four-minute mile, 6 May 1954.

1954

Bannister's dream mile

I F A BOOK WERE TO BE WRITTEN about the 10 most memorable sporting achievements of the twentieth century, it is a sure bet that the mile race involving six men at a meet between the Amateur Athletic Association and the University Athletic Association on the Iffley Road track, Oxford, would figure in it. This was the occasion on which Roger Bannister overturned one of the greatest landmarks in athletics – the 4-minute mile. His time of 3 minutes 59.4 seconds shattered the history books. Over 40 years later, this still stands out as a most remarkable achievement.

Although athletes had dreamt about it for years, the first sub-4-minute mile was close to becoming a reality in the early to mid-1950s. However, Roger Bannister, a 1.85-m (6-ft 1-in), 25-year-old medical student at St Mary's Hospital, Paddington, was by no means assured of being the man to make history. In 1953, he had run his previous best time of 4 minutes 2 seconds. But that time had been matched by the Australian John Landy in the same year, and the American Wesley Santee recorded a time just 3/100ths of a second outside. The world record of 4 minutes 1.4 seconds had been set nine years earlier by Sweden's Gundar Haegg. Now a group of runners bunched on the verge of history.

Bannister lined up for the AAA with colleagues Chris Brasher and Chris Chataway. What was to follow looked distinctly implausible given the windy conditions and the threat of rain. Brasher and Chataway set the pace. Brasher took the trio along for the first two laps, but then dropped back. Chataway took over and led at the bell. Bannister, though, was the stronger and by the end of the race had opened up a 50-yd lead. His split times were 57.7 seconds for the first lap, 60.6 for the second, 62.4 for the third, and 58.7 for the final lap. After the race, an excited crowd rushed on to the track hoping for the best. The time-keeper was a young Norris McWhirter, who 'with no more emotion than a porter announcing the next train to Crewe', according to one paper, announced the in-credible time of 3.59.4.

Amazingly, just a few weeks later, John Landy broke the 4-minute mile and Bannister's record. But although his record never stood, Bannister's achievement did. This fact was missed by a report the next day in *The Times* which 'feared' the general match between the AAA and the UAA 'was rather forgotten in the excitement'. For the record, Bannister's AAA won by 30 points, but who remembers that?

Roger Bannister breaking the winning rope after 3 minutes, 59.4 seconds.

1962
Records fall to the man in black

SEVERAL YEARS AGO, 20 leading track-and-field experts were asked by the *Los Angeles Times* to select the 'winner' in a dream race involving every 800-m Olympic- and world-record holder of the twentieth century. All 20 ended up choosing New Zealand's Peter Snell.

Snell is certainly one of the greatest middle-distance runners of the last hundred years. He first came to prominence outside New Zealand in 1960 at the Rome Olympics. There, he took the gold even though the final was expected to be a battle between Belgium's Roger Moens and Jamaica's George Kerr. Snell won with a time of 1 minute 46.3 seconds to set a new Olympic record. Moens, who thought he had taken the gold until the final few strides, was devastated. 'As I approached the finish line,' he said later, 'I ... closed my eyes and said to myself, "Roger, it is certain. You are the Olympic champion." Then a black uniform flashed past me. It was Peter Snell.'

Left: Peter Snell accelerating his way to middle-distance world records in the '60s.

Right: Peter Snell setting the world mile record in his native New Zealand, 27 January 1962. His time was 3 minutes, 54.4 seconds.

Snell had established himself as the greatest middle-distance runner of his generation by the time he reclaimed his 800-m title at the 1964 Tokyo Olympics and took the 1500-m title as well. This was largely due to an astonishing week in January 1962 when he had shattered not only the mile world record but also the 800-m record. At the time, Snell was living at home with his parents in the potato-growing town of Pukekohe, 35 miles south of Auckland on New Zealand's North Island. A year before he set the world mile record of 3.54.4, he had told a journalist that he would 'really love to have a serious crack at the mile. I believe I'm far from my potential over four laps'.

In December 1961, Snell had, in training, run under the magic four-minute mark for the first time, clocking a time of 3.59.3. On a grass track at Cook's Gardens, Wanganui, the following January, he went even better. In front of a partisan crowd of 15,000, he broke the existing record held by Australian Herb Elliot. In a field of seven runners led by Britain's barefoot champ Bruce Tulloh, Snell ran the first lap in 60 seconds at the back of the field. At halfway, he pulled himself up to third in a time of 1 minute 59 seconds and proceeded to take over the race, destroying the field and the record. He is said to have finished 'full of running'.

A few days later, Snell obliterated the 800-m record, running in 1 minute 44.3 seconds. Two years earlier at London's White City, he had run the same distance in 1 minute 44.9 seconds in a relay race. The existing world record at the time was 1 minute 46.8 seconds. His double-winning performance at the Tokyo Olympics made him the first runner since Britain's Albert Hill in the 1920 Antwerp Olympics to take a gold in both distances.

1968
Bob Beamon leaps into history

BOB BEAMON did more than break the long-jump world record on 18 October 1968; he leapt into history. His incredible jump of 8.9 m (29 ft 5 in) at the 1968 Mexico City Olympics has been described as the greatest athletic achievement of all time. Since Jesse Owens had broken the long-jump record 33 years earlier, the world record had moved forward just 20 cm (8 in). In a matter of seconds, Beamon moved it forward another 55 cm (22 in), completely bypassing the 8-m (28-ft) barrier. The record was to stand for over 22 years before fellow American Michael Powell broke it in June 1991.

Beamon's leap broke all the barriers and practically re-defined the sport of long jumping. Incredibly, just like Jesse Owens 32 years earlier at the Berlin Olympics, Beamon almost lost the chance to create history. Like Owens, he had fouled on his first two jumps in the qualifying round and faced elimination. Again, just like Owens, he received crucial advice from one of his main competitors. The American Ralph Boston, who finished with the bronze medal, helped Beamon with his notoriously erratic run-up. Beamon made sure he qualified for the final by making a legal jump on his third and final attempt.

Although Beamon, then a 22-year-old from the Bronx, New York, had entered the competition as favourite, his victory was not assured. All three medalists from the 1964 Tokyo Olympics were competing; and despite winning 22 out of 23 events in 1968, Beamon entered the Olympics under a cloud. In April, he had been suspended from the track team at the University of Texas after refusing to compete, in a protest against the racist policies of another university. This meant that he had no regular coach, a factor which further affected his run-up. Incredibly, he used no markers, relying instead on his blistering speed and instinct to hit the jump board.

The day of the Olympic final was overcast, which was supposed to favour other competitors. By having sexual inter-course the night before the final, Beamon also believed he had ruined his chances. He could not have been more wrong. His incredible jump in the very first round destroyed the competition. But because the official distance was given in metres and Beamon was accustomed to feet and inches, he was one of the last people in the stadium to realize what he had done. When Ralph Boston told him, Beamon's legs gave way and he suffered a seizure. He made only one more jump that day and throughout his whole career would never again jump further than about 8 m (26 ft 11½ in). At the time of Beamon's leap, the Russian jumper Igor Ter-Ovanesyan said, 'compared to this jump, we are as children'. He was right.

Bob Beamon setting a new world record in long-jump – 1968 Olympic Games, Mexico City. He jumped 8.9 m (29 ft 5 in).

1972

Elfin gymnast tumbles into public's affection

AT THE 1972 OLYMPICS, Soviet gymnast Ludmila Tourischeva won the gold medal for the all-round championship. That she went home virtually unknown was due to the captivating performances of a 17-year-old Soviet girl who finished only seventh in the all-round championship but who won the popularity contest by a mile.

Olga Valentinova Korbut, a 1.5-m (4-ft 11-in), 37.8-kg (6-stone) gymnast from Grodno in Belarus, so captured the public's imagination that she instantly became a superstar. Her room at the Olympic Village became a shrine for flowers and telegrams sent from fans all over the world. When she walked around Munich, buses stopped so passengers could get her autograph. Shop-keepers refused to take her money, and eventually she had to buy a wig and hat to get round town. Back home, she received 20,000 letters in one year after the Olympics; a special clerk had to be assigned to deal with her post. Her effect on gymnastics was extraordinary. Prior to Munich, there were fewer than 15,000 American female gymnasts. After Munich, there were 50,000. President Nixon told Korbut at the White House in 1973 that her performances in Munich had reduced the Cold War tension between the USA and USSR more success-fully than diplomats had over the previous five years.

There were many reasons for Korbut's immense popularity. There were the tears she spilt after failure on the bars in the all-round competition meant that she had lost her chance of a gold medal. Then there were her innocent, stylish perfor-mances on the floor, which contrasted greatly with those of many of her com-patriots. Finally, there was her appearance – 17 going on 12. Korbut was dubbed the 'Munich Munchkin'.

Korbut had already claimed gold in the team event by the time the individual events began. Halfway through the all-round event, she was in the lead and

threatening the favourite, Tourischeva, as she went to her next piece of apparatus, the asymmetric bars. But then disaster struck. She scuffed her mount, slipped off the bars and fluffed a simple remount. Korbut was given the lowly mark of 7.5, destroying her chances of victory. Immediately, she burst into tears, a scene which was picked up by the TV cameras and which endeared her to the public even more. Two days later, Korbut reappeared in the individual events to claim two golds, one for the balance beam and the other for the floor exercise, at which she excelled with her dazzling display of somersaults, showbiz, and smiles. She also won a silver medal on the asymmetric bars. Munich launched Korbut's career, and she went on to become the first-ever gymnast to do a back somersault on the beam. She later married a Belarussian singer and was living in Grodno, near Chernobyl, when the nuclear tragedy struck in 1986. Korbut moved to Atlanta, Georgia, and established a foundation for Chernobyl victims.

Left: *the amazing Olga Korbut of the USSR at the 1976 Olympic Games, Montreal.*

Top right: *Olga Korbut, the 'Munich Munchkin' at the 1972 Olympics, where she became an instant and much-adored celebrity.*

1972
Spitz's magnificent seven

ARNOLD SPITZ FROM CALIFORNIA, father of record-breaking swimmer Mark, used to tell his young son that 'swimming isn't everything, winning is'. In 1972 in the smooth waters of the Munich Olympic pool, 22-year-old Mark Spitz lived up to his dad's maxim, swimming his way into history by claiming seven gold medals and as many world records. Despite the Games being overshadowed by the murder of 11 Israeli athletes by Palestinian terrorists, Spitz's records in the pool still stand out. He took the gold in the 100-m and 200-m freestyle, the 100-m and 200-m butterfly, and three team events: the 4x100-m freestyle relay, 4x100-m medley relay, and 4x200-m freestyle event.

For Spitz, it was second time lucky. As an 18-year-old, he had predicted that he would win five medals at the Mexico City Olympics. He ended up with two, and both came in team events rather than individual races. In 1972, Spitz won his first event, the 200-m butterfly, by almost two seconds, smashing his own world record by almost a second, coming home in 2 mins 00.70 secs. That same afternoon, he swam the anchor leg in the 4x100-m freestyle relay and claimed his second gold medal. The team set a new world record of 3 mins 26.42 secs, over two seconds better than the previous record. Next to fall was the 200-m freestyle, which Spitz won in a

world-record time of 1 min 52.78 sces, knocking over half a second off his own record. Second in the race was fellow American Steven Genter, who – incredibly – led with 50 m to go, having been released from hospital the day before after surgery on a partially collapsed lung. The 100-m butterfly followed soon after, as did yet another world record. Spitz, who had taken the silver in the event at Mexico City, won in a time of 54.27 secs, breaking his previous world record of 54.56 secs. That same afternoon, he captured his fifth gold, swimming the anchor leg in the 4x200-m freestyle event. The world record of 7 mins 43.3 secs was smashed by almost seven seconds.

Five gold medals and five world records represented an amazing performance, and for a while it seemed to satisfy Spitz. He told his coach Sherm Chavoor that he was tired and did not want to compete in the 100-m freestyle, saving himself for the 4x100-m medley relay. Chavoor told him that if he did not swim in one he would not swim in either and would be called 'chicken' for avoiding arch-rival Jerry Heidenreich in the individual event. Spitz duly entered, beat Heidenreich, and set a new world record of 51.22 secs. Finally, in the medley event, Spitz captured his amazing seventh gold and seventh world record when the Americans won in a time of 3 mins 48.16 secs.

Left: Mark Spitz on his way to winning one of seven gold medals at the 1972 Munich Olympics.

Right: Mark Spitz held aloft by his US team mates at the 1972 Olympics in Germany.

Steve Ovett at the 1980 Olympic Games in Moscow after winning the gold in the 800 m, beating compatriot competitor Seb Coe.

1980
Ovett beats Coe ... Coe beats Ovett

THE 800-m AND 1500-m COMPETITIONS in Moscow in 1980 were two of the most eagerly awaited races in athletics history. Brought together for the first time in two years were a pair of the greatest middle-distance runners the world had ever seen, Britain's Sebastian Coe and Steve Ovett. The two had dominated middle-distance running in the late 1970s and early 1980s, beating every other contender and smashing or equalling five world records between them in the run-up to Moscow.

The only doubt which remained was who was the better of the two. The last time they had met was in the 1978 European Championships, where their fear of each other had let in East Germany's Olaf Beyer to win the gold. The rivalry between Coe and Ovett was given a sharper edge by the British media, which claimed that it was bitter indeed and portrayed Coe as the golden boy of British athletics while not knowing what to make of the more aloof Ovett. Coe arrived in Moscow the hot favourite for the 800-m title, Ovett the slight favourite for the 1500 m.

Ovett, though, had other ideas. Both qualified with ease for the final on 26 July. A slow first lap of 54.3 seconds saw both men floundering towards the back of the pack, waiting for one another to make the first move. Ovett pushed his way through on the inside to second place by the final bend, while Coe had to go all the way round the outside to try and peg him back. It was too late. With just 70 m left, Ovett flew past the Soviet Kirov and claimed the 800-m title. Coe, who took the silver, was shattered, saying afterwards that he had run the worst race of his life.

Six days later, though, Coe took his revenge. Once again, both men qualified for the final, but this time Ovett was the favourite at the longer distance. He had won 42 consecutive races at 1500 m and the mile since 1977. He seemed so confident that in the semi-finals he gave the crowd his trademark victory wave *before* he had taken the lead. Coe's path was less smooth. He had struggled in his first-round heat and was now under even more media pressure to win the gold in his less favoured event. Between the British pair stood East Germany's Jürgen Straub, who led for most of the race. This time, though, Coe stayed near the front, anxious not to repeat his mistakes in the 800 m. On the final bend, he kicked for home and held

off the challenge of both Straub and Ovett, who took the bronze. When he passed the finishing line, Coe's face was a mixture of ecstasy and relief. After the race, the two men shared a drink. The question of who was the best would never be answered conclusively.

Sebastian Coe in his victorious 1500 m race at the Moscow Olympics, 1980.

1981

Mennea sprints into the record books

PIETRO MENNEA is the greatest and most consistent sprinter Italy has ever produced. The 200-m champion at the Moscow Olympics, he also held one of the most enduring world records in track and field.

In September 1979, at the World Student Games in Mexico City, he ran the 200 m in a time of 19.72 seconds to break the existing world record by a little over a tenth of a second. The previous record had been set by the American sprinter Tommie Smith at the 1968 Olympics in winning the gold medal. Smith's record was lost in the fuss created by his and his colleague John Carlos's Black Power salutes on the podium when they were presented with their medals; but his record stood for 11 years.

Mennea's lasted even longer. It was June 1996 – almost 17 years later – when Michael Johnson finally bettered his time. Despite the fact that Mennea's record was set at altitude, the amount of time it took for the record to be beaten is testament to the run he produced. Prior to Johnson beating the world record, Mennea's run had set another record, having become the oldest record in athletics. Celebrated widely in Italy, it was regarded by many as a national treasure. When it was finally beaten, the president of the Italian athletics body, Gianni Gola, said, 'I have congratulated Johnson but above all I would like to express the warmest affection of the Italian sporting world for Pietro Mennea'. The Italian head of the International Amateur Athletic Association, Primo Nebiolo, said Mennea had 'a legendary record that honoured athletics, but also honoured Italy'.

Mennea, from Torino, secured his popularity among many Italians when he took the gold medal in 1980, just ahead of Britain's Allan Wells, who had already won the 100 m. This was Mennea's third attempt at winning the 200-m Olympic gold. In 1972, he had failed to make the Munich final, while in 1976, he had finished fourth, just outside the medals, in a time of 20.54 seconds. Later, he qualified for the 1984 Los Angeles final, finishing seventh. Mennea spanned out his career by regularly shunning the smaller tournaments in preparation for the bigger events. His strength traditionally was in the final 100 m, where his speed over the straight was legendary, as Allan Wells found out when Mennea beat him in a time of 20.19 seconds.

A twist to the Mennea tale was that prior to the 1980 Olympics in Moscow, he had been a member of the Social Democratic Party, which supported the boycott of the Games. Mennea, though, found the possibility of a gold medal too alluring and so took his place in Moscow and, ultimately, in sprinting history.

The finish of the 200 m final – Italy's Pietro Mennea beating Britain's Allan Wells.

1983
Daley Thompson defies injury to win gold

DALEY THOMPSON is the finest athlete Britain has ever produced and one of the best the world has ever seen. The fact that he became famous for winning numerous titles and breaking world records in one of the least glamorous events – the decathlon – demonstrates the extent of his achievements. During the first half of the 1980s, he dominated the event and proved himself the ultimate competitor. Every time it looked like he might lose to any of his arch-rivals, particularly Germany's Jürgen Hingsen, Thompson triumphed again. He thrived in crucial moments, gaining those vital seconds which made the difference between winning and losing.

Thompson was a double Olympic champion, world champion, European champion and Commonwealth champion. Prior to his 1983 triumph at the first World Athletics Championship, he had broken the world record three times and the Commonwealth record nine times. When he won the title in Helsinki in 1983, Thompson became the first athlete ever to hold all four major titles. Allied to his amazing ability and incredible determination to win was an exuberant personality with a ready smile. The son of a Nigerian father and Scottish mother, he found himself in hot water at the 1984 Los Angeles Games for wearing T-shirts emblazoned with controversial messages and got into trouble in Britain for whistling through the national anthem after claiming yet another gold medal.

Britain's Daley Thompson winning the gold in the Decathlon discus event; 1983 World Championships, Helsinki.

Helsinki, 1983 – Daley Thompson winning the gold for Britain in the World Championship's Decathlon javelin event.

Thompson's entrance into big-time athletics had been low-key, when, as an 18-year-old, he came last in the Montreal Olympics. By 1980, though, he had broken the world record for most points in the decathlon – 8622 – and although he lost that record before Moscow, he took the gold medal. In 1982, he won at the European Championships, in the first of his major battles with Hingsen at the top events. In 1983, Thompson entered the tournament not knowing if he would be able to compete, claiming that there was an 80 per cent chance he would withdraw due to a niggling injury. This time, he faced a three-pronged German attack, headed as ever by Hingsen and including Siegfried Wentz and Gido Kratchmer. Thompson was later to ascribe the motivation for his success to the fact that all three ignored him in the athletes' village.

Even with his injury, Thompson got off to a flyer. In atrocious conditions on the first day, he finished 120 points clear. He got the two highest scores for the 100 m and the long jump and came third in three other events, finishing on 4486 points. The next day, he maintained his lead, ending on 8666 points, 106 ahead of the unfortunate Hingsen, who had entered the championships as the world-record holder.

The next year, Thompson won gold at the Los Angeles Olympics despite Hingsen once again entering as the world-record holder. Thompson became the first man since the USA's Robert Mathias had claimed gold at the 1948 and 1952 Olympics to win decathlon golds consecutively.

1984
First Owens, then Lewis

INCREDIBLY FOR A MAN who grew up to become one of the most prodigious athletes of his age, Carl Lewis was thought to be the least athletic person in his family. Born the third son of two track coaches in Birmingham, Alabama, he was to become the best athlete of his generation and leave his mark on athletics forever. His place in the sport's hall of fame was assured after his performance at the Los Angeles Olympics, where he won four gold medals in the 100 m, 200 m, and long-jump and as a member of the US 4x100-m relay team, thus emulating, 48 years on, his hero Jesse Owens.

Lewis went to Los Angeles after winning three gold medals at the 1983 World Championships in Helsinki. His first gold medal in 1984 came in the 100 m. This event was thought to be his weakest, but he ended up winning by a huge margin – 8 ft. His time was recorded as 9.99 seconds and his speed at 28 mph.

The Olympic sandpit has produced several legends, and in 1984 Lewis put his name alongside those of Owens and Beamon, among others, in securing the gold medal. Prior to the Olympics, he had won 36 straight long-jump competitions and was regularly jumping over 28 ft. In Los Angeles, he secured the gold with his very first jump, which was given an official distance of 28 ft ¼ in, almost a foot ahead of second-placed Gary Honey from Australia. Lewis's victory was controversial, however. He jumped only one more time, completing just two of his six allotted jumps. He was booed by spectators unhappy at his reluctance to jump again, despite his punishing Olympic timetable. Although Lewis was proved right, the incident is an example of how he has somehow failed to gain public favour, being perceived, unfairly in this instance, as aloof.

Lewis's third medal was secured back on the track, where he set an Olympic record time of 19.80 seconds to claim the 200-m title. His victory was based on a blistering start, and he eventually won by 1½ m as the USA took all three medals. His medal tally was rounded off with the only track-and-field world record of the Games, as the US 4x100-m relay team produced a stunning time of 37.86 seconds.

After emulating Owens's 1936 achievements, Lewis said that the earlier athlete had acted as his inspiration. He went on to win gold medals at four different Olympics, thus joining a very exclusive club.

*America's Carl Lewis at the 1984 Olympic Games in Los Angeles – **top**: winning the 200 m race; **bottom**: taking the gold in long-jump.*

1992
Cacho's golden run ends Spain's Olympic drought

THE SUMMER 1992 OLYMPICS in Barcelona will always be remembered fondly in Spain, not just because they were the most successful Olympics in two decades. Spain finished the Games with a total haul of 22 medals. Of these, 13 were gold, seven were silver, and two were bronze. The country finished sixth in the medal table, sandwiched between Cuba and South Korea. Previously in the Olympics, Spain had had a dismal record, having won only 25 medals in its entire history, four of these being gold. The first medals, two silvers, had come at the 1920 Antwerp Olympics. At the 1928 Amsterdam Games, Spain had won its first gold, but then had to wait another 52 years before claiming its next one at the boycott-affected 1980 Olympics in Moscow. Two more gold medals followed in the next two Olympics. In 1988 at Seoul, Spain finished in 26th place, tied with Finland.

The organizers of the Barcelona Olympics were faced with the prospect of the host nation having little or no chance of winning many medals. The response from the Spanish government was swift, pumping money into large-scale training programmes. The policy worked beyond their wildest dreams. The greatest home victory was that of Fermin Cacho Ruiz in the men's 1500-m race. Cacho's victory was Spain's first in the event, and he became the first Spanish runner to win a gold medal. It immediately propelled him to national hero status. Before he had a chance to shower after his victory, he was granted an audience with King Juan Carlos at the stadium.

Prior to the Olympics, Cacho had finished fifth in the 1991 World Championships. Although the man from Agreda, near Zaragoza, was given the chance of a medal, no one was given a chance of gold except the hot favourite, Noureddine Morceli of Algeria. Throughout 1991, Morceli had remained undefeated at 1500 m, but early in 1992 he had injured his hip. Despite his problems, he qualified for the final, as did Mohamed Ahmed Sulaiman of Qatar with the fastest qualifying time in Olympic history, 3 minutes 34.77 seconds.

Cacho won his first round in 3 minutes 37.04 seconds and qualified second to Sulaiman in his semi-final. The final was the slowest since 1956, and the 400-m and 800-m splits were slower than those in the women's final, won by Hassiba Boulmerka of Algeria. Cacho took the lead midway through the final lap after being allowed through the inside by Kenya's Joseph Chesire. With his powerful finish, the Spaniard was able to hold off the challenges of Rachid El Basir of Morocco and of Sulaiman, who took the bronze. Cacho's final lap was run in just 50.4 seconds as he came home in a time of 3 minutes 40.12 seconds. Morceli, who finished seventh, later claimed that he could not eat or sleep for a week afterwards.

1992
Dieter Baumann sprints to the tape in 5000 m

LONG-DISTANCE RACES rarely throw up as many exciting finishes as the men's 5000-m final at the Barcelona Olympics. Usually fought out by a couple of runners after many tense laps, this event was dramatically contested by five runners on the final straight. In the end, the first four runners were separated by just over a half-second.

The title went to the talented German runner Dieter Baumann, whose extraordinary sprint finish gave his country its first-ever men's gold medal at the 5000-m mark. Baumann's win marked the first time the title had been won by a non-African since the 1976 Montreal Olympics, when the legendary Finnish runner Lasse Viren had picked up the second of his 5000-m gold medals.

For Baumann, from the small town of Blaustein close to Stuttgart, it was a moment to savour and made up for losing out on the gold medal at the 1988 Games in Seoul, where he had finished second behind Kenya's John Ngugi. His powerful sprint at the finish had proved decisive, making it possible for him to pass Portugal's Domingos Castro with the finishing line in sight. Castro was also pipped for the bronze medal in the final few strides and burst into tears immediately after. Baumann's time of 13 minutes 15.52 seconds would not have got him a medal at Barcelona, however.

In 1992, Baumann's main adversaries were once again the African runners: Kenya's Paul Bitok and Yobes Ondieki and Ethiopia's Fita Bayisa and Moulay Brahim Boutaib all provided stiff opposition. Baumann made his way easily into the final nonetheless. In heat three, he qualified in a time of 13 minutes 20.82 seconds. His pre-race tactic seemed to be to rely on his terrific finishing speed whilst keeping a wary eye on the talented group of Africans who were his main source of danger.

Baumann's fear was that somebody would take up the pace early, rendering his fast finish useless. But the other runners played into his hands. A gentle pace was taken up by the field with everyone too anxious to make an early stab for the medal. As the runners came to the final bend, five moved in for the kill. Baumann was in the worst position. Boxed in at the back of the pack containing Bitok, Bayisa, Boutaib and Ondieki, his only escape was to go on the outside and pick off the leaders one by

one. Despite his incredible finishing powers, it seemed impossible for Baumann to win the gold from that position. But that is exactly what he did. He finally overtook Bitok with just a few strides left to leave the others shattered, winning in a time of 13 minutes 12.52 seconds and running the last 200 m in 24.9 seconds.

Germany's Dieter Baumann in his astonishing victory burst to win the 5000 m race. Barcelona Olympics, 1992.

1993
Christie's Grand Slam

LINFORD CHRISTIE is the best-ever European sprinter. His form in the early 1990s broke American dominance in the sprints. Prior to his win in the Barcelona Olympics in 1992, only four non-Americans had won the gold medal in 11 Olympics since the Second World War. Christie, the only European to have run under 10 seconds, has won more major championship medals – 23 – than any other British male athlete. Until 1996, he remained unbeaten by a British athlete for eight years. Although he has never held the world record for the 100 m, his fastest time of 9.87 still stands as the European record.

Christie's record is matched by very few. But it was not until the early 1990s, that – already in his 30s – he produced his best form and was recognized as the supreme runner on both sides of the Atlantic. By 1993, Christie had won athletics' coveted grand slam, taking first place in the Commonwealth Games, European Championships, Olympics and World Championships. The Commonwealth title was the first one he gained, winning in the 1990 games. The same year, he won the European title, the first of six he would win. His form was confirmed the next year, when he took part in one of the most extraordinary 100-m races in history. For the first time ever, six men ran under 10 seconds at the World Championships in Tokyo. The American Carl Lewis won in a world-record time of 9.86. Although Christie ran 9.92, he finished fourth and without a medal. Apparently, he was so disenchanted by this that he thought of retiring. But he did not, and the following two years proved to be the most successful of his career.

The biggest title of all, the Olympic title, came next. Aged 32, Christie was in the best form of his life. He had lost only once all season. His greatest threat seemed to come from the American Leroy Burrell, who had beaten him 10 consecutive times. Christie beat Burrell in the quarter-finals only for Burrell to return the compliment in the semis. But in the final, Christie produced one of the performances of his life. After 60 m, he was clear of the field and pulled away to claim Britain's second 100-m gold medal in 12 years. Christie was the oldest man by four years to win the Olympic gold medal.

In Stuttgart in 1993, he completed the set. Lining up against his fiercest rivals, Christie again triumphed, taking the gold and setting his fastest-ever time. At the end of 1993, he was voted BBC Sports Personality of the Year. Although he was unable to retain the world title in 1995, being hampered by a hamstring injury, or the Olympic title in 1996, when he false-started twice, he continues his involvement with athletics, training stars such as Jamie Baulch and Darren Campbell.

Opposite: a victorious Linford Christie flying his country's flag after taking the 100 m gold, in the Stuttgart World Championships.

Right: Britain's Linford Christie warming up at the 1993 World Championships in Stuttgart.

1997
Coe's 800 m record finally beaten

7 July 1997 – Wilson Kipketer running to victory for Denmark at Stockholm's Olympic stadium.

ON 5 JULY 1979 IN OSLO, Sebastian Coe ran the 800 m in a world-record time of 1 minute 42.33 seconds. He smashed the record held by Cuba's Olympic champion Alberto Juantorena by a full second. Two years later in Florence, the prodigiously talented Briton

brought the record down again, this time by more than a half-second to 1 minute 41.73 seconds. His record was to stand for a further 16 years, defying all comers until August 1997. Wilson Kipketer, a Kenyan-born 24-year-old running for Denmark, finally ended Coe's term as world-record holder.

The nearest anyone had came to lowering the record before Kipketer was Brazil's Olympic champion Joaquim Cruz, who in Cologne in August 1984 had run 1 minute 41.77 seconds, making him only the second man in history to clock a time under 1 minute 42 seconds. A decade later, Kipketer became the third. Incredibly, after breaking the record in Zürich with a time of 1 minute 41.24 seconds, Kipketer broke it again in the same month, lowering it to an amazing 1 minute 41.11 seconds. Given his age, he looks set to break the record several more times yet. Steve Cram, the former British world champion at 1500 m, has predicted that Kipketer could be the first man to run under 1 minute 40 seconds.

Kipketer's running potential was spotted when he was only 10 years old. Kenya's 1968 1500-m Olympic champion, Kip Keino, was the first to recognize his promise. But his chance of an athletics career was almost lost before it started. Keino recommended him to the Irish priest, Father Colm O'Connell, who runs St Patrick's school in Kenya's Rift Valley, a school which has nurtured many world-class runners. Keino could not afford to sponsor the young Kipketer because of his commitments to other young stars, and it was only because the boy helped to paint the school during the summer holidays that he was allowed to stay. In 1990, he went to Copenhagen as an exchange student and was made to feel so welcome that he never left. This arrangement was to lead to disappointment, however. Despite being world 800-m champion, he was banned from running for Denmark in the 1996 Olympics because he was not yet a Danish citizen.

He put disappointment behind him in 1997. Having smashed Coe's record in Zürich, he said, 'everything was perfect – the weather, the pace, the crowd', but added ominously that he was 'satisfied – for now'. A few weeks later, however, he proved that his thirst for breaking the world record remained undiminished. Already he has run the second-highest number of 800-m times under 1 minute 45 seconds. It is surely only a matter of time before he breaks that record as well.

1997
Bailey or Johnson? The Great Debate

The controversial head-to-head race between Canadian Donovan Bailey and American Michael Johnson in June 1997 was intended to put an end to the long-running rivalry between the two sprinters, and answer the fundamental question: which of these two was the world's fastest man?

During the 1996 Atlanta Olympics, both athletes had fulfilled their quest for glory and indisputably established themselves as the greatest runners of their time. In July 1996, Bailey smashed the world record for 100 m with a time of 9.84 seconds. In the 4 x 100 m relay, with fellow Canadians Robert Esmie, Glenroy Gilbert and Bruny Surin, he provided a storming finish to the race, taking his team to gold. Just five days later Bailey's arch-rival, Michael Johnson took the gold, and the world record, for the 200 m, clocking 19.32 seconds.

The arguments began to rage. They were both fast, but who was the fastest? Canada and the US locked horns, each country convinced its own star could lay claim to the title. The only way to find out was to run a one-on-one hybrid race of 150 m.

The setting was the SkyDome in Toronto, giving Bailey the advantage of home support. 25,000 fans gathered to encourage their national hero, certain of his eventual victory. The atmosphere was electric, the tension between the runners unprecedented. The race started. It was over in five seconds. Johnson pulled up injured before the race was even half-run, and Bailey crossed the line alone. The controversy began before the two men had even left the track. Was Johnson really injured? Bailey had certainly looked the most likely victor and he wasn't the only one to suggest that Johnson had thrown it. Whatever the truth, the outcome of the race had satisfied no one, and the rivalry between the runners increased.

The World Championships, held in Athens just a few weeks later, brought further success for both: Johnson winning the 400 m and Bailey taking the gold as part of the 4 x 100 m relay, although he only achieved silver in the 100 m. Both men continue to prove themselves the heroes of their individual events, but the debate is unresolved. The talk of a rematch, and public enthusiasm for one, must eventually result in a race that will decide once and for all who is the Fastest Man on Earth.

Bailey's sprint success restored athletic pride to Canada.

Michael Johnson about to win the
400 m at the World
Championships, 5 August, 1997.

1997
Golden Johnson

MICHAEL JOHNSON – 'SUPERMAN' – is one of the most incredible athletes the world has ever seen. The fastest man in the world over 200 m and 400 m, a double Olympic champion, triple world champion, and double world-record holder, his supremacy is unquestioned. His unique running style, that seems to break every rule in the book, making him appear as if he is running leaning back, makes him an even more fascinating performer. Currently, he is arguably the world's best-known athlete and certainly track-and-field's biggest draw.

This claim is borne out by the events of the 1997 World Championships held in Athens and Johnson's controversial appearance there. The 30-year-old from Dallas, Texas, had not been selected for the American team, after injury had forced him to withdraw from the US trials in Indianapolis, Indiana. The strict American qualifying rules, which decree that only the first three in the trials qualify for the championships, left Johnson out of the team and the world without one of its biggest athletes at one of its biggest tournaments. That proved no problem for the International Athletic Federation's president, Primo Nebiolo, however. Nebiolo gave the talented American a wild-card entry to the championships to run the 400-m event, by creating a rule that every defending champion should be allowed to compete at the World Championships even if they had not qualified for their national team. Other athletes were furious, but Johnson was allowed to go to Athens to defend the title he had won in Gothenborg in 1995. 'It's good for me and it's good for athletics,' he declared.

Johnson did not let Nebiolo down. Despite almost failing to qualify in one of the heats, and amidst accusations that he was not taking the tournament seriously enough as he went straight from the track to his place in an American TV commentary booth, Johnson defended his title successfully. He won the final in a time of 44.12 seconds, passing the Ugandan athlete Davis Kamoga, who led for much of the race and who clocked 44.37 seconds. Johnson, the man who had not qualified for the US team, was now the world champion for the second

time. To celebrate, he did a lap of honour waving a Superman shirt in the air. 'People used to say Michael Johnson can only win from the front, but I showed I can win from the back, from any place on the track. I can be good when I'm good and good when I'm bad,' he said. This performance came just a year after two world-record runs at the Atlanta Olympics, when he took the gold medal in both the 200 m and 400 m.

Michael Johnson showing off his superman shirt at the 1997 World Championships in Athens.

Boxing

3

If I can't beat this bum, take my name off the record books. **Jersey Joe Walcott** before losing to Rocky Marciano in 1952.

1919
The Champ throws in the towel:
Willard v Dempsey

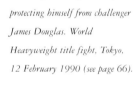

JACK DEMPSEY, one of the greatest heavyweights of all time, first claimed the world title which was to be his for the next seven years on 4 July 1919.

Born in Manassa, Colorado, in 1895, the son of Mormons who had migrated west from Virginia, Dempsey derived his famous ring-name, 'The Manassa Mauler', from the little-known town of his birth. Jess Willard was almost 15 years older than Dempsey when they met to contest the title, which Willard had held since 1915, having only defended it once due to America's entry into the First World War. Dempsey, in contrast, had spent the previous few years working his way up from boxing booths and back-room bouts and was hungry for the title.

After much haggling between the fighters' managers, it was agreed that the fight would take place in the Toledo Arena in Ohio. Sources put the crowd at anywhere between 20,000 and 45,000, and whilst there is no denying that they were in for a

great fight, few expected it to go the distance. A surprisingly light boxer for the heavyweight division, Dempsey hovered around 83 kg (13 stone 4 lb) for most of his career. Willard, in contrast, weighed in at over 108 kg (17 stone). The comparison between the fighters' reaches is as surprising as that between their weights. The best Dempsey could manage was 192 cm (77 in), whereas Willard's fists could reach out an impressive 210 cm (83 in).

Despite his weight and reach handicaps, Dempsey set about the hapless Willard like a man possessed, moving with the speed of a featherweight but punching like a steam-hammer. Willard had no answer for this whirlwind of punches and simply stood there whilst Dempsey pummelled him with punch after telling punch. After only two minutes of the first round, Willard's face was a mask of blood with deep cuts opened above both eyes and a badly broken nose. More punches landed, splitting his lip before a right to his jaw sent him down to the canvas. This was the first time Willard had been there in his entire professional career! There was nowhere else for him to go, and he hit the floor six more times before the first round was over. Referee Ollie Pecord raised Dempsey's hand only to discover that the bell had sounded, saving Willard from a first-round defeat.

An inexperienced Dempsey let Willard recover a little in the second round, but when the fighters came out for the third he destroyed Willard with a violence rarely seen in the ring. By the time Willard's corner threw in the towel at the end of the third, the crowd were chanting 'Stop it, stop it!' In just nine minutes, Dempsey had become one of the most famous names in America!

Overleaf: a sweaty Mike Tyson protecting himself from challenger James Douglas. World Heavyweight title fight, Tokyo, 12 February 1990 (see page 66).

Below: Jack Dempsey bringing down Jess Willard on 4 July 1919, in Toledo, Ohio.

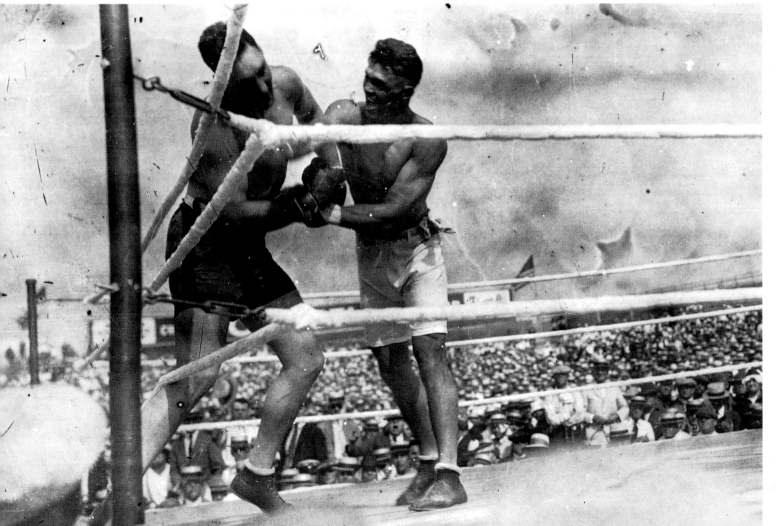

1923
The 'Wild Bull' fights back:
Dempsey v Firpo

SINCE WINNING THE WORLD TITLE in 1919, Jack Dempsey had defended it only four times. The first three fights had all been won inside the distance, but the fourth, against Tom Gibbons, had been a bruising affair that had gone the whole way. That bout occurred just two months before one of Dempsey's most remarkable fights.

Luis Angel Firpo, nicknamed 'Wild Bull of the Pampas', was a huge fighter from Argentina, and whilst generally regarded as having little boxing brain, he was blessed with an enormous punch. In advance of the match, held at the New York Polo Grounds, no one gave Firpo much of a chance. They were all very nearly proved wrong.

In his years as champion, Dempsey had become a very popular draw, and close to 85,000 spectators turned up to watch what they expected would be a walk-over, the only real speculation being on how long it would take Dempsey to knock his opponent out. On the bell, Dempsey came out of his corner and, as was his style, set about Firpo with a vengeance. But where his previous opponents had reeled back, Firpo stood his ground and twice in the first minute caught Dempsey with swinging rights to the head and body. The second of these attacks brought Dempsey to his knees and left him hanging on to Firpo with both gloves. This humiliation seemed to bring the American to his senses. Back on his feet, he moved in close and got Firpo with a left hook, dumping him straight on the canvas. Firpo got straight up and blundered back towards Dempsey, who promptly delivered a smart upper cut which put him back down again. In an amazing sequence of events, Firpo was floored no less than five times in quick succession, each time bouncing back to his feet like a Jack-in-the-box. The crowd was already going wild when the unthinkable happened. Firpo suddenly lunged towards his tormentor and with an enormous swing brought his right fist crashing through Dempsey's guard to impact squarely on the champ's jaw. Dempsey's feet were lifted clear off the canvas as he fell back through the ropes and out of the ring.

No doubt stunned by these events, the referee did not seem to notice the pack of ringside reporters helping Dempsey back into the ring, something which should have seen him instantly dis-

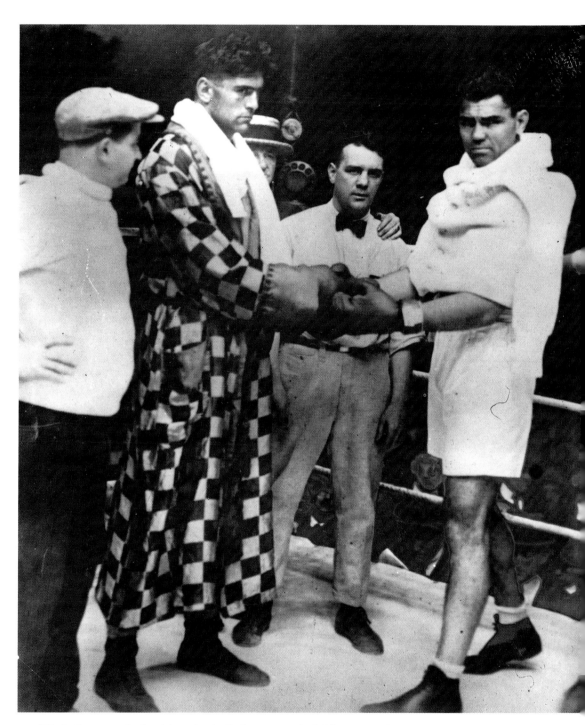

qualified. Fortunately for him, the bell then sounded. The second round lasted just 57 seconds, during 10 of which Firpo lay flat on the deck, having given his all and found it wanting.

This was Dempsey's last successful defence, although he would remain champion for three more years.

Luis Angel Firpo and Jack Dempsey shaking hands before their big fight in September 1923.

1938
This is personal:
Louis v Schmeling

JOSEPH LOUIS BARROW was born in 1914 in a small cabin in the cotton country of Lexington, Alabama. Brought up by loving parents in abject poverty, he recognized early on that boxing offered a way out.

By the time he was 19 years old, Barrow had won the Golden Gloves of America title at light-heavyweight. He promptly turned professional. It took Louis (he had by now dropped the name Barrow) just three short years to climb the ladder to the world championship, losing just once on the way, when he was knocked out by one Max Schmeling in the 12th round of their 1934 bout. In 1937, Louis won the world heavyweight title from James Braddock with an eighth-round knockout. Despite being severely tested by the Welshman Tommy Farr two months later, Louis, now known affectionately as the 'Brown Bomber', held on to his title.

Two title fights later, the inevitable bout took place. Schmeling had felt aggrieved that he had not been given a chance to challenge Braddock for the title himself. This, coupled with the fact that Schmeling was a strong supporter of Hitler and the Nazis, meant that the fight was going to be a humdinger. Louis, who hardly ever took anything personally, hated Schmeling, who had been saying some very unpleasant things about him in the media. Not only that, Schmeling was the only person to have beaten him, and that had to be avenged!

The big fight finally took place in New York, but the proceedings were not destined to last long. As soon as the bell sounded, Louis went after Schmeling like a man possessed and quickly put three quick jabs into his opponent's face, followed by a right to the body. Schmeling staggered back into the ropes and was caught by another right hook to the body, forcing an involuntary shriek of pain. For the next two minutes, Louis stood over his opponent and battered him practically senseless, sending Schmeling to the canvas twice. In desperation, the German covered up and turned away from Louis, receiving a swinging body blow in the left kidney as he did so. The referee had seen enough and stopped the fight with the clock on 2 minutes 4 seconds, declaring Louis the winner.

To the ardent Nazi, defeat by Louis was unthinkable, and much to his shame he complained bitterly that the champion had fouled him by punching his kidneys. No doubt worried by what an embarrassed Führer might do, he was still cowering on his stretcher when he was carried off the ship in Hamburg several weeks later.

Louis defended his title a total of 25 times, more than any other boxer. From a personal point of view, his win over Schmeling was probably the most satisfying.

1934: Joseph Louis Barrow slumbering on the canvas while referee Arthur Donovan gestures 'lights out'. Max Schmeling can be seen exultant in the background.

1951
A shock win, a gallant defence:
Robinson v Turpin

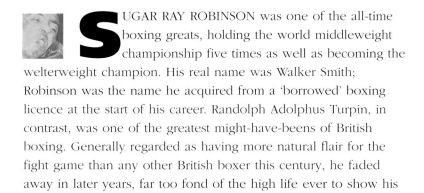

SUGAR RAY ROBINSON was one of the all-time boxing greats, holding the world middleweight championship five times as well as becoming the welterweight champion. His real name was Walker Smith; Robinson was the name he acquired from a 'borrowed' boxing licence at the start of his career. Randolph Adolphus Turpin, in contrast, was one of the greatest might-have-beens of British boxing. Generally regarded as having more natural flair for the fight game than any other British boxer this century, he faded away in later years, far too fond of the high life ever to show his

best. But he was at the peak of his powers when he met the great Sugar Ray Robinson.

Robinson had lost only once since turning professional in 1940. This single defeat, inflicted by the great Jake 'The Bronx Bull' LaMotta, had been avenged when Robinson took his middleweight crown in 1951, in a fight remembered as the 'Saint Valentine's Day Massacre'. Just a few months later, at the end of a seven-fight European tour, Robinson came to Wembley Stadium, London, to fight Turpin for the middle-weight title. Despite fighting on his home turf, Turpin was not expected to win. Robinson, at the time regarded as unbeatable, had fought eight days earlier in an Italian exhibition match.

Strange things can happen in the ring, though. Cheered on by a full house of 18,000, the deadpan Turpin carried out a masterful piece of boxing strategy and out-pointed a flabbergasted Robinson with considerable ease. It was almost as if Robinson was asleep. The fight was a classic example of an underdog victory, and Britain went wild, as did Robinson and his management, but in a rather different way. No doubt because the rest of the world still regarded Robinson as the champion, despite his defeat by this virtual unknown, a rematch was arranged in double-quick time – in America.

Just 64 days later, the two boxers met again in the New York Polo Ground, this time in front of 61,370. Much to everyone's surprise, Turpin continued to have the slight advantage and by the ninth round had cut Robinson into the bargain. Perhaps spurred on by the taste of blood, Robinson dug deep into his reserves; putting together a wicked combination, he finally put Turpin down in the tenth with a left hook. Turpin staggered to his feet almost on the count of 10, but after another 30 seconds the referee, Ruby Goldstein, stepped in and stopped the fight, despite Turpin's protestations. There was some controversy over the decision, which many viewed as being premature. However, just the previous week a young fighter had died in the ring, and caution was very much the watchword.

Robinson was to go on for nearly another 10 years at the top level. Turpin, who had promised so much, never recaptured his top form.

American Sugar Ray Robinson regaining the world middleweight championship from Britain's Randolph Turpin.

1952
The end of the road:
Jersey Joe Walcott v Rocky Marciano

UNLIKE MANY OF THE FIGHTS described here, this bout was a gruelling battle which went almost the whole distance. Walcott, the defending champion in this world heavyweight contest, for many years held a record as the oldest boxer to become world champion (he was 37 at the time). His road to the world crown had been a slow and arduous one with more than a few setbacks, as can be deduced from the fact that out of 72 fights he lost no less than 18.

Rocky Marciano's was a very different story. It has often been said that all you need to know about Marciano is 49–0 – that is, 49 victories out of 49 fights, 46 of which had been knockouts. At 1.77 m (5 ft 10 in) and 83 kg (13 stone), he was small for a top-class heavyweight, and surprisingly slow as well. What he lacked in size he more than made up for in power, aggression and the ability to take a punch.

In the run-up to the fight, Marciano came out as the favourite, despite a famous quote from Walcott: 'If I can't beat this bum, take my name off the record books.' When the fighters met, Walcott was 38 years old and Marciano 29. Marciano weighed in at 82 kg (6 stone) to Walcott's 87 kg (14 stone). Despite Walcott's wealth of experience, the fight was not expected to go the distance. Everyone was amazed, then, when in the first round Walcott caught Marciano with a left hook and sent him slumping to the floor. This was the first time that he had been on the canvas, and despite shouts from his corner to take an eight count, Marciano was up in three. The bout now turned into a real brawl, Walcott scoring consistently with solid shots and Marciano swarming all over him swinging away like a madman.

Despite withstanding everything that Walcott was throwing at him, Marciano was not scoring enough on his own account. By the 12th round, it was apparent that the only way

he could win would be by stopping or by knocking out his opponent. In the 13th and final round, Marciano continued to look for that one winning punch and at last found his opportunity. Walcott backed away from an attack on to the ropes, momentarily dropping his guard and allowing Marciano to deliver one of the hardest punches ever thrown in a world championship. Walcott slumped backwards on to the ropes and down to the floor and was out cold for several minutes.

Marciano went on to make six successful defences of his title before being forced to quit due to a recurring back injury. The first of these, a rematch against the ever-keen Walcott, ended in a humiliating first-round knockout for the former champion that signalled the end of Jersey Joe's career.

Above: a determined Rocky Marciano giving a pounding to Jersey Joe Walcott in 1952.

Opposite: a portrait of Rocky Marciano showing his undefeated fists, taken in August 1953.

1963
The crowd's favourite floors the Louisville Lip:
Cooper v Clay

THIS WAS THE FIGHT which set Muhammad Ali, or Cassius Clay as he was then, on the road to challenging Sonny Liston for the heavyweight championship of the world. It was also the fight in which Henry Cooper dumped Clay on the canvas, with Clay being saved from defeat only by the timely intervention of the bell!

Cassius Marcellus Clay was just 22 years old when he went to London to face Henry Cooper at Wembley Stadium. Having first come to public notice when he won the US amateur light-heavyweight title aged 18, he went on to win the Olympic title in 1960, turning professional straight afterwards. 'The Louisville Lip' soon acquired a reputation for being as quick with his wits and his tongue as he was on his feet. Clay's repartee made him a big draw at any fight and also helped to unnerve many weaker-willed opponents. By the time he had compiled eight straight wins, Clay was starting to predict the round in which he would beat his opponent. Much to many people's annoyance, he got it right nearly all the time.

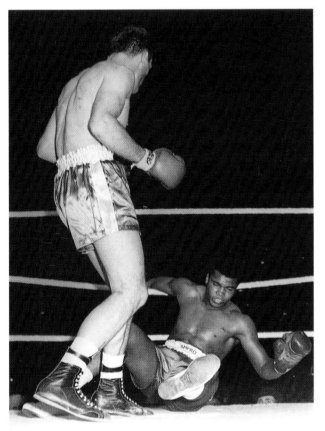

Left: Cassius Clay crashing to the canvas after a hefty blow from Cooper in the fourth round.

Right: British challenger Cooper with a badly cut eye – it caused the referee to stop the fight.

So it was that Clay went to London to take on Henry Cooper, promptly prophesying, 'After all the jive, Cooper will fall in five'. Clay had now amassed 18 straight victories, quite a record. Cooper, however, was no push-over and had the distinct advantage of fighting in front of his home crowd.

The fight itself was scheduled for 10 rounds and proceeded without much incident until the closing seconds of round four. Cooper's favourite left hook arced out and caught Clay squarely in the face, sending him collapsing into the ropes. A roar rose from the Wembley crowd fit to raise the roof! Clay struggled to his feet on the count of four, but was suffering and desperately trying to cover up as Cooper closed for the kill when the bell went for the end of the round.

Over in Clay's corner, his second, the hugely experienced Angelo Dundee, now took a hand, literally, in shaping history. There was a small tear in one of Clay's gloves which needed minor attention. Dundee later admitted to making this tear worse, so that a new glove had to be found. This delay gave Clay time to recover, and he came out for round five like a new man. Cooper absorbed all that Clay could throw at him, but unfortunately his suspect eyebrows, not for the first time, proved his undoing. A cut which appeared over his left eye forced the referee to stop the fight. Clay's prediction proved half-right, and he was on his way to his first championship. But for that bell, things might have been different.

1971
The Fight:
Ali v Frazier

FOR THE FIRST TIME in the history of professional boxing, two undefeated world heavyweight champions were matched for the world title. Each boxer was to receive the then unheard-of purse of $2.5 million and the fight would be watched by a worldwide audience of 300 million!

Joe Frazier had become world champion while Muhammad Ali was absent from the ring fighting to avoid the Vietnam draft on religious grounds. Frazier was 27 years old, two years younger than Ali, and had won all 26 of his professional fights, only three of them even going the distance. Ali was very rusty after his enforced absence.

On the night of the fight, the ring in Madison Square Garden, New York, was surrounded by a who's who of boxing. Ali was being his normal self, taunting and jibing at Frazier. The early rounds saw Ali dancing around the ring using his familiar jab, with Frazier stalking him and ignoring every blow. When these tactics failed, Ali started to lie back on the ropes, hoping that Frazier would wear himself out. By the time the eighth round arrived, Ali looked all in and took a real thumping blow from Frazier's left hook. It appeared to be pretty much over in the

ninth until Ali suddenly unleashed a volley of blows that sent Frazier reeling backwards to be saved only by the bell.

Both fighters continued to batter each other despite their obvious exhaustion, and it became clear that it was Frazier who was leading on points. The drama was not over, however. Frazier, despite his fatigue, caught Ali with a left hook and dumped him unceremoniously on the canvas. Ali managed to get back up before the count of 10 and, backing away, saw out the round, but it was Frazier who was the clear points winner in the fight. Ali's jaw swelled up to gigantic proportions, and indeed both fighters ended up in hospital.

Before the fight, Ali had said, 'If I loose, I'll crawl across the ring and say, "You're the real champ of the world"'. In a telling testimony to the ferocity of the encounter, Frazier grabbed Ali a few moments after the final decision and said to him, 'You fought one hell of a fight ... You don't have to do no crawling.' Back in his dressing room, Ali made it clear that he wanted a return match. As it happened, there were to be two more fights with Frazier, both of which went to Ali, and both of which were violent and bloody affairs. Ali v Frazier fights were always thrillers. This one was so famous in its time that it was called, simply, 'The Fight'.

***Top**: Joe Frazier versus Muhammad Ali in 'The Fight', Madison Square Garden, New York.*

***Bottom**: Ali punched to the floor by a heated Frazier – Ali was soon up on his feet again.*

1973
Gone in two: Frazier v Foreman

GEORGE FOREMAN, born into poverty in Texas in 1948, was, at just under 2 m (6 ft 4 in), a giant of a boxer. Although he dropped out of school at 14, it was not until he was 18 that he first put on a pair of boxing gloves, though from then on he hardly looked back. Winning the Olympic heavyweight title in 1968, he turned professional in 1969 and won all of the 38 fights he had before his 1973 meeting with Joe Frazier.

Frazier, who had held the world title since 1968, had also been the Olympic champion in 1964. Despite being physically a smaller man, he had the advantage of experience, and with Foreman rated at 3–1 was very much favourite to win.

The fight took place at the National Stadium in Kingston, Jamaica. As soon as the bell sounded for the first round, Frazier came bounding out of his corner just as he always did. Foreman simply stood his ground, and an enormous fight erupted in the centre of the ring. Frazier, who had a distinct disadvantage in reach, tried to punch his way towards Foreman, but was kept at bay by a constant barrage of long punches. Foreman then appeared to take deliberate aim with a clubbing right which smashed into Frazier's jaw and sent him to the canvas. Frazier rose on two, but looked distinctly wobbly for the standing eight count. Seemingly unaffected, Frazier pushed forward again and caught Foreman with a few hard blows, but with apparently no effect on the giant Texan. The round finally came to an end with Foreman very much on top.

The second round commenced much as the first had. Frazier exploded out of his corner, but managed only to tumble straight into a stinging two-punch combination which again sent him on to the deck. This time, he stayed there for all of the eight count. From then on, he was in a daze; unaware of what was going on, he was sent to the ground for a fifth time. Battered and bleeding, Joe Frazier had become a pathetic sight.

By now, even Foreman was begging Frazier to stay down, but despite all this he somehow managed to drag himself to his feet for the sixth time, though mercifully the referee stopped the fight just 35 seconds later. It was just 1 minute 35 seconds into the second round! After the fight was over, Frazier made what must be one of the biggest under-statements ever in boxing: 'We were fooled into thinking it would be easy.... I guess we underrated him'. Both fighters' careers continued. Foreman held the world title for just over 18 months.

Left: Joe Frazier ready to face George Foreman in Kingston, Jamaica, 1973.

Right: George Foreman began boxing at the age of 18, just two years later, he won the Olympic heavyweight title.

Opposite: George Foreman, a giant of a fighter who measured 2 m (6 ft 4 in), towering over his opponent, Joe Frazier.

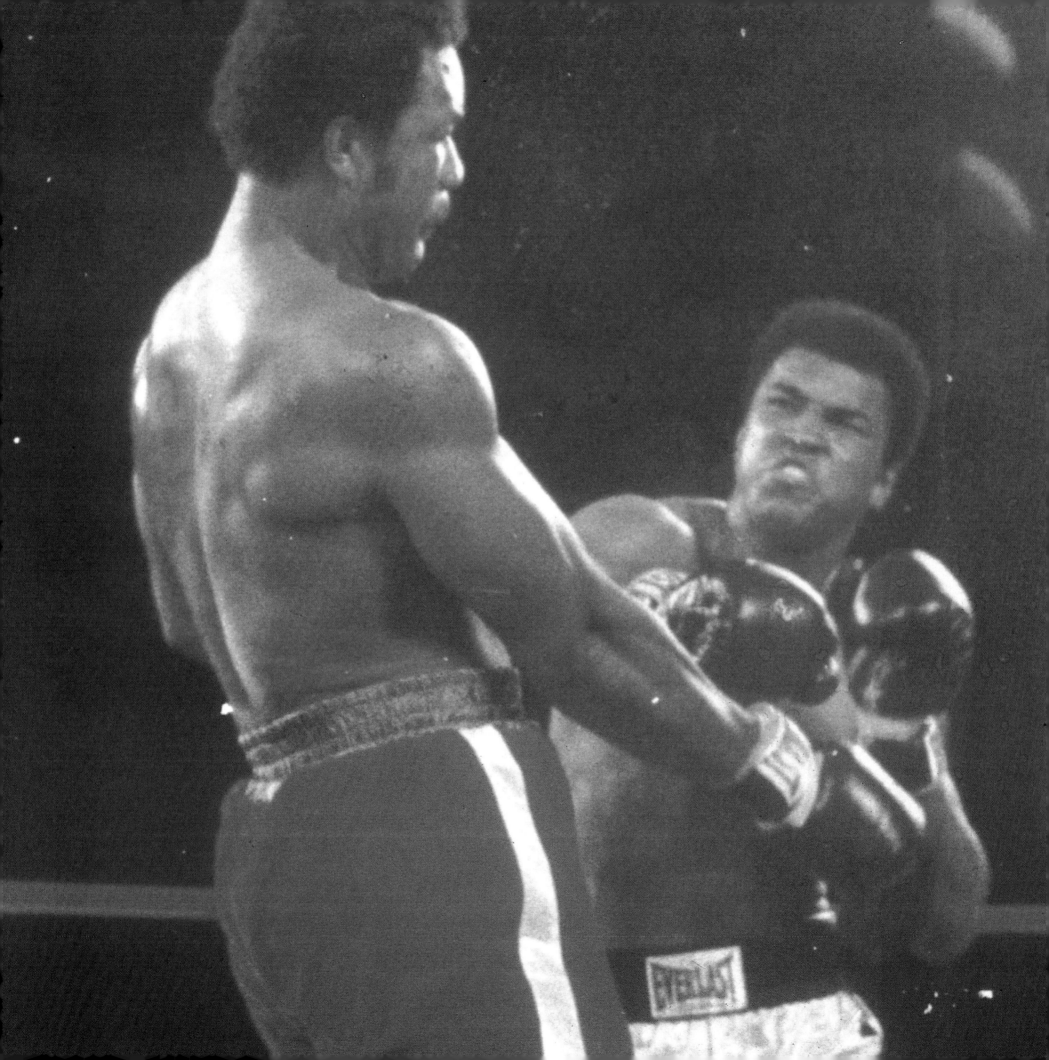

1974
The Rumble in the Jungle:
Ali v Foreman

NO MATTER WHICH WAY you look at it, this fight has to be one of the most remarkable in the history of boxing.

To start with, there was the location. The stadium was built in what amounted to a jungle clearing just outside Kinshasa, the capital of Zaire. President Mobutu of Zaire took a personal hand in the promotion of the fight.

Despite the fact that George Foreman was the reigning world champion, Muhammad Ali's popularity was the driving force behind the bout, with the government of Zaire agreeing to put up $12 million only if Ali was the title challenger.

In the run-up to the fight, many of those claiming to be in the know fancied Foreman, a fighter with an enormous punch who had victoriously completed his last eight bouts in only 15 rounds! Ali, despite the adulation of the general public, was 32 years old, late middle age in boxing terms.

Just eight days before the bout was due to commence, Foreman suffered a cut eye during a sparring session, forcing the postponement of the fight for five weeks, which at least gave both boxers time to acclimatize to the incredible heat and humidity. When the fight finally started, it was 4.00 in the morning, a time chosen so that the maximum peak-time TV audience could be reached worldwide. For $5 million each, neither of the boxers was about to complain. The local populace were solidly behind Ali for the whole fight, chanting after each round, 'Ali! Ali! Bomba-ya!' or 'Ali! Ali! Kill him!'.

For a fighter renowned for being light on his feet, Ali was surprisingly sluggish. Everyone had expected him to try to avoid Foreman's huge punches, but it seemed that he was trying to do just the opposite, forever edging back to the ropes whilst Foreman threw in punch after punch. All the time this was going on, Ali kept taunting Foreman about his 'light punches'. Quite how Ali survived these blows remains a mystery, since although he managed to block most of them, his body still absorbed an enormous amount of punishment without noticeable effect.

As the fight progressed, the apparent failure of his punches and the draining heat began to have their effect on Foreman, and by the eighth round he was almost dead on his feet. Ali, on the other hand, who had spent much of the fight in comparative inactivity, was suddenly his old self. Bouncing off the ropes, he caught Foreman squarely on the chin with a crashing right fist. Foreman managed to get off the canvas on the count of 10, but the fight was stopped anyway. Ali was once more back where he belonged as champion of the world.

Opposite: Muhammad Ali and George Foreman in their famous 'Rumble in the Jungle', Zaire, 1974.

Left: David and Goliath: the comparatively diminutive Muhammad Ali faces an enormous George Foreman.

1985
Marvellous Marvin KOs the Hitman:
Hagler v Hearns

 MARVIN HAGLER, WHO INCIDENTALLY had his name legally changed to Marvellous shortly before this fight, was another of the great middleweights. Born in Newark, New Jersey, in 1954, he lost only two fights in his entire career. Hagler started his climb to the top when he won the American Athletics Union's national tournament at 18 and promptly turned professional the following week. By 1980, he had become undisputed world middleweight champion, defeating Britain's Alan Minter in just two rounds.

At more or less the same time, Hearns was making his way up the ladder, winning his first 17 fights by knockouts. Born in Michigan in 1958, this self-confessed 'skinny kid who got fed up with being bullied' came within a whisker of dethroning the great Sugar Ray Leonard from his world welterweight title. Moving up to super welterweight, he took the World Boxing Council title in 1982. By 1985, the inevitable was about to happen. Hagler and Hearns, the two toughest kids on the block, just had to see who was best.

The fight was arranged to be held in Las Vegas, Nevada, and from the moment Hagler muttered 'Hit Man, my ass', the world was in for a brutal spectacle. After a few seconds where both fighters just stood and stared at each other, a fight erupted in the centre of the ring the likes of which is rarely seen, and with neither boxer paying much attention to defence the injuries came quickly. Within seconds, Hagler received a cut over his eye, and for three solid minutes the two men pummelled each other without pausing for breath, willed on by the crowd, who were on their feet, howling for blood. It was not a dignified spectacle.

The second round continued in the same vein, with Hagler just gaining the ascendancy despite being caught by several telling punches from Hearns. In the third round, Hearns at last started to try boxing rather than fighting and managed to put together a few useful combinations. Several jabs reached Hagler's already injured eye, and Richard Steel, the referee, stopped the fight for a doctor's inspection. Perhaps intimidated by Hagler's snarling, the doctor indicated that the fight could continue. Probably aware that this injury would ultimately put him out of the fight, Hagler set about bringing the proceedings to a close. Hearns allowed himself to brawl with Hagler rather than use his skill. It took another two minutes for Hagler to destroy Hearns, who collapsed on to the canvas.

Sugar Ray Leonard and Marvellous Marvin Hagler in Las Vegas, April 1987.

This fight was far from the end of Hearns's professional career; he went on to hold the world light-heavyweight title. Hagler, of course, was destined to meet the great Sugar Ray Leonard in 1987

1987
Sugar Ray's finest day:
Leonard v Hagler

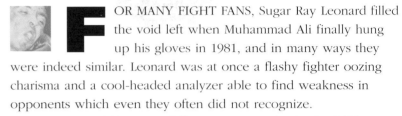 **F**OR MANY FIGHT FANS, Sugar Ray Leonard filled the void left when Muhammad Ali finally hung up his gloves in 1981, and in many ways they were indeed similar. Leonard was at once a flashy fighter oozing charisma and a cool-headed analyzer able to find weakness in opponents which even they often did not recognize.

Born in 1952, Leonard first came to notice in the 1976 Olympic Games, where he won a gold medal before turning professional. From there, he acquired the world welterweight title in 1979. By 1981, he had moved into the middleweight division and promptly won that title as well. In a remarkable seesawing of weights, he returned to welterweight to reacquire the title from Tommy Hearns.

There followed a remarkable series of retirements and comebacks, with a problematic and recurring detached retina giving cause for concern. During nearly three years of inactivity between 1984 and 1987, another remarkable fighter, one Marvellous Marvin Hagler, rose to prominence in the middleweight division. There can have been few better examples of 'chalk and cheese' than Leonard and

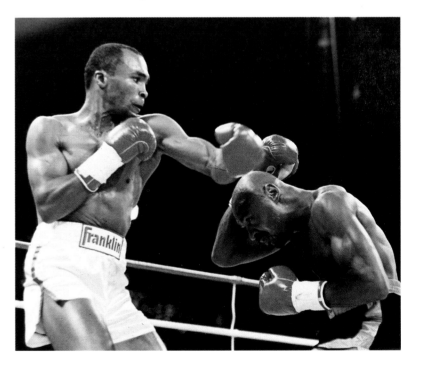

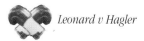

Hagler: Leonard, the sparkling and charismatic showman, and Hagler, the shaven-headed bruiser who had amassed no less than 52 knockouts out of 67 fights by the end of his career. Both were great boxers, and with hindsight it was inevitable that they had to meet, in what was to be one of the most controversial fights of the 1980s.

In the run-up to the fight, Hagler was enjoying the reputation of being unbeatable; indeed, he had not been defeated in over 11 years and was an odds-on favourite to win. In typical style, Leonard told his own critics, 'The reason I will win is because you don't think I can' – now you can't say fairer than that!

Surprisingly for a man with Hagler's reputation and history, he started the Las Vegas fight rather slowly and lost the first four rounds. At the end of the fifth, however, Hagler caught Leonard

on the ropes and was severely punishing him when the bell went. Leonard, however, continued with his containing tactics, doing his best to irritate Hagler, even sticking his head out and challenging Hagler to try and knock it off! Although Hagler came back strongly in the eighth and ninth rounds, Leonard survived everything thrown at him.

By the end of the fight, Leonard's clever tactics had paid off, and he won by a split decision, though a ridiculous score of 118–110 by one judge added fuel to what was already a controversial result. If ever there had been a fight which demanded a rematch, it was this one. But it was not to be. Leonard steadfastly refused, and Hagler retired in frustration. Sugar Ray, who was declared Boxer of the Decade in the 1980s, himself retired shortly thereafter.

A rematch was expected, but not forthcoming. Leonard and Hagler retired from the sport soon afterwards.

1990
Against the odds: Tyson v Douglas

 WHEN MIKE TYSON met James 'Buster' Douglas to defend his undisputed heavyweight crown, he had never lost a professional fight and was generally regarded as being unbeatable.

It is not surprising, then, that no one except Douglas and his team gave the underdog any chance at all. However, all was not well in the Tyson camp. He was now without Bill Cayton, his long-term manager, and had recently gone through acrimonious divorce proceedings. There was also a suggestion that Tyson was not quite as hungry as he had been and was beginning to slacken up on his training. Douglas, a polite and likeable person, had until recently been a carpet delivery man and was keen as mustard. His mother died shortly before the fight, an event which Douglas later admitted spurred him to even greater efforts to win the championship, if not for himself then for her.

On the day of the fight, it was possible to get odds of 42–1 on Douglas; some perceptive people were going to make a lot of money that night! By this time, a few boxing journalists had spotted that Tyson was not his old self, but hardly any of them could have foreseen what would happen.

Tyson started the fight as he always did, but Douglas spoiled every attack by pre-empting it. After five rounds, all of them won by Douglas, Tyson's left eye was cut. Unfortunately, his corner-men seemed to have forgotten the small metal device they used to reduce swelling and had instead to apply a condom filled with ice-water! Mistakes like this would never have occurred when Cayton was in charge.

Things continued in Douglas's favour until round eight, when against the flow Tyson landed a beautiful right which sent his opponent to the floor. Douglas was up on the eight count, immediately setting about Tyson again. Don King, Tyson's manager, was already screaming for the fight to be stopped, claiming that the referee was counting too slowly. Had his boy been winning, the time would no doubt have flown by! As it was, Tyson was only saved from defeat in the ninth round by the bell.

Just past the minute in the tenth, Douglas launched a devastating five-punch combination which sent Tyson to the deck. Obviously unaware of what was going on, he struggled to his feet, but was waved out by the referee. Douglas's first words at

James 'Buster' Douglas knocks down Mike Tyson as Tyson struggles to regain his heavyweight crown.

the end of the fight were 'My Mother, God bless her heart'.

Douglas had won ... or had he? Replay of the tape showed that Douglas had been down for 13 seconds, and Tyson had been down for 14 seconds! Ugly wrangling continued for a few days before Douglas was given the recognition he so rightly deserved.

*Tyson attempts to defend himself
from the Douglas onslaught –
Tyson lost in the tenth round.*

4 Cricket

That's not a six, it's a twelve.
TV commentator **Peter Walker**
on the last of Sir Garfield Sobers'
six sixes in an over against
Glamorgan in 1968.

1930

Don Bradman: A quite magnificent year

 MANY CRICKETERS might be thought of as the greatest. However, few have stood the test of time quite like Donald George Bradman, the jewel in Australia's cricketing crown for over 20 years.

Bradman's career batting figures speak for themselves: an all-time average of 95.14 and a Test average of 99.94, all-time records in both categories. Bradman missed out on a Test career average of 100 by just four runs! His top scores are equally impressive, with a first-class record of 452 and a Test record of 334.

Bradman made his international debut in 1928, but it was the 1930 season which made him a superstar. Things started off well when he set a record which still stands. In the domestic Australian league, he scored no fewer than six double centuries, four of them in consecutive games, beating a record which had stood since 1900. Then came a trip to England and a Test series against the old enemy. An unsuspecting England was in for a shock.

The conditions in England were damp that year, something the Australian batsmen were not used to. England had a strong and experienced side, enjoyed the advantage of playing at home and were also the defending champions. The first Test at Nottingham had been won without too much trouble – what could go wrong?

It was a different story at Lord's. Bradman made a splendid 254 out of a mammoth Australian total of 729 for 6 and set up a handsome seven-wicket victory. The next Test was played at Headingley in Leeds. The pitch was in good order, the outfield brisk, perfect conditions for a big score. Bradman duly obliged. He came in at the fall of the first wicket and had scored 309 runs by the close of play that

day, averaging no fewer than 52 runs per hour. He went on to make 334, a new Ashes record and even now the highest by an Australian Test player. The English bowlers had no answer to this kind of batting perfection. To their credit, they continued to set attacking fields and tried every weapon in their arsenal, but Bradman was just too good. Nevertheless, the match was drawn.

The fourth Test at Old Trafford, Manchester, was also drawn, so the fifth and final Test at The Oval became the decider. Bradman made 232; Australia won the match by an innings and 39 runs, and with it the series and the Ashes. Faced with such a phenomenon, England were going to have to rethink their entire strategy. A hint of what was to come appeared during this match. Harold Larwood, England's fast bowler, made the most of a damp pitch and sent down a few short balls which for the first time made Bradman appear uncomfortable. Douglas Jardine made use of the technique when he captained the England side to tour Australia in 1932–33, in what became known as the bodyline series.

Overleaf: England's Ian Botham on his way to 143 not out (see page 78).

Left: a 1938 Player's cigarettes collectors' card featuring top Australian batsman Donald Bradman.

Right: Don Bradman on 12 July 1930 – the day he scored 309 runs. His score was the highest ever for an Australian versus England.

PLAYER'S CIGARETTES

S.A.C.A.

D. G. BRADMAN

1938
Sir Len Hutton's 364 against the Aussies

SIR LEN HUTTON was one of England's finest batsmen of all time, a man whose influence went far beyond simple skill with the bat. Despite losing six years from his career due to the Second World War, suffering from a persistent injury to his left arm and taking early retirement at 39, only three other players have scored more runs. Sir Len was also the first professional to be made captain of England and did much to bring respect to the Players, as professionals were then known (to distinguish them from the Gentlemen, who were the amateurs).

Sir Len was a man of his time, a magnificent batsman in an era when the game was well and truly dominated by the bat. (Whether this was due to the brilliance of the batsmen, the mediocrity of the bowlers or the preparation of the pitches is an argument which has raged for decades.) The 1938 Test against Australia was a particularly extreme example of this, as is apparent from some of the early scores: Paynter 216 not out, McCabe 232, Hammond 240, Leyland 187. Today, it is doubtful if such games

PLAYER'S CIGARETTES

L. HUTTON

would hold the public interest, but in the 1930s things were different, and the battles with Australia attracted huge audiences.

The final Test match at The Oval in London in August 1938 saw one of the greatest innings of all time. England won the toss and elected to bat first on an ideal wicket. Throughout eight sessions and a total of 13 hours 17 minutes, Sir Len batted away to reach the staggering score of 364, beating the previous record of 334 set by Bradman. The innings itself was a slow and deliberate effort, mainly due to the exaltations of Wally Hammond, the England captain. Hammond was determined not to give the Australians, who still fielded the mighty Bradman, any chance of recovery. Bradman, who had unfortunately broken a shin when in the field, was a frightening spectre to the England team. By the time Hammond was satisfied, England had reached the almost ridiculous total of 903 for 7. Without Bradman, the Australians collapsed in just a day and a half, and suffered one of the most crushing defeats in their history, losing by an innings and 579 runs.

Despite his brilliant achievement, Sir Len did not view this innings as one of his best, believing that he had played many superior ones in far less favourable circumstances. Despite this, the record was to stand until Sir Gary Sobers, a worthy successor, made 365 nearly 21 years later. Sir Len received his knighthood in 1956, just a year after his retirement. He continued to play an active role in the game and will be remembered not only as a great player but also as a genuinely great sportsman.

Left: *a Player's cigarette collectors' card showing Yorkshire's hero Leonard Hutton. The card was issued in 1938.*

Right: *Australia versus England at the Oval, 1938 – Hutton and Edrich walking out to bat.*

MCC versus Yorkshire at Lords,
May 1937 – Dennis Compton
scoring through the slips off T. F.
Smailes

1947
Compton and Edrich:
The glorious summer of '47

DENIS COMPTON and Bill Edrich were two of England's finest batsmen, and it was to the great fortune of the game that they played at the same time and for the same county, Middlesex. Both enjoyed long and successful careers which bracketed the Second World War, careers which no doubt would have been even more successful had they not been interrupted.

Compton, perhaps the better known of the two, began his first-class career in 1936, at the tender age of 18. Rapidly showing himself to be supremely talented, he went on to play his first Test match for England the following year. Compton's batting style would best be described as cavalier; he often got away with strokes a lesser man would have missed. This devil-may-care attitude disguised a near-perfect defensive technique which ensured that once he was in, he was almost immovable. That is not to say that he was perfect. Compton was famous for his appalling judgement when it came to quick singles and was run out far more often then he should have been. Indeed, it was said that 'a call for Compton was merely a basis for negotiation'. As well as being a wizard with the bat, Compton could also bowl, returning a career figure of 622 wickets, a fair achievement in its own right.

If Compton was the suave and good-looking buccaneer, then Edrich was a study in serious application. The opposite to Compton in almost everything except the ability to score runs, he is often overshadowed by his contemporary. Edrich joined Middlesex just a year after Compton, although he had the advantage of having played for Norfolk for five years previously. Again a year behind Compton, he first played for England in 1938, the same year in which he scored 1,000 runs before the end of May.

The summer of 1947 saw a depressed, post-war Britain captivated by some of the finest cricket ever played in this country, and it seemed that Compton and Edrich were permanently at the crease. The figures returned by both of them are quite staggering. The record books show that Compton held records with 18 centuries and 3,816 runs for the season. However, Edrich was only just behind with 12 centuries and 3539 runs, a fact sadly forgotten by many.

Both men went on to captain Middlesex, for two years sharing the job. Both enjoyed long careers, having considerable success at football as well. Compton played for Arsenal and Edrich for Tottenham – another source of rivalry! Both men, however, were to look back at the summer of 1947 with fond memories of glorious cricket.

Bill Edrich photographed in June 1948 after being picked to play Australia in the first Test Match at Nottingham.

Jim Laker at Old Trafford, 1956. Laker took 19 wickets in two innings – a world record.

1956
Jim Laker takes ten in an innings

N THE 1913–14 series in South Africa, a 40-year-old English bowler by the name of Sidney Barnes finished one Test match with figures of 17 for 159. In the whole history of first-class cricket, no one had taken so many wickets in one match. In Test cricket, no bowler other than Barnes had taken more than 15 wickets. No one, including

Barnes, had taken 10 wickets in one innings until the incredible and rain-affected fourth Test between England and Australia in July 1956 at Old Trafford in Manchester.

There, Jim Laker, a 34-year-old spin bowler with Surrey, took nine wickets in the first innings and followed that with ten in the second. This achievement gave England victory and the Ashes. Laker ended with amazing match figures of 19 for 90 (9 for 37 in the first innings and 10 for 53 in the second). A newspaper report of the day concluded, 'J. C. Laker defeated Australia by an innings and 170 runs.'

Amazingly, it was the second time in the summer of 1956 that Laker had taken 10 wickets against the Australians. Playing for Surrey in May, the off-spinner had taken 10 for 88 as they became the first county for 44 years to beat the Aussies. He was the first man since 1878 to record such a feat against the Australians. After 78 years of waiting for another Englishman to record a clean sweep of wickets, Laker achieved it twice in the space of two months.

In the first innings of that Old Trafford Test, England amassed 459, needing a victory to secure the series. On a doubtful wicket, Laker set about his task brilliantly. He came on to bowl with the score on nine. Wicketless, he and his partner Tony Lock swapped ends, and the wickets started tumbling. Laker took the first two; then Lock had the Australian batsman Burke caught with the score on 62. Laker swept through the rest of the Australian order at a cost of just eight runs. Only 22 more runs were added to the total and, not surprisingly, the Aussies were asked to follow on.

There was little play on the Saturday and Monday because of rain, and Australia resumed the final day on 84 for 1 and a chance of saving the match. But after 36 overs from Laker, their hopes were dashed. He had entered the record books. Australia were bowled out for 205. One by one, Laker claimed the Australian wickets with only one batsman, Colin McDonald, putting up any resistance, scoring 89. With just an hour to go, Laker claimed the final wicket, trapping Maddox leg before, to spin his way into the record books.

1968
The D'Oliveira Affair

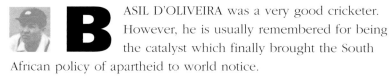

BASIL D'OLIVEIRA was a very good cricketer. However, he is usually remembered for being the catalyst which finally brought the South African policy of apartheid to world notice.

D'Oliveira was a South African, born in Capetown of Asian lineage, and as such was not a full citizen in the eyes of the South African government. In the parlance of the time, he was a Cape coloured, and whilst this afforded him more rights than a native African, he was still severely discriminated against.

Being unable to play at any senior level in his own country, the young D'Oliveira made his way to England in 1960 and began his professional career. A talented all-rounder, he soon made a name for himself, making his Test debut for England in 1966. In 1968, England were due to travel to South Africa for a Test series, just as they had for many years. However, public awareness of apartheid was growing, and the media were mounting an increasingly vociferous campaign against the South African authorities.

The British government found itself sitting uncomfortably astride the fence. On the one hand, it did not want to be seen to approve of apartheid, but on the other it did not want to alienate South Africa, a country in which it had a massive amount of investment.

Throughout 1967 and the first half of 1968, various meetings occurred between the British and South African governments which touched on the subject of D'Oliveira and the tour. Nearly all of these suggested that the South Africans would have no problem with him touring; indeed, on several occasions it was suggested that he should be playing for them rather than the English. However, as the tour drew closer and it became apparent that D'Oliveira, who was in sparkling form, would be part of the England team, things began to change. First he was approached by a South African businessman who offered him £40,000 to coach in his old country – as long as he did not join the tour. When this failed, the South

Africans let it be known that should D'Oliveira be included in the English side, the tour would almost certainly be cancelled.

Things were growing increasingly heated when D'Oliveira was left out of the touring squad, only to be readmitted when the unfortunate Tom Cartwright had to drop out due to injury. By now the media were alive with the story, and the allegations of government interference in the team's selection were rife.

On 17 September, the South Africans denounced the selection of D'Oliveira as politically motivated. The MCC (English cricket's governing body at the time) deafened by the clamour of the press, called off the tour. The South Africans were invited to England for a Test series in 1970 but this provoked such protests and political debate in the wake of the D'Oliveira affair, that the tour was cancelled and the South Africans entered a cricketing hiatus which was to last into the 1990s. D'Oliveira himself remained calm throughout and continued to enjoy a splendidly successful cricketing career.

Left: South African cricket ace Basil D'Oliveira in action.

Right: Basil D'Oliveira playing for MCC against Yorkshire at Lords, 27 April 1968.

1968
Sir Gary Sobers hits six for six

SIR GARFIELD ST AUBRUN SOBERS is without doubt one of the finest cricketers who ever lived. Many, including the entire population of Barbados, would say that he was the finest.

From the age of 17, when he made his first appearance for the West Indies, Sir Gary was a dazzling batsman, an effective bowler and a brilliant fielder. His versatility with the ball was awesome. Such have been his achievements within the game that he was recently voted the greatest cricketer of all time, receiving over 65 per cent of the total votes cast! During his Test career, he appeared in 93 matches, bettered Sir Len Hutton's record by scoring 365 runs in a single innings, captained his country a record 39 times, made 110 catches and took 235 wickets.

Sir Gary was blessed with two vital attributes: he was a great natural athlete, and he was possessed of a wonderful sense of timing. These two qualities allowed him to get away with many shots which would have seen lesser men out. His use of unorthodox shots made Sir Gary a great player to watch.

Like many West Indian players, Sir Gary played his club cricket in England, representing Nottinghamshire, and it was whilst playing for them that he compiled one of cricket's most memorable batting records. Playing against Glamorgan at their Swansea ground during the summer of 1968, he faced Malcolm Nash. Nash, more of a batsman than a bowler, was very much a second-rate spinner; bowling against the likes of Sir Gary, he did not expect to do particularly well. He was right. Sir Gary walloped Nash for six straight sixes. On the fourth delivery, Sir Gary was actually caught, but the umpire ruled that the fielder's foot had gone over the boundary rope, thereby nullifying the catch. For the record, the shots were over: 1. long-on, 2. long-on, 3. long-off, 4. mid-wicket, 5. long-on, 6. mid-wicket – in short, smashed all over the ground. Fortunately for the world, this game was televised, and as the last ball sailed out of the ground, commentator Peter Walker exclaimed, 'That's not a six. It's a twelve!'

Malcolm Nash, ever the gentleman, took comfort in the fact that he would be immortalized in the pages of Wisden, if not for exactly the right reasons. The last six had been so powerful that the ball had been temporarily lost, only to be found by a small boy several days later, thus fortunately being preserved for posterity. Sir Gary, as ever, remained modest about the whole thing. After all, there were plenty more sixes where those had come from!

Garfield Sobers for Nottingham playing at Lords versus Middlesex, 14 June 1968.

1977
Geoffrey Boycott's hundred hundreds

IN 1977, THE WORLD OF INTERNATIONAL cricket was in turmoil. In May, 35 international cricketers from five different countries, including four from England, had 'defected' to Australian media magnate Kerry Packer's so-called TV circus. The future of international cricket was, at the time, thought to be seriously under threat. Throughout this period, one of the most controversial and talented figures English cricket has ever produced resurrected his Test career and provided one of the season's most memorable moments, scoring his 100th hundred in a Test match against Australia at his cricketing home of Headingley.

Geoffrey Boycott was an opening batsman of undoubted quality but also a man who was never far from controversy. To many, he appeared the epitome of a stubborn, bloody-minded Yorkshireman whose actions would leave most exasperated. To others, he was a genuine hero. Although recognized as a great batsman – Boycott is the third-highest-scoring English Test batsman of all time – his unyielding pursuit of runs often landed him in trouble. He can surely be the only England captain who was deliberately run out by his team-mates, as he was in New Zealand in 1978, for scoring runs too slowly when the match situation demanded a run chase.

In a Test career spanning 18 years (1964–1982), Boycott played in 108 Tests for England. But in 1977, he had not played for his country for a period of 30 games, mostly due to self-imposed exile. Then he was selected for the Trent Bridge Test match against Australia. England, with Ian Botham making his debut, won by seven wickets, and Boycott scored 107 and 80 not out. A complete success? No. Boycott remained immersed in controversy. On the first day's play,

with England struggling on 34 for 2, he was joined at the wicket by local hero Derek Randall. It wasn't long before Boycott called a suicidal run which resulted in Randall sacrificing his wicket. The Nottingham crowd were mortified. Boycott later said that he had no choice but to go on to make a hundred because of running out Randall.

All this had been forgotten by the time the teams reached Headingley. England were put into bat and made steady progress. On 22, Boycott was almost caught but survived and rarely gave another chance. On 75, he survived appeals for a leg-side catch off Ray Bright's bowling. At 6.10 p.m., the historic moment arrived. Boycott produced a textbook straight drive which the other batsman, Graham Roope, had to jump over to avoid – an image which will live long in the memory. By the time the ball reached the long-on boundary, Boycott had been joined at the wicket by hundreds of fellow Yorkshiremen anxious to take part in the celebrations. He went on to make 191 runs. England won the Test and took the five-match series 3–0.

Geoff Boycott on the brink of his 100th hundred at Headingley, versus Australia.

1981
Ian Botham's Test

IN THE 1980S, one man bestrode English cricket like no other in the modern era: Ian Botham. From the very beginning of the decade, when he was England captain at just 24 years of age, to its end, Botham's influence on English cricket was unparalleled. His achievements with both bat and ball will never be forgotten. An immensely talented all-rounder, deeply committed to winning and a genuine crowd-pleaser, Botham was an incomparable hero. He will always be remembered for how he destroyed the Australians in the summer of 1981 with performances which went beyond superlatives and assured for him a legendary status in English sport.

What made it all the more remarkable was the way the season started for Botham. He captained England in 12 matches without winning one game. In the first Test in 1981, Australia triumphed by four wickets at Trent Bridge. The second Test at Lord's ended in a draw, but Botham resigned the captaincy after being bowled first ball in the second innings, having scored nought in the first. Mike Brearley took control of the captaincy; Botham took control of the series.

In the third Test at Headingley, England were so certain of being beaten after just three days that they were ready to check out of their hotel. Just before tea on the fourth day, they were 135 for 7, still 91 runs behind the Aussies, and with the crowd filing out of the gates Botham was joined at the wicket by youngster Graham Dilley. Soon, thousands were checking back in. With an incredible display of big hitting, they added

Left: Ian Botham hits four off Geoff Lawson during his 143 not out.

Right: Botham in fine form playing Australia for the Ashes in 1981.

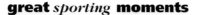

117 in 80 minutes for the eighth wicket. Then 67 more were added with Chris Old. Botham finished on 149 not out, scoring his hundred in just 76 balls. At one stage, he went from 39 to 103 with a six, 14 fours and two singles. Australia were set 129 to win, but an incredible bowling performance from veteran Bob Willis, who took 8 for 43, meant that England won by 18 runs to secure one of the most memorable Test victories ever.

Botham, though, wasn't finished with his heroics. In the fourth Test at Edgbaston, Birmingham, Australia needed 151 to win. Botham took five wickets for just one run in 28 balls after Australia looked set for victory on 114 for 5. But still he wasn't finished. At Old Trafford, he scored 118 of the best runs seen in Test cricket; indeed, *The Times* asked if it wasn't 'the greatest test innings ever'. England won the series 3–1 after looking certain to lose, ensuring that 1981 will always be remembered as Botham's summer. Botham himself went on to have an astonishing and at times controversial playing career. Off the pitch, he had his ups and downs with the press, but it didn't matter. To those in search of sporting heroes, they don't come much more heroic than Ian Botham.

1988
Graeme Hick's 405: A first-class record

F AN INNINGS is described as 'probably the greatest I have ever seen' by someone like Ian Botham, then something pretty special must have happened. On 6 May 1988, at Taunton cricket ground, something special did happen. Graeme Hick, the 21-year-old Worcestershire batsman, rewrote the record books that day, posting the highest score in championship cricket this century – at least until Brian Lara's exploits some six years later – by scoring 405 not out. Prior to Hick's magnificent knock, the only time the county championship had witnessed a score of more than 400 had been way back in 1895. Then, a 24-year-old Lancashire batsman by the name of Archie MacLaren had scored 424 out of a total of 801. Like Hick, he had scored his runs at Somerset's county ground in Taunton.

Born in Harare, Zimbabwe, in May 1967, Hick was being trailed in 1988 as the future great hope for English batting. Although southern African, by 1991 he would be eligible to play for England. In 1986, he had become the youngest-ever player to make 2,000 runs in a season. In April 1988, he scored 410 runs – a county record. By the time he had finished at Taunton, he had a batting average of 163 for the season.

Hick came to the crease at 78 for 1, but then Worcestershire collapsed to 132 for 5. Hick took control. In a nine-and-a-half-hour stint at the crease, Hick scored a phenomenal 405 runs out of the total 550 scored during that time. In 555 minutes and 469 balls, he shattered the record books, setting the highest-ever individual total for Worcestershire. He hit 35 fours and 11 sixes and batted at a remarkably even pace. He scored his first hundred in 153 minutes from 126 balls, his second in 189 minutes from 151 balls and his third in 142 from 134 balls, only accelerating for his final hundred, which was scored in 71 minutes and 58 balls. He shared a sixth-wicket partnership with Stephen Rhodes of 265 and an eighth-wicket partnership with Richard Illingworth of 177; Illingworth scored just 31 of those runs. Hick reached his 300 with two sixes from three balls, and during his fourth hundred he hit 72 in boundaries. He gave two chances early on and on 391 was dropped by Somerset's Colin Dredge. Hick then reached his 400 by hitting Dredge for a huge six. After his marathon stint at the wicket, he got two wickets with his off-spin. Worcestershire went on to win the match by an innings and 214 runs; Hick went on to play for England.

Top: Graeme Hick being interviewed during his 405 not out at Taunton, May 1988.

Bottom: the spectacular sight of Graeme Hick during his innings of 405 not out.

1990
Graham Gooch's 333:
The pinnacle of a remarkable match

AT LORD'S, THE HOME OF CRICKET, in July 1990, one of the most incredible Test matches of the decade took place. England beat India by 247 runs in a match littered with remarkable personal performances. That only one of these is usually remembered – England captain Graham Gooch's innings of 333 – demonstrates the extent to which his batting throughout the whole game was truly superb.

At 11.00 a.m. on 26 July, the 37-year-old England captain and opener walked to the crease for the start of the game. It was to be 5.00 p.m. on 27 July before he would leave the crease. In total, he batted for 10 hours, hit 43 fours and three sixes, and was out just 32 runs short of Sir Gary Sobers' Test record of 365. Although India's bowling attack was little short of mediocre, nothing should detract from Gooch's batting. His was the third-highest Test score by an English batsman. He was finally out, bowled by Manoj Prabhakar, in the final session of the second day. But Gooch's achievements during the game weren't confined to the first innings. In the second, he scored a further 123 runs, making an aggregate of 456, second only to Hanif Mohammad's world-record 499.

That Gooch's batting gave England victory in a one-sided Test doesn't do justice to a marvellous sporting occasion. After Gooch there followed a fantastic innings of 121 from his counterpart, Indian captain Mohammad Azharuddin, which was full of some of the most natural stroke-playing ever seen at Lord's. There was also a hundred from Ravi Shastri, and then with India needing 24 runs to avoid the follow-on and with just one wicket left, legendary all-rounder Kapil Dev scored four successive sixes off Eddie Hemmings. Just for good measure, 17-year-old Sachin Tendulkar, in his first Test appearance in England, pulled off one of the finest-ever boundary catches seen there.

But the match belonged to Gooch. Throughout a prestigious England career which spanned 20 years, he had never batted better. His distinctive, powerful hitting with his trademark heavy bat was never shown to better advantage. With 8,900 runs, Gooch is currently the highest-scoring Englishman ever in Test cricket, ahead of David Gower and Geoffrey Boycott. He averaged 42.58 runs in Test matches, not bad for somebody who started

with two noughts in his first match at Edgbaston in 1975 against Australia. In first-class cricket, the man from Leytonstone fared even better, averaging 49.57 runs. He retired from Test cricket in 1995 and from first-class cricket in the summer of 1997. His contribution to English cricket will be long remembered and he is now an England selector.

Top: Graham Gooch celebrates with champagne after scoring 333 at Lords, 1990.

Bottom: Graham Gooch in action — partway to his spectacular score of 333.

1993/94
Brian Lara's season

IN APRIL 1994, A SMALL, YOUNG, left-handed batsman from Trinidad set about rewriting the record
books. By the time Brian Lara had finished 49 days
later, they had run out of ink.

On 18 April, in the fifth Test against England at the
Recreation Ground, St Johns, Antigua, Lara broke Sir Gary
Sobers' Test record by scoring 375 runs. On 6 June, he broke the
world record for the highest number of runs scored in a first-
class match when he hit 501 not out for Warwickshire against
Durham. Lara became only the second man in history to hold
both records at the same time.

Aged just 20, Lara had made his Test debut against Pakistan
in December 1990, scoring 44 in his first Test innings. By the time
England arrived in the Caribbean four years later, his Test average
was up to 53.69. Before the series, he had stated his aim to score
a triple century. In 12 hours 46 minutes of sheer brilliance, Lara
set about breaking a 36-year-old world record. In March 1958, 21-
year-old Sobers had scored 365 for the West Indies against
Pakistan in Kingston, Jamaica. Lara came to the crease when the
West Indies were struggling at 12 for 2. He left the crease almost
two days later a national hero. In an innings of pure genius, he
didn't give his first chance to the English bowlers until he had
scored 347. He scored his 375 in 535 balls, scoring his 50s from
121, 59, 60, 52, 68, 52 and 77 balls. The record was secured when

he pulled Chris Lewis for a mid-wicket boundary to begin mass
celebrations. Sobers, who thought his record would never be
broken, was one of the first on the pitch to congratulate Lara.
When he was eventually out, Lara left the crease under a triumphal arch of bats and stumps.

Especially happy about Lara's batting that day was the
Warwickshire County Cricket Club who had signed him just the
week before. In his first six innings for the county that summer,
Lara hit five centuries. In June, he hit five more – in one match. At
Edgbaston, Lara equalled or surpassed 15 personal, county and
world records as he hit an incredible 501 not out. One of the most
remarkable of these moments was his scoring of the most-ever
runs in a day – 390. Dropped before he had made 20, and on 238
and 413, Lara scored his 501 from 427 balls in 474 minutes. He hit
10 sixes, 62 fours, four threes, 44 twos and 93 singles. He brought
the record up at 5.30 p.m. by driving John Morris to the extra
cover boundary which took him from 497 to 501, making him the
first man to score over 500 runs in one innings in first-class
cricket, breaking Pakistan Test star Hanif Mohammad's record of
499 set in January 1959.

Left: *Brian Lara walks off the
pitch through a triumphal arch of
bats and stumps.*

Right: *Brian Lara during his
historic innings of 375 for the
West Indies.*

5
Football

Some people are on the pitch. They think it's all over.... It is now.
Possibly the most famous piece of commentary ever from **Kenneth Wolstenholme** in 1966 as Geoff Hurst scored England's fourth goal in the World Cup final against West Germany.

1923
The White Horse final

THE FOOTBALLING 'MECCA' that is London's Wembley Stadium evokes many vivid images, and none more memorable than that of a policeman on a white horse attracting as much FA (Football Association) Cup final attention as any of the players.

It happened on 28 April 1923, when Bolton beat West Ham

2–0 in the first final to be played in the shadow of those famous twin towers. A police constable by the name of George Scorey and his steed played a major part in easing one of the most chaotic crowd scenes ever witnessed at a big sports event. But for them, it is possible that the occasion would have been marred by a disaster and the match cancelled.

PC Scorey and his 13-year-old equine partner, Billy, became the unlikeliest of FA Cup final heroes as a result of the authorities greatly underestimating public interest in the match. As the 1922 final at Stamford Bridge had attracted 53,000 spectators, less than half of Wembley's capacity, it was felt unnecessary to make the game all-ticket. Imagine the authorities' surprise when they were forced to close the admission gates an hour and a quarter before the 3.00 p.m. kick-off with 126,000 inside, and their horror as thousands more broke into the ground. The number of people inside the stadium swelled to an estimated 200,000, with thousands more outside. The crowd was good-natured and patient but the pitch was a mass of bodies, and it took some 45 minutes to push them back behind the touchlines so the game could start. Even then, play was held up twice through fans spilling on to the pitch, and the two teams, mindful of the difficulty in getting to and from the dressing rooms, stayed on the pitch at half-time.

Scorey, ironically a man who had no interest in football, was not the only mounted policeman at Wembley that day. But the *Daily Mirror* report of the fiasco, referring to the problems one mounted policeman experienced through fans coming on to the pitch again when he moved to a different area, stated: 'He [Scorey] dominated the crowd by the sheer force of his personality, and wherever he appeared, he received willing obedience.' In a BBC interview, the constable was nothing if not modest: 'The horse was very good, easing them back with his nose and tail until we got a goalline cleared. I told them in front to join hands and heave and then went back step by step until we reached the line. Then they sat down and we went on like that ... it was mainly due to the horse. Perhaps because he was white he commanded more attention. But he seemed to understand what was required of him.' Scorey's temperament also helped. Upon his return home, his girlfriend asked what sort of day he had had. 'Oh, just ordinary,' he replied.

1950
England is humiliated by the United States

ON A CLOUDY AFTERNOON in June 1950, during the World Cup finals in Brazil, a crowd of 10,000 turned up at the football stadium in the town of Belo Horizonte expecting to see England inflict one of the biggest international defeats of all time on the United States. This was not an unreasonable expectation. England, with stars like Stan Matthews, Stan Mortensen, Tom Finney and Wilf Mannion, were joint favourites with Brazil to win the trophy. The American amateurs, whose obscure line-up was led by a Scottish right-half – Eddie McIlvenny – who had been given a free transfer by Wrexham, were 500–1 outsiders. Even the American team, beaten 3–1 by Spain in their opening tie while England overcame Chile 2–0, felt that they were in for a hiding. On the eve of the match, one player asked an English journalist, 'Have you brought your cribbage board with you?' But the joke was very much on England as the US won sensationally 1–0 – arguably the most unexpected result in the game's history and one which long represented a source of inspiration for sporting underdogs everywhere.

How could a country where soccer was very much a minority sport bring off a triumph of this magnitude? Apart from England's stubbornness in adhering to a close-passing game on a hard, bumpy pitch, many felt that they also boobed in not selecting Matthews. He was not deemed fit enough to play against Chile, having joined the squad from a Football Association tour of Canada, and the England selection committee were unwilling to change a winning team. More to the point, this was a day when the American goalkeeper, Borghi, had good cause to think, 'Someone up there likes me'. In the first minute, Jimmy Mullen broke clear of the US defence and, with only Borghi to beat, fired over. From then on, in addition to the keeper's excellent saves, England hit the US woodwork no fewer than 11 times. In the 37th minute, the seemingly impossible happened – from a McIlvenny throw-in, Walter Bahr shot from 25 yards, and America's Haitian-born centre-forward Larry Gaetjens got his head to the ball to deflect it past England's astonished keeper, Bert Williams. According to the US fullback, Harry Keough, his team feared that this would 'wake up' England and lead to their 'raining goals on us'. But, as highlighted in the last 10 minutes, when Mullen hit the post and Mortensen the bar from the rebound, they were fated not to score.

The defeat left England needing a win against Spain in Rio to force a play-off for a place in the next round, but they lost 1–0. In the closing minutes, the Brazilians waved handkerchiefs and chanted 'Adios'. Goodbye to England – but not to the memories of their Stars-and-Stripes nightmare.

Bert Williams saving a US goal, 3 July 1950 – Williams' effort was not enough to prevent the US trouncing the English team.

1953
Stanley Matthews, the 'Wizard of Dribble'

THE TANTALIZING ball-playing skills which earned Stanley Matthews his nickname – not to mention a knighthood – thrilled millions over a period of some 35 years. But for all Matthews's mesmerizing performances between his first match at 17 in 1932 and his last in 1965 at 50 (when he became the oldest player ever to take part in a First Division match), his right-wing sorcery in steering Black-pool to their victory over Bolton in the 1953 FA Cup final stands out like a beacon.

Blackpool v Bolton: the magic of Stanley Matthews, the 'Wizard of Dribble'.

Stanley Matthews being congratulated by Bolton's captain, Billy Moir after the 1953 FA Cup final.

This was the first major sports event to be televized in Britain, and for the 38-year-old Matthews, it seemed his last chance of gaining an FA Cup winners' medal – his greatest ambition following his experiences of being on the losing Blackpool teams in the 1948 and 1951 finals. Such was his popularity that the dream was only marginally less pronounced among the general public, whose emotional support for him must have caused Bolton to think that the whole world was against them.

The manner in which Matthews inspired Blackpool to a 4–3 win after they had been 3–1 down with little more than 20 minutes to go also provoked the thought that the match had been controlled by a scriptwriter. It says much about the public's affection for Matthews that, although Stan Mortensen became the first player to score an FA Cup final hat-trick, the game has always been referred to as the 'Matthews final'. Many believe that he was helped by Bolton's tactical error when their left-half Eric Bell pulled a muscle in the 27th minute and was switched to the left wing in place of Bob Langton. The latter was moved to inside-left. Mortensen later claimed, 'That was a major blunder. Stan hated an opposing winger on his flank tackling back'. Bolton became even more vulnerable on that side when their left-back Ralph Banks was hit by cramp. However, their centre-forward, Nat Lofthouse, took a different view of Matthews' display. 'Even a bullet wouldn't have stopped Stan,' he has said.

Matthews, repeatedly fed by Blackpool's ingenious little inside-forward, Ernie Taylor, appeared to be playing Bolton virtually on his own. In the 67th minute, he supplied the cross from which Mortensen – with the help of a fumble by goalkeeper Stan Hanson – made it 3–2. Then, after a Mortensen equalizer from a free-kick three minutes from the end, Matthews, amid unbearable excitement among the 100,000 crowd, waved his wand again in injury time. He took the ball past the hapless Banks, beat Malcolm Barrass as the centre-half moved across to cover, and, a few yards from the goal-line, cut the ball back into the middle. There, waiting for it by the penalty spot, was Bill Perry. Blackpool 4, Bolton 3. Magic.

1953
The Magical Magyars

FOR SIX YEARS in the 1950s, the national team which would have been at the top of any international fantasy league was not Brazil or Italy or Germany, but Hungary. Between 1950 and 1956, the 'Magical Magyars', built round Jozsef Bozsik, a brilliant right-half, and the outrageously gifted inside-forward trio of Sandor Kocsis, Nandor Hidegkuti and Ferenc Puskás, lost only once in 48 matches – in the 1954 World Cup final against West Germany – and scored 210 goals. The most famous of those goals were the six they put past England at Wembley Stadium on 25 November 1953. The 6–3 victory gave Hungary, then the Olympic champions, the distinction of being the first continental team to beat England on the latter's home soil. The manner in which they achieved this sparked a major rethink among home managers and coaches concerning the methods by which their players were developed.

The Hungarians, with their mastery of the ball, speed of thought and movement, and fluidity as a team, looked as if they had come from a different planet. England, who had taught the world how to play, had suddenly been revealed as the pupils. One aspect of Hungary's approach that inspired many raised eyebrows was their finishing. For some time, English professionals had enthused over the build-up play of continental teams, but been dismissive of their ability to get the ball in the net. Before the start, one English player, referring to the opposition's lightweight boots, remarked, 'This is going to be easy – they're wearing carpet slippers'. How incongruous that remark seemed in the very first minute, when centre-forward Hidegkuti beat centre-half Harry Johnston and shot home from 20 yards.

Even more disconcerting to England was that Hidegkuti, who went on to score a hat-trick, did not operate in the way they had come to expect of a centre-forward. Instead of staying up the field, as the last attacker, he would drop deep and involve himself – with imagination and intelligence – in the build-up. Johnston, whose failure to cope with Hidegkuti resulted in the curtain being drawn on his international career, explained: 'Hidegkuti put me in two minds. If I had followed him all over the field, it would have left a huge gap in the middle of our defence. With the other Hungarian forwards [Kocsis and Puskás] coming at us down the middle we couldn't afford that. We would have done better if we'd appointed one of our other players to mark Hidegkuti. Instead, we all ended up marking space.'

Ironically, the Hungarians attributed their success partly to the influence of a Lancastrian – Jimmy Hogan – who had coached in their country in the 1930s. Hogan, who watched Hungary's remarkable win from the Wembley stands, must have felt that he had a lot to answer for six months later, when Hungary met England in Budapest and won 7–1.

The Magyars in action in 1954, on their way to beating England 7–1 in Budapest.

1954
Popular Hungarians fail at the last

IN ADDITION TO BEING EUROPE'S most consistently successful national team, West Germany (or Germany as they are now) could also be described as the game's ultimate party poopers. Many of their World Cup and European Championship successes have been achieved at the expense of more flamboyant – and popular – teams. But few would deny that the fitness, strength and discipline which has earned them such triumphs has been little short of awesome. German teams traditionally play with their heads rather than their hearts. Machine-like is the most popular description of them – and never more so than when they achieved the first of their three World Cup triumphs, against Hungary.

Hungary, acknowledged as the best team in the world at the time, had scored 25 goals on their way to the final, a path which included a 4–2 win over the other highly fancied team, Brazil, in the quarter-final. Even more remarkable in light of what was to follow was that in the preliminary group, from which two teams went through to the last eight, they had an 8–3 win over West Germany. But the Germans invited this massacre by deliberately fielding a weakened team. It suited them not to finish top of the group because they knew that they would need to beat only Turkey in a play-off for second place (which they did 7–2) and that the position would cause them to avoid meeting Brazil at the next stage.

The one drawback for Hungary in their win against the Germans was that Ferenc Puskás, their captain and arguably the most dynamic of their attacking players, sustained a damaged ankle. The Hungarians claimed that the challenge which caused it, by centre-half Walter Liebrich, was deliberate, and there was some doubt that Puskás would make the final.

A poignant reminder of the Magyars greatest moment – just months before their crashing defeat by West Germany.

That he did so, when clearly not 100 per cent fit, was a Hungarian gamble which appeared to have paid off when he and Zoltan Czibor gave Hungary a two-goal lead in the opening nine minutes. Most teams would have been destroyed by this – but not a machine as strong and resilient as Germany. By the 16th minute, Max Morlock and Helmut Rhan had capitalized on Hungarian mistakes to make the score 2–2. The Hungarians responded vigorously, causing the Germans to be grateful for having a goalkeeper, Toni Turek, in top form, and the luck of Nandor Hidegkuti missing a golden scoring chance 12 minutes from the end. Five minutes later, Germany's Hans Schaefer crossed from the left, and Rhan drove the ball into the net.

At the final whistle, it was difficult not to feel sadness for the Hungarians. At the same time, one had to admire West Germany's strength of character.

1960

Real Madrid: Worthy champions of Europe

ALFREDO DI STEFANO and Ferenc Puskás were both 33 when they operated together in Real Madrid's great European Cup team. Physically, Di Stefano was characterized by a bald patch, Puskás by his tubby build; but appearances can be deceptive, as Eintracht Frankfurt discovered to their cost when they faced the two in the European Cup final on 18 May 1960. That night, before a

Hampden Park crowd of 127,000, Real produced what is generally considered to be the greatest performance by any club team, beating Eintracht 7–3 to lift the trophy for the fifth successive time.

To this day, the European Cup (or European Champions' League, as it is now called) still evokes the thrilling images of that famous all-white Real Madrid strip and the extent to which the men wearing it outclassed their German opponents in Scotland. Real, indeed, appeared the footballing equivalents of the Harlem Globetrotters. Di Stefano and Puskás pushed themselves to the forefront with their exhibition of extraordinary attacking skills. Di

Stefano scored a hat-trick, and Puskás got Real's other goals, one from a penalty, bringing the team's goals in the 1959–60 competition to 31 in seven games. It said much about the entertainment Real provided that, despite the one-sided nature of the contest, hardly a soul in the crowd – then the biggest ever officially recorded for a match in Britain – left for home until the victory parade had been completed. The *Glasgow Herald* spoke for them all when it stated, 'Thank you, gentlemen, for the magic memory'.

Eintracht were clearly no slouches themselves. Scottish fans were particularly conscious of this because Eintracht had twice put six goals in the Rangers' net in the semi-finals. Real, too, had good cause to take them seriously when the Germans took a 19th-minute lead against them. But shortly afterwards, Di Stefano scored twice in five minutes, and Real were on their way. Eintracht's problems were best emphasized towards the end, when they pulled one back to make it 6–2 only for Di Stefano, from the restart, to run straight through their defence to complete his hat-trick.

Di Stefano, who had played in Colombia before joining Real in 1953, was the player who caught the eye the most. The Argentinian was more than a centre-forward – his all-round ability and tendency to pop up in defence and midfield as well as attack made him the conductor of the whole Real team. This was a sore point with Real's arch-rivals, Barcelona, who had also wanted to sign him. Both claimed to have secured an option, and the Spanish Federation ruled that Di Stefano would have to spend alternate seasons with the two clubs. But Barcelona, unimpressed by his contribution to their game, sold Real their interest in the player. Still, it could have been worse for Barcelona. At least they weren't in Eintracht Frankfurt's position at Hampden.

Real Madrid goalkeeper Dominguez leaps to save a potential Eintracht Frankfurt goal.

1961
Tottenham do the double

THE 1961 FA CUP FINAL, when Tottenham beat Leicester 2–0 with second-half goals from Bobby Smith and Terry Dyson, was not the best of matches – but to millions of football followers this did not matter a jot.

Tottenham, after all, had achieved the impossible, having become the first team this century to win the championship and the FA Cup in the same season. This feat had only been matched by Aston Villa in 1897 and Preston in 1889. With the physical and mental pressures on teams having increased considerably since those days, it was understandable that Tottenham were not able to use their last match fully to illustrate their talents, talents which had, however, been in sufficient evidence throughout the season to cause even the most demanding of observers to forget the dull note on which Tottenham ended it.

English football benefited greatly, because those 'Super Spurs' blazed a double trail which has since been trodden by Arsenal (1971, 1998), Liverpool (1986) and Manchester United (1994, 1996). How could it be otherwise for a club whose motto is 'To be bold is to accomplish'? Tottenham set a First-Division record at the start of the season by winning their opening 11 matches, and it was not until the 17th, against Sheffield Wednesday, that they suffered their first defeat. They also set new milestones in terms of their number of league victories (31), away wins (16) and goals (115). Their final total of 66 points equalled Arsenal's 1931 record and brought them the title by a margin of eight.

Perhaps the only man who did not go overboard about all this was Tottenham's Bill Nicholson, a dour Yorkshireman and the hardest of task-masters. His temperament and personality were hardly reflected by his team's stylish,

ingenious attacking play. Nicholson's captain – the whimsical Irishman, Danny Blanchflower – complemented him perfectly. Upon his appointment as manager in 1958, Nicholson promptly restored Blanchflower to the captaincy, a position the player had lost because of a clash with the previous manager, Jimmy Anderson. It was an inspired decision. Blanchflower, the master strategist among British players, thrived on responsibility.

The blend of Nicholson and Blanchflower – of pragmatism and idealism – was similarly potent in the team. Winger Terry Dyson said, 'I think we had five really great players [Blanchflower, Dave Mackay, John White, Cliff Jones, Bobby Smith] and the rest of us just seemed to blend around them. This business of blend is what every manager dreams of getting'. Blanchflower summed it up, as only he could, when the Tottenham and Leicester teams were being presented to the Duchess of Kent at Wembley Stadium. 'The other team have their names on their tracksuits,' she remarked to him. 'Yes,' Blanchflower replied. 'But we know each other'.

Opposite: A jubilant Tottenham Hotspur run to the end of Wembley Stadium to give loyal Spurs fans a glimpse of the coveted FA Cup.

Below: Leicester City's stricken goalkeeper tries valiantly to save a spectacular goal from Spurs' Dyson.

1966
England: World Champions at last

**A**LF RAMSEY, a man noted for not showing his emotions, showed a self-restraint remarkable even by his standards on the afternoon of 30 July 1966. At the final whistle in his England team's World Cup final against West Germany, Ramsey was approached by the trainer, Harold Shepherdson, who tried to lift him off his touchline seat. Ramsey was unmoved. 'Sit down, Harold,' he commanded.

It's a pity that others were not able to follow his example. England's 4–2 victory, sealed in a gripping 30 minutes of extra-time, created so much excitement that the St John's Ambulance Brigade members on duty at the match reported several cases of fainting – even heart attacks – amongst the 100,000 crowd. As an estimated 400 million watched this epic contest on TV, the mind boggles at what the overall total of suitable cases for treatment – psychological as well as physical – could have been. But who would have wanted to miss the sight of Ramsey's troops, controversially pushed into action with no orthodox winger and no Jimmy Greaves, producing the greatest two hours in English soccer history?

The memory has remained particularly vivid in East London, given the impact of Ramsey's West Ham trio of Bobby Moore, his imperious central defender and captain; Martin Peters, a player whose versatility caused Ramsey to describe him as being '10 years ahead of his time'; and striker Geoff Hurst, who justified his inclusion at the expense of Greaves by becoming the first player to score a World Cup final hat-trick.

England's finest hour – Bobby Moore, held high by the England squad, raising the World Cup for all to see.

With Hurst having cancelled out Helmut Haller's opening goal for Germany, Peters put England ahead initially 13 minutes from the end of normal time. But in the last minute, England suffered another blow when Wolfgang Weber brought the teams level again. The England players inevitably looked shattered, yet before the start of extra time, Ramsey, later to be knighted, implored them: 'You have beaten them once, now do it again. Look at them. They're more tired than you are.'

Ten minutes into extra time, Hurst hit the underside of the bar with a shot from a cross by the indefatigable Alan Ball. The ball bounced almost straight back down. Hurst and Hunt, who was following up, wheeled away, arms raised, claiming the goal. But did the ball cross the line? The goal stood, sparking a controversy that still rages to this day. Deep into the last minute, with Germany giving the whole home nation palpitations with their efforts to save the game, Moore hit a long ball into the path of Hurst on the halfway line. Hurst somehow summoned the strength to go forward with it ... and then hit an explosive left-foot shot into the roof of the net. No mistake there. England had won, 4–2. 'They think it's all over,' observed the BBC's match commentator, Kenneth Wolstenholme, referring to spectators on the pitch as Hurst was about to swing his boot at the ball. 'It is now,' he added.

Gordon Banks leaps to save a West German goal at the 1966 World Cup final, Wembley.

*England's jubilation –
celebrating their glorious win over
West Germany at Wembley,
30 July 1966.*

1967
Celtic conquer Europe

THE MOST BEAUTIFUL DAY in Celtic's history came on a sunny afternoon in May 1967, in the Portuguese national stadium in the hills overlooking Lisbon. It was a beautiful day for football, too, because in becoming the first British club to win the European Cup, with a 2–1 victory in the final there against Inter Milan, Celtic struck a massive blow for attacking play. One did not need to be a Scot to rejoice in Celtic's performance. When, for example, Tommy Gemmell made the score 1–1, a policeman ran some 40 yards to the Celtic touchline bench to congratulate manager Jock Stein.

The match had been billed as being between the good guys and the bad guys. Celtic were in the former category, because of their positive attitude and sense of integrity. Stein, a former Celtic centre-half who had become manager only two years earlier and who was to become one of the game's most revered figures, might not have had the most gifted team in Europe. But they attacked with such commitment and pace – especially on the flanks, where the full-backs, Jim Craig and Gemmell, repeatedly supported the wingers, Jimmy Johnston and Bobby Lennox – that opponents must have thought they were facing a tidal wave.

In contrast, Inter, under the management of the authoritarian Argentinian Helenio Herrera, were masters of the ultra-negative. 'It only takes one goal to win a game,' he was fond of saying. Thus, once Inter had gone ahead, they were quite content to concentrate on holding their lead.

They tried to do it against Celtic, even though only eight minutes had gone when Sandro Mazzola put them in front from a penalty. As Celtic's captain, Billy McNeill, said later, 'They underestimated our attacking ability.' Inter also underestimated the tactical know-how of Stein, who at half-time told Lennox and Johnston to move into the middle to allow Craig and Gemmell to use the flank space.

In the 60th minute, with Celtic having come close to scoring on a number of occasions, they got the breakthrough their wonderful spirit deserved, with Craig going down the right and then providing the pass from which Gemmell hit a stunning shot into the net from 25 yards. Psychologically, Inter were now a beaten team. Celtic turned up the heat on them even more; five minutes from the end, another Gemmell forward burst led to Steve Chalmers clinching victory.

Celtic captain Billy McNeill being presented with the European Cup at Lisbon.

Stein went on to steer Celtic to nine championship wins in a row, a record which seemed impregnable until Celtic's arch-rivals, Rangers, equalled it in 1997. But even Rangers have yet to provoke the European Cup ecstasy which engulfed Celtic in 1967. Two fans who might remember it more than most are the gentlemen who reportedly flew back to Glasgow the next day, following a night of uninhibited celebration ... and then remembered that they had driven to Lisbon by car.

Celtic come home with the European Cup – showing it to an ecstatic crowd at Celtic Park, Glasgow.

1968

Manchester United win the European Cup

THERE WAS NOT A DRY EYE in the house at Wembley Stadium on 29 May 1968. That night, 10 years after the Munich air disaster which had destroyed Matt Busby's dream of leading Manchester United to the European Cup and plunged millions into mourning, Busby and United finally succeeded with a 4–1 win over Portugal's Benfica after extra time.

fateful day in Germany, a great team had died, a team packed with outstanding young players who had graduated through the club's youth system. Having reached the semi-finals in their first attempt at the European Cup the previous season, they were returning from a quarter-final victory over Red Star Belgrade in Yugoslavia when their aircraft crashed on take-off. Eight players lost their lives, including the England triumvirate of Roger Byrne, Duncan Edwards and Tommy Taylor, and Busby was critically injured. So there was a special place for him in the public's hearts when United beat Benfica, as there was for Billy Foulkes and Bobby Charlton, the only Munich survivors on the team.

It was Charlton who put United ahead in the second half, but then the team suffered the agony of an equalizer by Jaime Graca 10 minutes from the end – and a lucky escape when the great Benfica forward Eusebio failed to score with only goalkeeper Alex Stepney to beat. In the first minute of extra-time, however, George Best, who had been having a quiet game, suddenly reminded Benfica of the magic which had enabled him to destroy them in a remarkable 5–1 United win in Portugal in 1966. Stepney's long kick was headed on by Kidd, and Best, United's European Footballer of the Year, made the rest look ridiculously easy. He took the ball forward, beat the keeper with a dummy, and put it into an empty net. Within eight minutes, United had scored two more, with Brian Kidd marking his 19th birthday by making it 3–1 from Charlton's cross and setting up Charlton for his second goal.

Pat Crerand (left) and George Best (right) flank an emotional Matt Busby to show Manchester United fans the European Cup.

This was the first time that an English club had won the European Cup, and it was entirely fitting that United, who in 1956 had become the first English club to take part in the competition – against the advice of the Football League – should achieve the distinction. It was a particularly appropriate moment of glory for Busby, who, unlike the League, recognized the potential of the European Cup, and who would surely have brought the trophy to Old Trafford much earlier but for the Munich tragedy. On that

England has produced other impressive European Cup teams, notably the Liverpool sides who won the trophy in 1977, 1978, 1981 and 1983. But it was United's success – encapsulated by the poignant post-match sight of Busby and Foulkes embracing each other and Charlton in tears – that made the biggest impact. Both Busby and Charlton later received knighthoods.

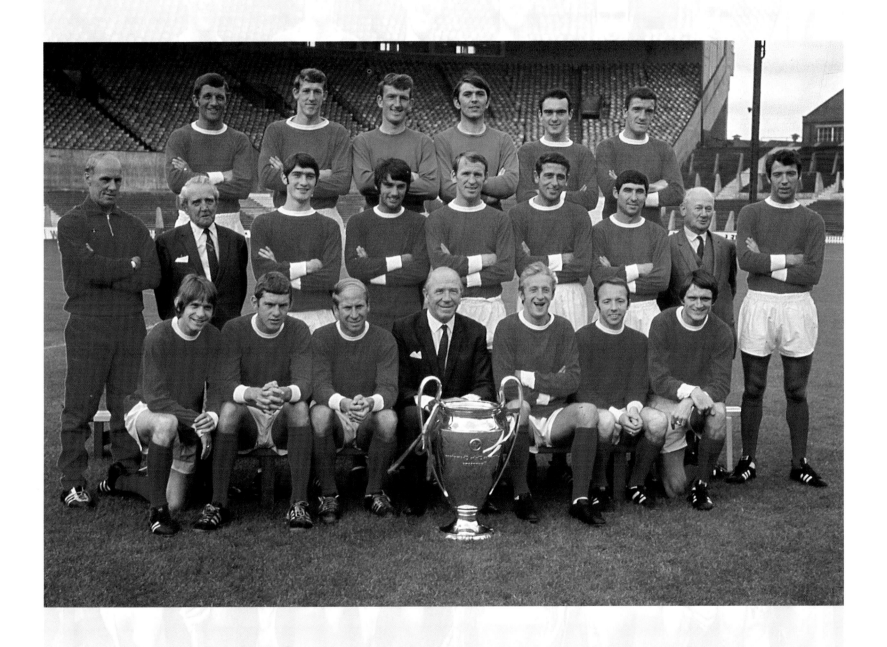

The Manchester United squad with their well-deserved European Cup, photographed in July 1968.

1969
Pelé's 1000th goal brings
jubilation to the Maracana

IT WAS ONLY A GOAL from a penalty, but when the incomparable Edson Arantes do Nascimento scored it for his Brazilian club, Santos, in Rio's Maracana Stadium, it brought the house down.

The player – otherwise known as Pelé – and his adoring public had waited some weeks for that strike. When it came in the 2–1 win against Vasco de Gama on 20 November 1969, it brought Pelé's total to an astonishing 1000 in 909 competitive matches and sparked wild scenes of rejoicing amongst his millions of worshippers. For Pelé, who reached the 1257-goal mark in 1321 games before his retirement in 1977 at the age of 36, such adulation was nothing new. He was arguably the most feted player of all time, not just because of his record, but also because of the quality of many of his goals.

Brazilians have long cornered the market in the latter respect. In recent years, the goals which have caused a particular stir have included Roberto Carlos's 35-yard strike for Brazil against France in June 1997, when he bent the ball around the defensive wall and into the right-hand side of the net with the outside of his left foot, and the long Ronaldo dribbling run which preceded his goal for Barcelona against Compestella the same year. Notable non-Brazilian goals were made by Spain's Nayim and England's David Beckham, who had the temerity to lob the ball over the keeper from around the halfway line. Nayim did it for Real Zaragoza against Arsenal in the 1995 European Cup-Winners' Cup final, Beckham for Manchester United in the premiership match against Wimbledon the following year. No stage was too big for Pelé to produce such acts, as he emphasized in the 1970 World Cup finals in Mexico, when he failed by centimetres to do what Nayim and Beckham did, against Czechoslovakia.

One wonders what Beckham and Nayim would have made of Pelé's part in helping Brazil win the World Cup for the first time with their 5–2 win over Sweden in the 1958 final in Stockholm. At 17 the youngest player to appear in the finals (Ireland's Norman Whiteside narrowly beat the record in 1982), Pelé later recalled: 'I was just a skinny little black and I am sure that some were faintly amused to see a child on the field for a match of this importance, if not outraged.' Some child. Pelé, noted as much for his modesty off the field as for his brilliance on it, scored Brazil's fourth goal by taking the ball on his thigh, with his back to the goal, and then ingeniously knocking it over his head and spinning round his marker to volley it home. He also got their fifth, with a leap which belied his height of 1.72 m (5 ft 8 in) and a header which went in like a shot.

Right: *Brazil's commemorative stamp celebrating Pelé's 1000th goal, scored on 20 November 1969.*

Opposite: *jubilant fans invade the pitch after Pelé scores his 1000th goal for Santos.*

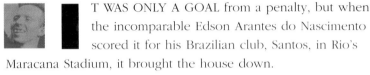

1970
Brazil entrance the world

PELÉ WAS FOND of describing football as the beautiful game. He was not referring to football in general, but to the uninhibited, artistic attacking play which has long characterized his national team.

Brazil played Italy in the 1970 World Cup final in Mexico's intense heat and altitude. No fan who witnessed their 4–1 win, which put the Jules Rimet trophy in their custody for a record third time and enabled them to keep it permanently, could have avoided falling head over heels in love with the Brazilians. In Europe, the era of flair football was dawning with the emergence of Holland's Ajax as the most successful – and attractive – club team. To Ajax and others, the mesmerizing skills of those 1970 Brazilian stars Pelé, Gerson, Jairzinho, Tostão and Rivelino provided the perfect lead.

Brazil had been disappointed in the previous World Cup finals in England in 1966, when an ageing team had found it difficult to cope with the physical pressure and did not even get to the quarter-finals. This was a particularly unhappy competition for Pelé. The extent to which he was fouled caused him to vow never to play in the World Cup again. How Brazil's 1970 World Cup opponents – most notably Italy – must have wished he had not changed his mind!

Left: Brazil's Rivelino tackled by an Italian defender – to no avail, Brazil won 4–1.

Right: an exultant Pelé after scoring his first goal against Italy in the 1974 World Cup.

Brazil's confidence in their attacking skills did cause them to be vulnerable in defence at times, and the Italians, having beaten West Germany 4–3 in extra-time in the semi-final, were well equipped to exploit this. Indeed, after Pelé had risen superbly to a Rivelino cross to head Brazil in front after 18 minutes, careless play by midfielder Clodoaldo in trying an impudent back-heel in his own half gave Boninsegna the chance to equalize. Italy then retreated into their renowned shell of caution ... and Brazil, in perfect harmony with the evocative samba beat emanating from the

drums of their fans, ran rings around the Italians. When Gerson put the Brazilians 2–1 ahead with a shot from outside the box in the 66th minute, Brazil's play was switched into carnival mode. Five minutes later, a Gerson free-kick was touched on by Pelé to enable Jairzinho, the electric winger who had succeeded Garrincha, to maintain his record of scoring in every game in Mexico.

But the best Brazil goal was saved for last. The move leading up to it began with a Gerson dribble past five players. As the attack developed through Rivelino, Jairzinho and Pelé, Brazil's right-back and captain, Carlos Alberto, pushed forward to join in the fun. Pelé waited for him to arrive and played the ball into his path to allow the skipper to thunder the ball into the net.

Brazil's World Cup team ready to face the England squad, 7 June 1970.

1973
Ajax v Bayern Munich:
Total Football at its best

BEARING IN MIND that British football has often been said to be too insular, something very strange happened in the 1972–73 season. A London travel company chartered a plane for a trip to a match involving Dutch and German teams in Amsterdam, and it was packed with Football League managers and coaches.

The match was the European Cup quarter-final first leg between Ajax, the holders of the trophy for the previous two years, and Bayern Munich. As the teams contained the most important figures in their countries' national teams, it was virtually Holland v Germany. But, notwithstanding the presence of super-star-players like Ajax's Johan Cruyff and Johan Neeskens and Bayern's Franz Beckenbauer and Gerd Müller, the real impact of this confrontation was that it involved the finest exponents of Total Football.

This was the name given to an exciting style of play – pioneered by Ajax and their coach Rinus Michels – that demanded a high level of intelligence and versatility from players. The style had its roots in the ability of players to be comfortable in any position or area of the field. In the Ajax team, the right-back was liable to pop up in the outside-left role, and vice versa. No one was more adaptable than Cruyff, whose all-round skills – and potential for winning a match virtually on his own – brought him the honour of becoming the first player to win the European Footballer of the Year award three times. To watch Cruyff and his colleagues was tantamount to attending a masterclass on the finer points of team play – especially on that night in Amsterdam. Although Cruyff was a man inspired, Bayern, stretched to the limit by Ajax's bewildering movement, somehow managed to hold out for an hour. Then, the roof caved in on them. Aarie Haan scored twice, and Gerrie Muhren and Cruyff added the others to give Ajax a 4–0 win.

Ajax, who eventually eliminated Bayern 5–2 on aggregate, went on to clinch their European Cup hat-trick by beating Real Madrid in the semi-final and Juventus 1–0 in the final. But the real final had been that clash with Bayern. Moreover, the memory of how easily Bayern were brushed aside became a sore point with Ajax fans when their team – beset by off-the-field disagreements – broke up. Particularly hard to take was the

transfer of Cruyff to Barcelona and the fact that Bayern themselves won the European Cup over the next three years. The revenge of Bayern's captain, Beckenbauer, also included his leading West Germany to victory over the Dutch in the 1974 World Cup final.

Still, the Ajax influence was not lost. AC Milan owed much to their triumvirate of Dutch stars, Frank Rijkaard, Ruud Gullit and Marco van Basten, for the transformation which brought them the European Cup in 1989 and 1990. Ajax did win the European Cup again in 1995 – against Milan.

Ajax players celebrate a goal during their victorious match against Bayern Munich, 7 March 1973.

1973
FA Cup final:
The underdogs of Sunderland beat mighty Leeds

AS THE FINAL WHISTLE sounded in the Sunderland v Leeds 1973 FA Cup final, Sunderland's manager, Bob Stokoe, with one hand on his head to keep his trilby in place, sprinted on to the pitch at Wembley Stadium to hug his goalkeeper, Jim Montgomery. It was one of the most memorable sights in the history of the competition – as was the stunning double save from Montgomery which had helped Sunderland stun the soccer world by becoming the first Second-Division team to win the trophy since West Bromwich Albion in 1931.

Sunderland's achievement was a giant-killing act to savour every bit as much as the other notable shock results which have done so much to give the FA Cup its magic appeal, such as Walsall's 2–0 third-round win over Arsenal in 1933 and Yeovil's 2–1 fourth-round win against Sunderland in 1949. Few can have quibbled with Montgomery's right to attract the most applause. He was not the first, however, to show millions of televiewers that goalkeepers deserved as much praise as goalscorers. Despite England's defeat by Brazil in the 1970 World Cup finals, Gordon Banks put himself into football folklore by thwarting Pelé. Banks's stop, when Pelé directed a powerful close-range downward header towards the keeper's right-hand post and Banks somehow leapt across his goal and knocked the ball over the bar, was rated the greatest save of all time. Pelé, who was so sure that he was going to score that he screamed 'Goal' as he made contact with the ball, has often described it as such.

But there was some argument about this when Montgomery emerged as Sunderland's saviour at Wembley Stadium, against a Leeds team who were the FA Cup-holders and acknowledged to be the outstanding team in England. Leeds, the hottest final favourites for years, got their first shock in the 30th minute, when, from a corner, Sunderland's Ian Porterfield pivoted on his left foot and struck a volley into their net. Even then, it seemed only a matter of time before Leeds took control. Certainly, no one in

Sunderland goalie Jim Montgomery makes a miraculous save from Leeds' Peter Lorimer.

their right mind would have bet against Leeds United scoring midway through the second half when Montgomery made a diving save from Trevor Cherry, only for the ball to go straight to Peter 'Hot Shot' Lorimer – the player reckoned to have the hardest shot in the game. Lorimer, with the goal at his mercy just six or seven yards out, struck the ball perfectly. He has said, 'As the ball was coming to me, I thought: "You don't have to blast the ball. Just a nice little contact will do." Really, I hit the ball exactly as I wanted to hit it.' But to Lorimer's astonishment, Montgomery raised himself quickly enough to deflect it on to the bar with his elbow.

Leeds were demoralized, and Sunderland, with the north-east chant of 'Ha'way the lads' booming out from the throats of their large army of fans, went on to spark some of the most ecstatic Wearside celebrations the region had ever known.

Sunderland's Ian Porterfield and Dennis Tueart with the FA Cup after the team beat Leeds 1–0 at Wembley.

1986
The Hand of God

ARGENTINA'S DIEGO MARADONA was the best player in the world in the 1980s, but unlike his fellow South American who had previously worn that crown – Brazil's Pelé – he was also controversial. The two sides of Maradona were particularly evident in the 1986 World Cup finals in Mexico, where acclaim for his football genius – which played a major part in Argentina winning the trophy – were offset by the widespread conviction that he had cheated his way to glory. Maradona's penchant for attracting outrage as well as admiration was summed up by Argentina's 2–1 win in their quarter-final clash with England on 22 June in Mexico City's Azteca Stadium, when he put his team ahead just after half-time with his left hand.

referee Ali Ben Naceur or his assistants. Apparently unsighted, they allowed it to stand. Maradona himself described it, tongue-in-cheek, as scored by the 'Hand of God', a phrase which will forever evoke stronger memories of him than anything he did with his feet. Just four minutes later in the same game, however, Maradona proved his exceptional ability. He burst through the heart of the England defence in an amazing dribble past Gary Stevens, Terry Butcher and Terry Fenwick to score the goal that put Argentina 2–0 up. Despite the outrage incited by his earlier actions, no one could deny that this goal ranked amongst the best of all time. It still does. Maradona went on to inspire Argentina to their 3-2 victory over West Germany in the final.

The incident occurred in the first match between the two countries since the Falklands War. England's Steve Hodge gained possession on the right – from an Argentinian attack initiated by Maradona – and hooked the ball over his head towards goalkeeper Peter Shilton. Maradona challenged Shilton for it in the air, and as he was not tall enough to get his head to the ball, he used his hand. For all Maradona's dexterity, it was obvious to many that the goal should have been disallowed, but it was not obvious to

All teams need one extra-special player, and there is no doubt that at national team level, Maradona, short but exceptionally strong, was as valuable to Argentina as was Pelé to Brazil, Johan Cruyff to Holland, Eusebio to Portugal and Michel Platini to France. In terms of one player dominating a major competition, Platini's impact in helping France win the 1984 European Championship in France – when he was the host team's captain and their top scorer – was especially impressive.

For his part, Maradona, in addition to his starring role in 1986, was similarly prominent in guiding Argentina to the 1990 World Cup final against Germany (which they lost 1–0) in Italy. But as if that 'Hand of God' controversy was not a big enough blot on his image, he was banned for two 15-month spells for failing drug tests, the second in the 1994 World Cup finals in the USA.

Top: Maradona's first goal in Argentina's World Cup match versus England in 1986 – using his hand to gain the ball from England's Peter Shilton.

Bottom: Maradona's 'Hand of God' goal gave Argentina the lead in a match that would otherwise have ended as a draw.

1990
Gazza's tears grip a nation

FOOTBALL IN ENGLAND has never been more popular than it is now. The game has been transformed into family entertainment, with a greater percentage of women watching and playing the game. Spear-headed by BSkyB, television companies are handing out millions of pounds for the rights to cover it. In fact, in the late 1990s, English football at its top level has become a glamorous business. All of which goes to show what effect it can have when a star player breaks down in tears.

England's Paul Gascoigne's failure to control his emotions in the thrilling World Cup semi-final against West Germany in Turin on 4 July 1990 was one of the most potent of all sporting images, showing that the game's stars had the same human vulnerability as everyone else.

To a great extent, the public impact of Gazza's agony (not to mention England's) was like that of a gripping soap opera. The reason for his anguish – inevitably highlighted by TV bringing a close-up view of his face into millions of homes – was that he was booked for a rash tackle. It was not the first time that Gazza, England's most gifted player, had been guilty of indiscipline. Not for nothing had the then-England manager, Bobby Robson, referring to his schoolboy-type pranks and wayward, self-destructive streak, described him as being 'as daft as a brush'.

On this occasion, Gazza's remorse sprung from the fact that it was the second time he had been booked in the competition – and that, in the event of England reaching the final for only the second time, he would miss the match because of suspension. He was inconsolable. Suddenly, he seemed so lost that mothers of sons everywhere must have found it difficult to avoid sharing his pain. There were more Gascoigne tears at the end when England

and Germany were locked at 1–1 after extra-time. England, having matched the Germans in every aspect of the game and helped produce one of the competition's most enthralling matches, lost the penalty shoot-out.

It was particularly difficult not to sympathize with Gazza because his passing and dribbling skills, allied to his insatiable appetite for playing, had been a major factor in England getting so far. Having joined Tottenham from his home-town club, Newcastle, this so-called 'man-child' who tried so hard to be liked – and who had a Tottenham manager, Terry Venables, who did not try to crush his individuality – was at his match-winning best.

'Gazzamania', public interest in Gazza after the finals, helped broaden support for the game in England. Gascoigne himself continued to make himself the centre of attraction, often for the wrong reasons, but he will be remembered the most for those tears.

1996
Southgate's agony

NOTHING IN FOOTBALL can compare with the drama of a penalty shoot-out.

The idea of using penalty tie-breakers to unearth the winners of Cup matches in which the scores are level after 30 minutes of extra-time was put into operation in the 1970s. It seemed a good idea, given the problems of finding space for replays in increasingly crowded fixture lists, and it is certainly exciting to watch. But, notwithstanding the argument that the system reduces matches to lotteries, it is an experience that players would much rather do without.

On the face of it, scoring from a penalty should be easy for a professional footballer. But the bigger the prize at stake, the more torturous the task becomes. As a result, few would have relished being in the shoes of the outstanding Italian forward Roberto Baggio when he took his spot-kick in the penalty finale to the 1994 World Cup final against Brazil in the United States – least of all when Baggio, needing to score with Italy's last kick of the five to keep their hopes of victory alive, blasted the ball over the bar. England's Stuart Pearce and Chris Waddle both suffered this nightmare in the 1990 World Cup semifinal against West Germany. If there is one player who epitomizes the heart-stopping nature of such moments, it is Gareth Southgate, the Aston Villa and England defender in the 1996 European Championship semi-final – again against the Germans – at Wembley Stadium.

England's success in the competition, in front of their home fans, had created a level of excitement and expectation not witnessed in the country since that World Cup triumph in 1966. So it is not difficult to appreciate the pressure on Southgate when the five nominated penalty-takers on either side all scored – and he became the first of the rest to have a go. The contest was now a sudden death affair, and Southgate actually volunteered for the job, even though the only previous spot-kick he had taken had hit the post, and even though the other England players available for the task included the captain, Tony Adams.

Southgate was too brave for his own good. He was on target with his shot, to the right of the German keeper, Andreas Kopfe – but the ball was not hit cleanly enough, and Kopfe, anticipating its direction, was able to save. Amidst unbearable tension, Germany's Andy Moller put Southgate out of his misery by

converting his kick to give his team victory. While Germany went on to win the trophy, the debate about whether this was a fair way to decide important matches became more intense than ever. Southgate himself took some time to stop asking himself the question his mother posed to him when he telephoned her after the match: 'Why didn't you just belt the ball?'

A dejected Gareth Southgate holds his head in despair after missing the final penalty against Germany.

6 Golf

*You little son-of-a-bitch, you're
something else. I'm proud of you.*
Jack Nicklaus, conceding the
1982 US Open to Tom Watson.

1955

US Open: Fleck pulls a Major surprise

ALL SPORTS RELY on surprise for moments of great drama, on the ability of David to slay Goliath, and golf is no different. In June 1955, at that year's US Open, the sport was to witness one of its greatest-ever shocks. A virtually unknown municipal golf-course professional, Jack Fleck, beat the most famous golfer of his day and one of the legends of the game, Ben Hogan, in a play-off.

Overleaf: Tiger Woods playing the 15th hole at the US Masters in 1997 (see page 126).

Right: Jack Fleck wins the 1955 US Open, after a play-off from Ben Hogan.

In fact, Fleck seemed the most shocked of all by his win. He appeared to play both his last and play-off rounds in a trance. Immediately after his victory, he was struck dumb, leaving the previous year's winner, Ed Furgol, to conduct his post-tournament interviews for him.

Fleck had arrived at the tournament at the Olympic Country Club in San Francisco, California, as a complete outsider. He was in his first full season on the PGA (Professional Golfers' Association) tour, but had originally turned professional before the Second World War. Little was known of the golfer from Davenport, Iowa, and he had only won just over $7,000 in prize money from 41 tournaments.

Hogan, in contrast, took over $207,000 during his career and was then at the height of his fame. Just two years previously, he had won the US Masters and US and British Opens all in the same year. At the 1955 US Open, he was attempting to win for a record-breaking fifth time. An intimidating man who shunned publicity, the Texan was nevertheless intensely popular due in no small part to his incredible recovery from a near-fatal car crash in 1949.

But reputation counted for nothing during the 1955 US Open, though there was little sign of the shock ahead in the first round. On a notoriously hard course, Fleck posted a six-over-par 76, four behind Hogan. However, the second day saw Fleck shoot a 69, leaving him on 145, tied with Hogan and one shot off the lead. A third-round 75 seemed to scupper Fleck's chances, and he was three off the lead held by Hogan. When the great man scored 70 on his final round, everybody assumed he had taken his fifth title. TV commentator Gene Sarazen, twice winner of the tournament himself, even announced to viewers that Hogan had won while Fleck was still playing. Transmission closed down, and the galleries started emptying. Fleck had other ideas, however, and birdied the last to shoot a 67 – 287 in total – and force a tie.

The popular opinion was that Hogan had been delayed the championship for just 24 hours. But Fleck was always in control during the play-off and at one stage led by three shots before securing his famous and unbelievable victory on the 18th. Hogan could take some consolation from the fact that the 32-year-old Fleck won the tournament playing with a set of Ben Hogan golf clubs.

1970
US Open: Jacklin never in danger

N 1920, TED RAY, a 43-year-old Jerseyman famed for wearing a battered hat and constantly smoking a pipe, won the US Open by a single stroke at Inverness, Ohio. For 50 long years, no other Briton was able to win the celebrated title until the son of a Scunthorpe steelworker blew away the field in exhilarating fashion, taking the title by seven strokes in 1970.

Tony Jacklin's victory and its influence on the next generation is seen as a watershed in British golf. Some have even remarked that his stunning victory at the notorious Hazeltine National Golf Club, near Minneapolis, Minnesota, was the golfing equivalent of England's 1966 World Cup footballing triumph, such was its influence on the game back home.

Jacklin, 25, arrived at the tournament at the peak of his career. Between 1968, starting with the Jacksonville Open, and 1973, he won six major tournaments. In 1969, he had won the British Open, the first home winner for 18 years. He was to add the Italian Open, the Dunlop Masters, and another Jacksonville Open to his successes, but in 1970 came what was probably his greatest playing triumph when he obliterated the field to take the US Open.

Although his victory was not a massive surprise, no one could have guessed at the manner in which Jacklin would win on a course famed for its treacherous conditions. He was the only player to come in under par and lead throughout. Winning at a canter, he gave the impression that he was the only competitor who enjoyed the long and windy conditions. His nearest challenger, the American Dave Hill, who finished on par at 288, was fined $150 for saying 'they ruined a good farm when they built this course' after the second round. He was not alone. Greats such as Jack Nicklaus opened with his worst-ever score – 81 – in the US Open. Gary Player went round in 80, and Arnold Palmer hit 79.

Jacklin, however, opened with a one-under-par 71, his worst round of the four, even though this gave him an initial lead of three shots. Despite gusts of about 64 km/h (40 mph), Jacklin consolidated his lead during the second and third rounds, shooting 70 in both, opening up a four-stroke lead for the final day. He appeared to be in trouble on the final day, scoring successive bogeys at the seventh and eighth, but a slice of luck at the ninth virtually secured the title. An overhit putt which appeared to be sailing past the hole hit the cup, flew into the air, hovered on the lip, and fell in for a birdie. There was no looking back for Jacklin, and he posted his third successive 70 to finish on a seven-under-par 281.

His victory was also a watershed for the US Open. It marked an increasing challenge to American supremacy from Europe, Australia and southern Africa for all of golf's major titles over the next three decades.

Left: Tony Jacklin after winning the US Open in 1970 – the first Englishman to win the tournament in 50 years.

Right: Tony Jacklin and his wife Vivien, with the US Open trophy and the winning cheque.

1973

US Open: Johnny Miller's final round
makes history

COMING INTO THE FINAL round of the 1973 US Open at Oakmont, Pennsylvania, four men tied for the lead. Jerry Heard, John Schlee, Julius Boros and golf legend Arnold Palmer all stood on three under par.

That none of them took the title was due to one of the most fantastic rounds of golf ever seen. Starting a full six shots behind the leaders, Johnny Miller, a lanky Californian, shot an astonishing eight-under-par 63, including nine birdies, to win the Open and inscribe his name in sporting history. His final round, which gave him the tournament by one shot from Schlee, has yet to be beaten as the lowest-ever recorded at the climax of the Open. Even allowing for the wet conditions which made the famous old course a much easier test than normal, his round stands out as a piece of pure golfing genius.

Miller was one of the biggest draws of his day, the nearest thing the 1970s had to Tiger Woods. Between 1971 and 1976, he won 20 tournaments, 16 of those on the US tour. But his success was not confined to his own continent. In 1976 at Royal Birkdale, he took the British Open in glorious fashion by six shots from two of the game's greats, Jack Nicklaus and Severiano Ballesteros. Miller also played twice in the Ryder Cup. He had turned professional just four years before his win at Oakmont, which event appeared to confirm the belief that this was a golf great in the making. He never fulfilled his promise, however, due largely to his inconsistency and his devotion to his family and Mormon faith. But his win at Oakmont will live long in the memory.

Miller's first three rounds had been unexceptional. He opened with a par 71, followed that in favourable conditions with a 69, but then added a disastrous 76 in the third round to leave him floundering in the pack. Nothing in those three rounds suggested that he was about to make history, but on the first four holes on the final day, he opened with successive birdies to put him among the front runners. With the leaders still in the clubhouse, Miller was given no chance, but his form held. He parred the fifth, sixth and seventh and then dropped his only shot of the day at the eighth. A birdie at the par-five ninth and Miller was out in 32 and in with a chance of winning. He eagled the 11th and birdied the 12th, thanks largely to his wonderful iron shots from

Johnny Miller exhibiting some of the golfing genius that won him the 1973 US Open.

the fairway. Another birdie at the 13th left him level with Palmer and seven under for the day. His final birdie came at the 15th, and he finished with three solid pars. Back in 31, Miller had completed the most amazing final round in the US Open to win his first Major despite late challenges from Schree and Tom Weiskopf.

1977
US Open: Death threat fails to deter Hubert Green

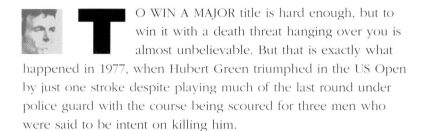 **T**O WIN A MAJOR title is hard enough, but to win it with a death threat hanging over you is almost unbelievable. But that is exactly what happened in 1977, when Hubert Green triumphed in the US Open by just one stroke despite playing much of the last round under police guard with the course being scoured for three men who were said to be intent on killing him.

Green, a competitive golfer from Birmingham, Alabama, entered the final day at the Southern Hills Country Club in Tulsa, Oklahoma, one shot ahead of Andy Bean on 208 – two under par. Green and Bean were the last pairing out on to the course, and as he came to the turn Green was beginning to struggle. He bogied the ninth, then the 10th, and was coming under increasing pressure from Lou Graham. Graham had hardly been inspiring over the first nine himself, going out in 37, but his form improved drastically. He shot four bogies in five holes and followed that up with a fifth at the 16th to pull within one shot of Green, who was now on the 13th.

The drama on the course was nothing to what was going on behind the scenes, however. That afternoon in the Oklahoma City office of the FBI, a clerk had taken a call from a desperate woman who claimed that three men were on their way to the golf course to kill Hubert Green. She said she had seen their guns and the threat was serious. It was certainly taken seriously. Despite the call being kept secret, uniformed policemen suddenly appeared around the course, as did plain-clothes detectives. The clubhouse was closed, and television crews covering the event were told to scan the crowd, particularly around the 15th green.

On the 14th, Green, who was hanging on precariously to his one-shot lead, was told of the death threat and given three options. He could continue to play, ask for play to be suspended, or withdraw from the tournament. Green chose to play on. After a par at the 15th, he birdied the 16th. He just about made par at the 17th, but then was in trouble, needing a five on the final hole to take the Open. His approach shot to the green was short and ended up in a bunker. He then left himself needing to get down in two putts from 6 m (20 ft). He won with one shot to spare, scoring a par 70 and beating Graham, who had finished on 279, by a single stroke.

The death threat was thought to be a hoax, and Green later joked that it had probably been made by an ex-girlfriend. From there on in, Green confined the drama to the golf course. In 1978, he held a seven-stroke lead over Gary Player in the US Masters only to lose by one stroke. In 1985, he took the US PGA in Cherry Hills, Colorado, by two strokes from Lee Trevino.

Hubert Green – undeterred by a death threat – on his way to winning the 1977 US Open.

1981
British Open: Bill Rogers confounds the pundits

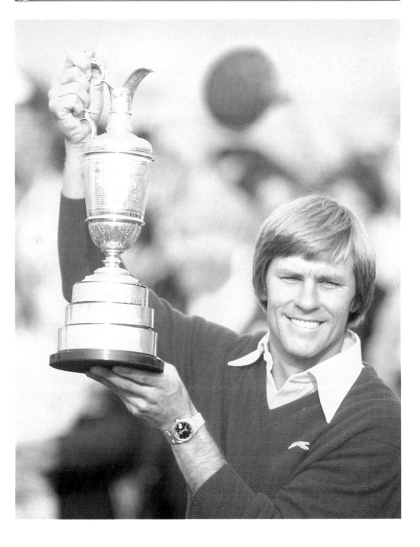

IN 1981, THE BRITISH OPEN returned to Royal St George's at Sandwich on the Kent coast after an absence of 32 years. The last man to win the Open there had been the South African Bobby Locke, who had won by 12 shots in a play-off.

As the players assembled for the 1981 tournament, the public and media eagerly anticipated a clash between the heavyweights of the day, Tom Watson, Jack Nicklaus, Hale Irwin and Ben Crenshaw. Home hopes rested with the 24-year-old Nick Faldo. No one gave much thought to a tall 29-year-old Texan called Bill Rogers, but 1981 was to prove his year as Rogers pulled off one of the greatest surprises in a Major in the modern era.

Rogers' success came as a surprise to many golf pundits as well. Despite obvious talent, he had been labelled the man who could not win a Major tournament. He had turned professional in 1974. Despite limited success in winning the Australian Open and World Matchplay at Wentworth in 1979, one of the big four titles was thought to be beyond him.

He started at Sandwich steadily, scoring a first-round two-over-par 72. But he really found his form during the second and third rounds, when he posted a 66 and then a 67 to give him a five-shot lead over his nearest competitors, Germany's Bernhard Langer and Britain's Mark James. The famous old claret jug seemed destined to go back to Texas, but because he was not a big name, many thought Rogers could be caught or would choke under the pressure. This looked like happening when he double-bogeyed the seventh, leaving him just a stroke ahead of Langer.

To lose the title then would have been a travesty. With his Open obituary already being written, Rogers produced three birdies over the next four holes to close the door on any challengers. The burst of birdies made his position unassailable. He could walk the final few holes knowing that, barring a disaster, he had won his first Major and proved the critics wrong. He finally finished with a round of 71 – one over par – to win by four shots on a total of 276. His nearest challenger was Langer, who finished four shots back. Rogers' penchant for drama at the British Open was not used up, however; at Royal Birkdale two years later he scored a rare albatross, though he could not sustain his challenge against the eventual winner, Tom Watson.

Top: Bill Rogers at the 18th green, at the 1981 British Open in Kent.

Bottom: Bill Rogers holding up his British Open trophy at Royal St George's, in 1981.

1982
Pebble Beach: Tom Watson's miracle shot

MOMENTS OF GREATNESS are by their very nature few and far between, but when they occur, they live long in the memory. Say the words 'Pebble Beach' to any golf fan, and they will immediately conjure up the picture of Tom Watson chipping in from the rough at the 17th to claim the 1982 US Open.

The shot, described as one of the three greatest golf shots ever played, is certainly the most talked-about of the modern era. Watson approached the 17th hole level with Jack Nicklaus, who had already completed a final round of 69 to finish on 284 and was watching nervously from a television monitor in the scorer's tent.

For Watson, this was uncharted territory. Despite having established himself as one of the game's greats with three wins in the British Open and two in the US Masters over the preceding seven years, by 1982 he had still not triumphed in the US Open. This time, he would be fine as long as he made no mistakes. But on the 17th tee, he did. A 190-m (209-yd) par-three hole, it offered few chances of birdies but plenty for bogies. Watson pushed his 2-iron shot into the rough left of the pin, about 6 m (20 ft) from the hole. His best chance of victory now seemed to be to take Nicklaus to a play-off. Nicklaus later said that he thought Watson only had a 1,000–1 chance of holing the chip. But as he approached the ball to play his second shot, Watson noticed that he had a good lie and his ball was sitting up rather than plugged in deep grass. He took his sand wedge and lined up the shot. Just before the shot, his caddie had told him to get it close. Watson replied, 'I'm not going to try and get this close. I'm going to hole it'. Played with an open club face, the ball pitched just on the green, broke right, hit the flag, and dropped in the hole.

Watson, who normally kept his emotions in check, danced around the green with his arms held aloft. The Open, thanks to one moment of brilliance, was his for the taking. Another birdie followed at the 18th, and Watson had claimed the title by two shots. After completing his round, he was met at the 18th by a smiling Nicklaus, who said, 'You little son-of-a-bitch, you're something else. I'm proud of you'. Later that year, Watson went on to claim his fourth British Open. The next year, he won his fifth and lost his US Open title by just one shot.

Legend has it that Watson was approached by a TV company to re-enact the shot, but refused, and that he tried on many occasions to repeat the shot but always failed. Whatever the truth, he made the shot the only time it mattered.

Tom Watson at perhaps his most memorable game of all time, chipping in from the rough at the 17th to claim the US Open title.

1984

British Open: Ballesteros wins it at the 17th

OF ALL THE MANY MEMORABLE sights in modern golf, surely one of the greatest is an ecstatic Severiano Ballesteros repeatedly punching the air in triumph on the 18th green at St Andrews in 1984 after clinching his second British Open. The image of an exultant and victorious golfer celebrating a birdie putt is one which will live long in the memory. Veteran commentator and former player Peter Alliss has called it 'one of the most joyous moments in golf I've ever seen'.

Left: Seve Ballasteros at the 1984 British Open, with the imposing building of St Andrews Golf Club in the background.

Right: triumph – Seve Ballasteros having just holed a putt on the 18th to win the 1984 British Open.

The great Spaniard won the title with a superb exhibition of stroke-play which saw off the strongest competition. Bernhard Langer and Tom Watson finished two shots adrift, Fred Couples and Lanny Wadkins four behind. It even pegged back the challenge of Australian Ian Baker-Finch, the surprise early leader. Ballesteros's win was to prove one of the most popular in the Open for many years.

The Spaniard, though, had entered the tournament under a cloud. It had been five years since the 27-year-old had won his first British Open, and although he had claimed two US Masters since then, the last in 1983, he was still thought to be out of form. He had yet to win a tournament in 1984 as he set off in pursuit of the claret jug at the Old Course.

But he had taken encouragement from modifications made to his swing by two fellow professionals, Jaime Gonzalez and Vincente Fernandez. Ballesteros opened with a three-under-par

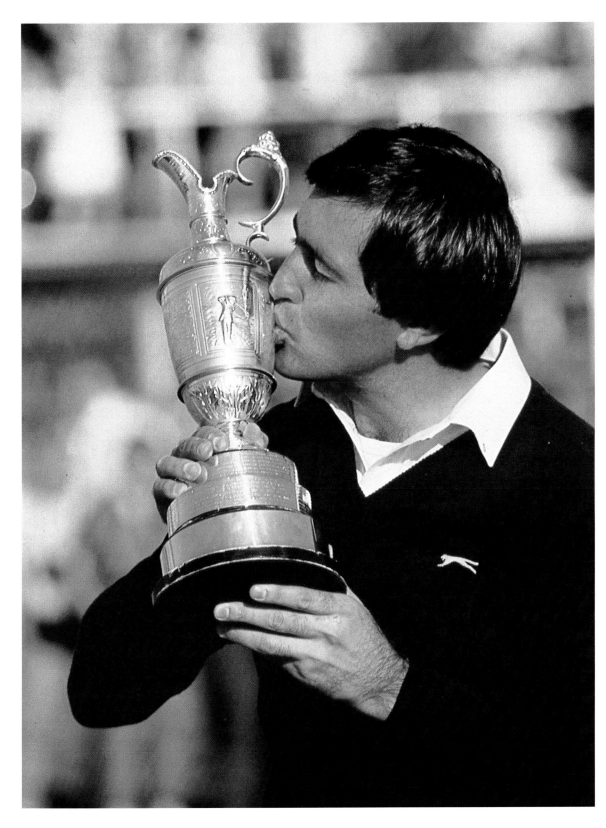

69, then on the second day went round in 68. A third-round 70 left him on 207, the same as Langer and two behind Watson and Baker-Finch. Ballesteros went out in 34 strokes, three better than Watson, who was to prove his main adversary throughout the final day. But the real test lay ahead. Apparently the night before the final round, Ballesteros had said that the championship would be decided at the famous – many say infamous – 17th Road Hole.

Ballesteros played the hole well, scoring a par four. Watson, playing in the final pairing, found himself the latest in a long line of victims at the 17th. In a good position for his second shot, Watson's 2-iron went through the green, ending up close to the road which gave the hole its name. A bogey five was the best Watson could do.

Meanwhile at the 18th, Ballesteros was putting successfully for a birdie and the 1984 British Open. He finished on a 12-under-par score of 276 to secure his fourth Major. In a touching speech afterwards, he claimed that he had beaten the world's best player – Tom Watson – on the world's greatest golf course. The irony was that that year, the 17th Road Hole had been described as being at its least lethal for many years. Unfortunately, they forgot to tell Tom Watson.

Spain's champion: Seve Ballasteros kissing his well-deserved British Open trophy, 1984.

1987
The Masters:
Sudden-death triumph for Larry Mize

DESPITE FOUR DAYS of thrilling play, the 1987 US Masters will always be remembered for just one shot, an incredible chip from 32 m (35 yds) on the second sudden-death hole which gave the 28-year-old American Larry Mize his first win in a Major.

If luck was with Mize, it was certainly against the Australian Greg Norman once again. The then British Open champion had suffered a similar fate at the previous year's US PGA at Inverness. There Bob Tway had chipped from a bunker to claim the title on the final hole and defeat Norman. At Augusta, Georgia, Norman was the victim of an even more outrageous shot.

Both Mize and Norman had tied on 285 stokes with Severiano Ballesteros to force a sudden-death play-off. Norman had only made the play-off with a blistering run of form on the back nine. From the 12th he birdied three out of four holes, dropped a shot at the 16th, and then birdied the 17th. A birdie at the final hole would have given him the title. Agonizingly, his putt shaved the hole and with it went his chances of winning the Masters.

On the first play-off hole, Mize was in control. He outdrove both Norman and Ballesteros, and a birdie putt from 10 feet just missed. Both Mize and Norman parred the hole, but it was the end for Ballesteros. He three-putted and was knocked out, leaving the course in tears. On the par-three second hole, it seemed as if Norman was the most likely to win. He had a birdie putt to win while Mize pushed his tee shot to the right of the pin. The man from Augusta looked as if he would be lucky to get his chip close to the pin, let alone hole the shot. His chip from 32 m (35 yds) was hit with pace. Rolling towards the pin, it suddenly looked like it was going to be close. The ball hit the pin and dropped in, setting off wild scenes as the player celebrated and the gallery went crazy with delight.

Norman still had a chance to halve the hole, just like at Inverness, but, again, his putt missed. Mize's victory seemed harsh on the Australian. In his career, Norman has gained the un-enviable record of losing in play-offs in all four Majors. He has often been labelled a choker after squandering seemingly winning positions in Major tournaments. But the 1987 Masters was never an example of that. There he was just the victim of an outrageously fortunate or brilliant shot, depending on your personal view.

For Mize, it was a victory which would throw off his image as an unknown. After the victory, a local newspaper said it would rid Mize of his reputation of being a choker. Another journalist replied cuttingly that he was unaware Mize had a reputation. Now, after his thrilling victory, there was another golfing reason for Augusta to be famous.

Top: *Larry Mize chips in – on his way to victory.*

Bottom: *Mize holes his chip shot during the play-off and wins the tournament, US Masters 1987.*

1991
Ryder Cup:
The 'War on the Shore'

THE RYDER CUP COMPETITION played at the Ocean Course in South Carolina in September 1991 was one of the most remarkable tussles in the long history of golf. After three days of gruelling competition, the USA finally won back the trophy on the final hole of the final singles game with a missed putt by Bernhard Langer.

The competition was a potent mixture of skill, bravery, high-level drama and rampant nationalism. Despite the sheer sporting tension of the event, it left a bad taste in the mouth of many. It took place just a few months after the Gulf War, and many references were made to the American-led successes over Iraq. Kiawah Island demonstrated just how big the pressures to win had become since the introduction of continental European players in the 1980s.

Throughout the three days, there was little to choose between the sides. After the first-day foursomes, the USA led by just one point, four-and-a-half to three-and-a-half, despite the inevitable early successes of Severiano Ballesteros and Jose Maria Olazabal. By the end of the second day, the scores were tied on 8–8. That morning, Nick Faldo, partnering Dave Gilford, suffered his heaviest Ryder Cup defeat – losing by seven holes with only six to play – at the hands of Paul Azinger and Mark O'Meara.

The final day's singles were perfectly poised, but the drama began before play started. The American captain, Dave Stockton, pulled out Steve Pate, who had been hurt in a car crash the previous week. The scores were amended to eight-and-a-half each. As the day progressed, the tension became unbearable. Europe began well, taking two-and-a-half of the first three points available through Faldo, David Feherty and Colin Montgomerie. The Scotsman's half-point was achieved despite being four down with four to play. But back came the USA. Azinger, Corey Pavin and Chip Beck won three of the next four games.

Eventually, the whole competition came down to the match between Hale Irwin and Langer. The USA needed only a half. Europe had to win the match to claim the Ryder Cup. Two up with four to play, Irwin looked like he had done enough. But Langer came back to tie the match at the 17th. On the 18th,

America's Hale Irwin playing in the Ryder Cup at Kiawah Island. September 1991.

Langer incredibly had a tricky 1.2-m (4-ft) putt to win the match and the Ryder Cup. His putt, though well struck, hit the lip of the cup and stayed out of the hole. Langer and the rest of the European team looked aghast. The Americans began their celebrations. The match was tied and the USA had the cup. It would be harsh to blame Langer, though. His fine fight back had given Europe a chance of victory when there previously appeared to be none. The pressure to sink the final putt was so great that commentators later said that no golfer would have made it.

Top: Europe's Bernhard Langer misses the vital last putt, giving victory to the US team.

Bottom: Seve Ballasteros and Jose Maria Olazabal waiting in anticipation at the 1991 Ryder Cup, Kiawah Island.

1993
The Masters: Langer back on song

FOR TWO LONG YEARS, Bernhard Langer had lived under a golfing cloud. Ever since the agony of missing the final putt at the 1991 Ryder Cup at Kiawah Island which consigned Europe to defeat, the German had suffered taunts about his undoubted golfing talent. His 1993 Masters win put paid to any whispering campaign about his status as one of the premier golfers of his age and gained him entry to an exclusive club. He became only the 12th man to have twice donned the famous Masters green jacket, and only the third European. In 1985, Langer had taken the Masters by two shots from Curtis Strange, winning in a total of 282. In 1993, he was to win by four strokes, shooting 277.

There's no doubt that before his success in 1993, Langer had been through some bad times. As well as the Ryder Cup heartache, he had also suffered every golfer's great putting fear – the dreaded 'yips', which makes putting a time of anxiety. His solution was to adopt an unorthodox putting grip, clamping the handle of the putter with the right hand against the left forearm. His success also extended the run of European wins at Augusta. Since 1988, when Sandy Lyle had taken the title by one stroke, Europeans had won four out of the five Masters. Only Fred Couples had achieved a home victory in 1992. In 1993, Langer was to make it five out of six.

Langer was in touch with the leaders from the very first round. He went round in 68, just one shot behind a five-strong group of Americans that included Jack Nicklaus and Larry Mize. After a second-round 70, Langer found himself still one behind the leader, who by now was the American Jeff Maggert. The third round, though, was where Langer stamped his authority on the tournament. He was one of the very few players to break 70 – scoring 69 – to lead by four shots as he went into the final day. He was now chased by a group of Americans including Chip Beck, who was to finish second, and John Daly, who came in third with Tom Lehman.

Any chance that Langer might suffer from nerves on the final day was dispelled when he went round in 70. Only Lehman, at 68, and Daly, at 69, scored better. But the title was Langer's. The nearest he had been to being caught during the day was when playing-partner Chip Beck got within two shots of him by the 13th. But the German hung on to end a torrid time. Later that year at the Belfry, Langer played again in an unsuccessful Ryder Cup campaign. He scored two points out of a possible four, but it was not enough, as the Americans won another close match by 15 points to 13.

Left: Bernhard Langer back on form after his disaster just two years previously, at the Ryder Cup.

Right: a triumphant Bernhard Langer after winning the US Masters in 1993.

1997
The Masters: Tiger Woods comes of age

ON 13 APRIL 1997, Tiger Woods did not so much win the US Masters as begin a new era in golf. Quite simply, his victory was so breathtaking, so record-breaking, so complete, that he instantly made himself the biggest name in golf and one of the major sporting superstars in the world.

A look through the records he broke shows just how amazing his performance was. He went round the famous Augusta course in 270 shots, breaking Jack Nicklaus's and Raymond Floyd's total of 271. His victory margin of 12 shots was the biggest ever recorded since the beginning of championship golf in 1860. His victory, at 21 years old, made him the youngest champion in the 61-year history of the US Masters. During the whole tournament, he played the back nine without bogeying, shooting an incredible 16 under par, thus breaking Arnold Palmer's record, set in 1962, by four shots. Perhaps most significantly for a course and a sport dominated by whites, Woods became the first black player to win a Major championship. To emphasize this, immediately after his victory he became only the third ethnic-minority player to join the Augusta club.

The victory came in Woods' third Masters and was achieved just seven-and-a-half months into his professional career. His victory was assured after the third round, when he shot a seven-under-par 65, to follow his 66 on the second day. After the first round, he was three off the lead. At the end of the second, he was three ahead. By the end of the third round, he was nine shots ahead, before rounding off his victory with a three-under-par 69. His victory was sealed with a par on the final hole. For the last 63 holes, he went round in 22 under par. After his victory, golfing legend Tom Watson said Woods might be a player who 'only comes round in a millennium'. Jack Nicklaus said Woods had 10 Masters victories in him. At the heart of his victory was his astonishing power off the tee. His driving averaged 295 m (323.1 yds) throughout the tournament and his putting was superb.

Tiger Woods, America's latest golfing sensation and winner of the 1997 US Masters.

The victory gave a seal of approval to the already-growing Tiger Woods legend. At the age of six, he played two holes against Sam Snead and lost by just one stroke. Afterwards, he offered Snead, who won the US Masters three times, his autograph. By the time he was 10, he had broken 80 shots for a round. He missed qualifying for the Los Angeles Open by just three shots when aged 15. His 1997 victory was something the young Californian had been dreaming about his entire short life. After celebrating his victory on that Sunday night, Tiger Woods was found asleep in bed hugging the famous green jacket with which all Masters winners are presented.

Tiger Woods holes a four-foot putt on the 18th green to gain victory in the 1997 US Masters.

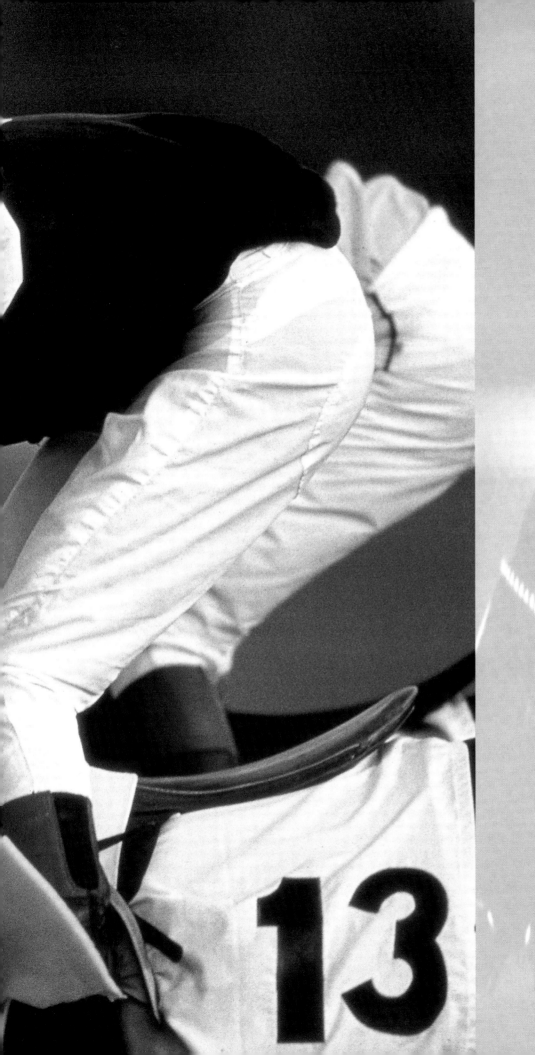

Horse Racing

7

I never heard anybody say it had been a false start and there were horses around me so I assumed it was a race.

John White, jockey of Esha Ness, winners of the 'Grand National that never was' in 1993.

1900
Sloan's last ride in the UK

ON 6 DECEMBER 1900, the *Daily Telegraph* reported that Tod Sloan, the most prominent of the American jockeys who had stunned the UK racing fraternity with their technique and speed, had been charged with fixing the Cambridgeshire. It had been reported to the Stewards of the Jockey Club that Sloan had accepted the offer of a large present from Mr F. Gardner in the event of Codoman winning and that he had bet on the race. Mr Gardner, who was unaware of the regulations forbidding such presents, expressed his regret at having broken the rules, and the Stewards, accepting his explanation, fined him £25 – a nominal penalty. They also fined Mr C. A. Mills, who acted as commissioner to Mr Gardner, the same amount. In addition, finding both charges proved against Sloan, they informed him that he need not apply for a licence to ride again in the UK. The charge resulted from a Steward over-hearing Sloan cursing the jockey who had beaten Codoman, the Irishman John Thompson; Thompson had refused to be corrupted by Sloan's accomplices, despite their having been successful at either fixing or nobbling all the other 'dangers' in the race. Sloan applied every year for 15 years for a renewal of his licence to ride in Britain, but was always refused.

Sloan had first arrived on English soil to ride for the American James R. Keene, but he was soon disputing the judge's decision after losing by a head in the Cambridgeshire, demonstrating the disregard for officialdom which would ultimately be his downfall. He was rarely out of the public eye, and his short-reined style was much admired and imitated. The American invaders had an aggressive style which put their English counterparts to shame. Sloan enjoyed a wonderful rapport with horses and appeared to inspire many of them to victory. He seemed able to burst out of the gate and race the whole distance, keeping just enough in hand for a sprint at the finish. But Sloan was also known as an arrogant gambler, and his 1900 coup was one of the most disreputable events in racing history. His gang went to extraordinary lengths to ensure that he would win. Thompson, on Berrill, refused to be moved and beat Sloan on Codoman by three lengths. The UK ban meant that Sloan missed riding what would have been his first Derby winner, Volodyovski, who was jockeyed by his compatriot, Lester Reiff. Reiff became the first American jockey to ride a Derby winner.

TOD SLOAN.

G.D.G.

Overleaf: Lester Piggott's first race since leaving prison for tax fraud (see page 139).

Right: an 1899 Vanity Fair illustration of American jockey Tod Sloan.

1913
Emily Davison, Derby martyr

ON THE MORNING of 4 June 1913, Emily Davison, one of the most militant members of the suffragettes, called in at the offices of the Women's Social and Political Union in London to collect two of the union's white, green and purple flags. Travelling to Victoria Station, she bought a return ticket to Epsom. Davison had joined the WSPU in 1906, embarking on a course of violence and destruction for which she was imprisoned several times, her offences including obstruction, brick-throwing, setting fire to pillar-boxes and smashing windows in the House of Commons.

Her intentions on the day of the 1913 Derby were unclear, but upon arriving at the track, she positioned herself on the inside rails at Tattenham Corner. Fifteen horses were competing that year for a first prize of £6,450, and the favourite was Craganour, jockeyed by the American Johnny Reiff; second favourite was Shogun. King George V's horse, Anmer, ridden by Herbert Jones, was an outsider at 50–1. The race began well, with Aboyeur taking an early lead, along with Craganour and Aldegond. With a mile to run, Anmer struggled to stay with the pace and started to drop back. In position at Tattenham Corner, Davison waited until the leaders raced past and then squeezed through the crowd and under the rails on to the course. She

avoided Agadir, one of the stragglers, and stepped out in front of Anmer, reaching up to clutch the reins of the King's horse. Witnesses claimed that she hung on to the reins for a split second as jockey Jones struggled to lose her, but the horse, travelling at over 48 km/h (30 mph) and weighing in at nearly three-quarters of a ton, hit her head, and the three went down in a heap. Playwright St John Ervine, describing the event for the *Daily Mail*, wrote: 'It was all over in a few seconds. The horse knocked the woman over with very great force, and then stumbled and fell, pitching the jockey violently on to the ground. Both he and Miss Davison were bleeding profusely.'

The crowds rushed on to the track as the race proceeded. Herbert Jones, Anmer's jockey, had injuries which proved not to be serious. While in hospital, he received a telegram from Queen Mary, who wrote, 'very sorry indeed to hear of your sad accident caused through the abominable behaviour of a brutal, lunatic woman'. Emily Davison never recovered consciousness and died four days later in Epsom Cottage Hospital of a fractured skull and brain haemorrhage. Her death created the suffragettes' first martyr. Buried in the churchyard of St Mary's at Morpeth in Northumberland, her gravestone was inscribed, 'Deeds, not words'. Five years after her death, women won the vote.

Top: Emily Davison attempts to catch the reins of the king's horse. in a fatal effort to draw attention to the women's suffrage movement.

Bottom: suffragette martyr Emily Davison, jockey Herbert Jones and King George V's horse, Anmer. lie injured on the race track at Epsom.

1953
Sir Gordon Richards rides Derby winner – at last

SIR GORDON RICHARDS was considered to be Britain's leading and most-loved jockey during his racing career, riding 4,870 winners out of 21,828 mounts. Twenty-six times, between 1925 and 1953, he was England's top jockey. In 1933, Richards set a record by riding 259 winners, improved on with 269 victories in 1947. In 1953, he was knighted by the newly crowned Queen Elizabeth II, the first jockey to be so honoured.

But for all his success, Richards had never managed to win the Epsom Derby, despite 27 attempts. Spirits and hopes were high on 6 June 1953 as the hour of the race approached. Few races have engendered such division of loyalties as did this one. High on the list of favourites was Aureole, trained by Captain Cecil Boyd-Rochfort and ridden by Harry Carr, who had scored a smooth victory in the Lingfield Derby, and which was owned by the young Queen Elizabeth. Richards, whose knighthood had just been announced, was another favourite on Pinza, owned by Sir Victor Sassoon, who had spent a huge amount of money over many years trying to win the Derby. A win by either party would be received with delight by the expectant crowd.

Pinza was a big horse, and many doubted whether he would be nimble enough down Tattenham Hill. He was also

highly strung, which further placed in doubt his chances of victory, despite the hopes pinned on Richards as jockey. In all, 27 runners went to post, and the early running was made by outsider City Scandal, who conceded the lead to Shikampur, with Pinza in sixth and Aureole further behind. At Tattenham Corner, Pinza slipped into second place on the turn for home, and with two furlongs to go, swept into the lead. Pinza galloped on relentlessly, winning by four lengths, with Aureole second.

The applause was uproarious, but Richards was strangely silent as he led Pinza to the saddling enclosure. He later wrote: 'My mind was in a turmoil, and my brain perhaps a little numbed ... the reception which the crowd gave me was something out of this world.' Pinza ran only once more, when Richards rode him to an easy victory in the King George VI and Queen Elizabeth Stakes at Ascot. Soon after, the horse broke down and was retired to stud, leaving the field open for Aureole, who went on to win the Coronation Cup, the Hardwicke Stakes and the King George. Richards was forced to retire during the 1954 season due to injury, so the 1953 Derby was not only his first win but also his last ride in the race.

Left: Pinza, ridden by Gordon Richards, striding ahead to win the Derby at Epsom in 1953.

Right: the winners' enclosure – Gordon Richards, surrounded by wellwishers, celebrating his first Derby win.

1954
A double first at the Derby

O N 2 JUNE 1954, 18-year-old Lester Piggott rode the American-bred Never Say Die to a spectacular victory in the Epsom Derby. Piggott was the youngest jockey to win in the history of the race. Never Say Die was also the first American-bred horse to take the title since Iroquoise had won in 1881, in a race from which he had very nearly been scratched.

Three weeks before the event, veteran American owner Robert Sterling Clark had received a cable from his English racing manager, Gerald McElligott, saying that Never Say Die had no chance in the Derby and seeking permission to scratch him. The horse had finished third to Elopement in the Newmarket Stakes on 12 May. Piggott, who should have ridden the colt at Newmarket, had begged to be excused as he had more promising mounts at Bath on the same afternoon. E. Mercer, who rode Never Say Die that day, reported that the colt hung badly, and it was suggested that he had no chance in the Derby. Clark decided to scratch the colt, but just after posting the letter he had a cable from the UK

saying that there had been a misunderstanding and that the horse was being left in the race.

In the *Daily Telegraph*, it was reported that Rowston Manor led around Tattenham Corner with Landau second and Darius third, followed by Blue Sail and Never Say Die. Rowston

Manor had run much too freely, and with a quarter of a mile to go, he and Landau were beaten. Darius took the lead, with Never Say Die moving up to challenge. With a furlong to go, Piggott sent Never Say Die into a clear lead, and with Darius now fading, Arabian Night took second place from the 2000 Guineas winner Darius in the last few strides. Never Say Die, with odds of 33–1, gave Piggott the Blue Riband, and the jockey went on to become the new king of racing, notching up four more classics by the end of a decade in which he was rarely out of the headlines.

Robert Sterling Clark was not present to see his colt win, but the 73-year-old trainer Joe Lawson was. This was his first Derby winner. Later that year, Stewards of the Jockey Club gave Piggott a severe warning as a result of their enquiry into a report on the King Edward VII Stakes when Piggott had ridden the same horse. Piggott was informed that Stewards had 'taken notice of his dangerous and erratic riding', and that he was continuing, in spite of frequent warnings, to show complete disregard for the rules of racing and the safety of other jockeys. Piggott lost his licence for six months, missing the St Leger at Doncaster in which he was to have ridden Never Say Die again.

Left: *Never Say Die riding to victory. Close behind are Arabian Night and Darius – they finished second and third in a photo finish.*

Right: *an 18-year-old Lester Piggott rides into the unsaddling enclosure after winning the Derby.*

1956
The mystery of Devon Loch

ON 24 MARCH 1956, celebrated English jockey Richard Stanley 'Dick' Francis rode the Queen Mother's horse Devon Loch in the Grand National, nearly capturing his first National win. The Queen Mother had two runners entered, M'as Tu Vu and Devon Loch, a 10-year-old son of Devonian with proven ability over fences. As a former steeplechase champion, Francis was a popular choice for jockey.

Francis and his mount Devon Loch were not the bookies' favourite, but the crowd was with them and the horse responded. Armorial III led at the first fence, but by the Canal Turn, Devon Loch was holding his own, while other rivals were struggling to hold their places for the last mile home. The final fence saw Devon Loch galloping strongly, one-and-a-half lengths in front of ESB, Mrs Leonard Carver's gelding and the mount of Dave Dick. From the stands came the loudest cheering ever heard on a racecourse as the crowds celebrated what looked likely to be the first Royal Grand National winner for 56 years.

The applause increased with every step taken by Devon Loch as he soared ahead of his pursuers. But with 55 yds to go and the Grand National at his mercy, Devon Loch, clear of all opponents, stumbled, skidded and fell for no apparent reason. The *Daily Telegraph* called it the 'most dramatic event ever seen on a racecourse'. Dave Dick, reconciled to finishing second, now drove ESB past the stricken Devon Loch to race first past the post. The cause of Devon Loch's fall has never been established. One of the racecourse vets who examined Devon Loch immediately after the race thought he might have suffered a sudden attack of cramp, but it was not certain. Francis led Devon Loch back through the paddock past an eerily silent and mystified crowd. ESB's time was only four-fifths of a second outside the record of 9 minutes 20 $\frac{1}{5}$ seconds set by Reynoldstown in 1935. Devon Loch, had all gone well, would certainly have beaten it.

Called the unluckiest National loser of all time, Devon Loch was the recipient of much public sympathy, and crowds bemoaned the cruel twist of fate that had denied the Queen Mother, Francis and trainer Peter Cazelet a well-deserved victory. After the race, the Queen Mother quietly approached the stables with becoming dignity and good humour, winning the hearts of everyone for the manner in which she hid her disappointment. She visited her horse and then went on to congratulate Mr and Mrs Carver, his rider and his trainer on their victory, as though nothing had happened. To this day, Devon Loch's collapse remains one of the unsolved mysteries of the turf. Francis retired from racing a year later, becoming the racing correspondent for the *Sunday Express* and achieving best-seller status as a novelist.

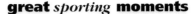

In 1956, crowds at Aintree waited with bated breath for what they hoped would be the first Royal Grand National win for 56 years.

1977
Red Rum's hat-trick

ON 2 APRIL 1977, Red Rum made National Hunt history at Aintree by winning the Grand National for a record third time, bringing his overall winnings total to £114,000 – another jumping record.

Red Rum, at 12 years of age, was widely considered to be one of the finest horses running, having won the National in 1973 and 1974 and come second in 1975 and 1976. The horse's success was largely due to the persistence and vision of trainer Ginger McCain, who had bought Red Rum for 6,000 guineas on behalf of owner Noel Le Mare and gradually made the horse into one of the best chasers in the north. Red Rum had also shrugged off the effects of damaging foot disease to become the King of Aintree.

Peter Scott reported in the *Daily Telegraph*: 'I cannot recall any Grand National winner showing less signs of fatigue after the race and the inevitable mobbing from his ecstatic admirers. It is said, with justification, that luck generally plays a bigger part in this race than any other, but Red Rum makes his own good luck. He nimbly avoids trouble, measures each of those now familiar fences with precision and runs on with ever-increasing power.' The favourite, Andy Pandy, had fallen at Becher's Brook on the second circuit, leaving Red Rum in front. Chased by What a Buck, Churchtown Boy, Happy Ranger, Sir Garnet and Pilgarlic, Red Rum stepped up the pace after jumping the Canal Turn, taking each subsequent fence in faultless style. Recrossing Melling Road, now four lengths in the lead, he ran into a crescendo of cheering from crowds aware that they were seeing history in the making. He strode majestically up the straight, drawing even further away from those in his wake, capturing his third victory by 25 lengths. McCain had been adamant that 'Rummy' would win, provided the ground was in his favour, and his words proved to be prophecy. The *Telegraph* observed that it was 'one of those days when the old cliché came true; strong men actually did weep, such was the emotional impact of Red Rum's historic achievement'. Jockey Tommy Stack was met with a jubilant reception in the winner's enclosure after the race, a moment he claimed he would never forget.

McCain was also outspoken in his views on the presence in the field of 21-year-old Miss Charlotte Brew, declaring that the 'National was no place for lady riders'. Partnering her own horse,

Barony Fort, on which she had completed one circuit of the course in the 1976 Foxhunters' Chase, Brew received intense media attention for being the first woman to ride the National. The odds were 200–1, but she rode a good race, struggling on bravely until the fourth from home, where Barony Fort refused, bringing Brew's National quest to an end.

Top: *death of a legend – Red Rum's grave at the finish line at Aintree, covered with floral tributes to racing's greatest name.*

Bottom: *the majestic and beautiful sight of Red Rum, being exercised over Southport Sands.*

1978
'The Kid' takes the Triple Crown

When eighteen-year-old Steve Cauthen, on Affirmed, ran away with America's Triple Crown in 1978, it shot him to superstar status. Cauthen was born into a family with a long history of racing and breeding and by 1977 he was already breaking records, winning over 400 races that season and walking away with more than $6 million in prize money. Nicknamed 'The Kid' by his increasing following in America, Cauthen knew he could do better still, and turned his thoughts to taking the most coveted prize in US horse racing – the Triple Crown.

Three classic races make up this prestigious event: the Kentucky Derby, the Preakness and the Belmont Stakes. Taking the Triple was the crowning glory.

The build-up to the races was touted as the ultimate duel between the three-year-old Affirmed and long-time rival Alydar. Alydar was favourite for the Derby, the first race of the three, but Affirmed and The Kid, showing characteristic determination, romped home a length and a half ahead. Cauthen did not let this go to his head, though, knowing that tougher challenges were to come. He was right. At the Preakness, Alydar dogged his every step and eventually Affirmed came in only a neck ahead of his rival.

All cards now on the table, and with the Triple Crown in his sights, Cauthen turned his attention to the final race – the Belmont Stakes. The Kid knew Affirmed could make it, but the horse had run two difficult races, and it would take all his reserves of energy – and an element of luck – to hold off Alydar for a third time. It was a nail-biting race. Then, on the final stretch Affirmed stumbled and it began to look as though Alydar might finally get his moment of glory. The Kid, seeing Alydar draw level, knew he had to find the strength to win just one more time. He had never used his whip on Affirmed before, but now he drew it out and hit the horse, begging him to make one final stand. It worked. Affirmed galvanized the last ounce of strength he had and crossed the line a neck ahead of the valiant Alydar.

It was always going to be a fight to the finish – but what a finish! Cauthen, celebrated as America's newest prodigy, was an unassuming young man off the racetrack and merely remarked, 'That is a moment in sports history ... it was an event ... and I was lucky to be part of it.'

1981
Aldaniti's Champion National

ON APRIL 4, 1981, the Grand National blazed an example of courage and perseverance round the world when Bob Champion and Aldaniti provided a triumphant ending to a tale of a three-times crippled horse and a cancer-beater. Champion, 32, had been given eight months to live in 1979 when doctors had diagnosed cancer. Two bouts of tendon trouble and a fractured hock bone had made Aldaniti's own prospects of Aintree glory appear just as remote.

Throughout his long and debilitating treatment, Champion had kept his eye on Aldaniti, who had been nine years old when Champion was diagnosed. Champion and Aldaniti had begun their partnership in January 1975, when the horse had won a novices' hurdle at Ascot on his racecourse debut. Despite his injury problems, he was clearly a candidate for the Grand National, and the idea of winning the Liverpool race on this horse became an inspiration for Champion as he underwent treatment. Josh Gifford, who had bought Aldaniti at the Ascot sales in May 1974, had performed wonders during training, and his achievement was matched on a more personal basis by his loyalty to Champion. Champion's long illness was made more bearable by Gifford's promise that his job of stable jockey would be there when he recovered.

The illness and treatment left Champion weak and bald, and it was nearly 18 months before he regained his fitness. Aldaniti, after 15 months of being laid off, was not expected to do well, but after easily winning the Whitbread Trial Chase at Ascot, he was second favorite for the Grand National at Liverpool. Champion had been advised to take a pull halfway to the first fence in order to prevent his mount from rushing at it, but Aldaniti could not be restrained. Champion later said, 'As we came to the fence Aldaniti stood off far too far away, pinged it, but came down much too steep. I slipped my reins to the end of the buckle. . . . What a waste for both of us. He was on the ground, down. His nose and knees scraping the grass. We'd had it.' But Aldaniti recovered his balance and continued. After another hiccup at the second, he jumped with perfect precision for the remainder of the course, pulling into the lead at the 11th. By Royal Mail, Champion let Aldaniti take his own time, while John

Thorne struggled to catch them on Spartan Missile, looking as if he might overtake on the straight. But Aldaniti responded gamely and kept up his gallop, leading the race to the post by four lengths. Their joint dream had come true. Not only had they overcome all to win the National, but Aldaniti was the first Grand National winner since Sundew in 1957 to lead throughout the final circuit.

In 1983, Champion founded the Bob Champion Cancer Trust, and four years later Aldaniti himself took part in the Trust's fund-raising activities.

Two sporting greats: Bob Champion and Aldaniti, photographed for the Bob Champion Cancer Trust.

1981
Shergar saunters to victory in the Irish Sweeps Derby

OWNED AND BRED by the Aga Khan and trained at Newmarket by Michael Stoute, Shergar had run only twice as a two-year-old, but he was soon proclaimed as a horse out of the ordinary, considered to be one of the very best of the post-war period, continually turning in devastating performances. Although his victory at the Derby in Epsom recorded the longest winning margin in the history of the race, it was the 1981 Irish Sweeps, where Shergar so completely dominated his rivals, which saw the horse at his peak.

His jockey was Lester Piggott, who had ridden Shergar in both his races as a two-year-old and had taken the mount from Walter Swinburn, who had been suspended after the King Edward VII Stakes at Royal Ascot. Piggott was under instructions not to pressurize the mount unless it was truly necessary, and he handled the horse with tenderness and supreme cool in a virtuoso performance. In the early stages, Shergar sauntered with his rivals, and his tongue lolled from his mouth in what appeared to be complete boredom. As the riders entered the straight with about three furlongs to go, Shergar was still coasting, eventually moving past them as television commentator Peter O' Sullevan enthused, 'He's only in an exercise canter!'. Shergar, with tail swishing and ears pricked, made for the finish, with no apparent effort whatsoever, as Piggott glanced from left to right, seemingly not believing their good fortune. The winning margin was four lengths from the second-placed Cut Above – a significantly smaller lead than at Epsom – but the astonishing fact remained that Shergar had got there without any obvious exertion. His performance marked him as an exceptional horse. After finishing fourth to Cut

Left: Shergar wins at Ascot in 1991, ridden by Walter Swinburn.

Right: the crowd's favourite – Shergar in his stables. The mystery of his abduction has never been solved.

Above in a gruelling St Leger later that year, Shergar was retired.

This was not, however, the end of the Shergar story. In 1983, the horse was abducted from the Ballymany Stud in County Kildare on the night of 8 February, a week before he was due to commence his second season as a stallion. Shergar's stud value was set at £10 million, and during the stud season, he would have covered a maximum of 55 mares, earning more than £2.5 million. Kidnapped from the stud farm near Newbridge by a gang of up to six men, he was never recovered, and it was assumed that his kidnappers, widely believed to be the IRA or part of a vendetta against the Aga Khan, killed the horse when they realized that their ransom demand of £2 million would not be met.

1990
'Come on, Lester!'

 ON 25 OCTOBER 1990, Lester Piggott stole the headlines at Belmont Park by swooping from behind on Royal Academy to win the Breeders' Cup Mile for Vincent O'Brien. This underlined Piggott's amazing return to the big time of international racing, just before his 55th birthday. John Oaksey wrote in the *Daily Telegraph*,

'Slowly away, Piggott was able to settle the Irish horse nearer last than first, until the turn for home; then, switching to the outside, he began one of those long, relentless challenges which used to be the trademark of so many winning years. The old cry "Come on, Lester!" resounded in the Belmont Press Room'. Racing correspondent Christopher Poole described this event as the most

Lester Piggott leading the race at Chepstow, 16 October 1990.

emotional occasion on any racecourse since Sir Gordon Richards had won the Derby. Piggott's comeback had been marred by two deaths – of Mr Nickerson, one of the 14-strong field, who collapsed and died of a heart attack as they jostled towards the turn, and of Go for Want, a brilliant three-year-old filly who shattered a leg and had to be put down – and an unlucky defeat for Dayjur, who made a jump at a phantom fence as two shadows were thrown across the field in the blazing autumn sun.

Piggott, who had just finished serving a prison sentence for tax evasion, had made his comeback just weeks earlier at the Hare Maiden Fillies Stakes in Leicester, where thousands flocked to watch racing's greatest living legend turn back the years in his own inimitable style, losing first by only 3 cm (1 ¼ in). Piggott had been sent to jail for three years (of which he served one) in 1987 after admitting tax evasion to the tune of £3 million. The Jockey Club Stewards had granted his wife a temporary licence to keep her husband's

Newmarket stables open, but made it clear that she would have to reapply for renewal. Piggott, whose personal fortune had been estimated at £20 million, had used different names to channel his earnings into secret bank accounts around the world. The illegal activities which landed him in court arose from his failure to declare the proceeds of a private contract under which wealthy racehorse owners met his demands for huge rewards on top of his officially registered fees and retainers. The nine-times Derby winner was prosecuted in the biggest individual tax-dodge case ever brought in Britain, and the sentence was the highest passed for a personal tax fraud.

Piggott, the grandad of racing, retained the admiration and support of his racing colleagues and fans throughout the trial and ensuing prison sentence, and there was genuine jubilation as he made his comeback, going on to ride his 30th Classic in 1992. Piggott became the greatest rider of his era, beating Richards' record of 5300 victories.

Number 13 proved lucky for Lester Piggott, back in the saddle in October 1990.

1993
The Grand National that never was

ON 3 APRIL 1993, the 150th Grand National at Aintree was declared void when, after one false start and a successful recall, almost the entire field failed to realize that a second false start had occurred. Racing Journalist of the Year, J. A. McGrath, reported in the *Sunday Telegraph*: 'The alleged failure of a casually employed flag man, paid £28 for a day's work, to signal a second false start – and the subsequent failure of seven jockeys to pull up their mounts before a second circuit of the course was completed – reduced the event to a farce ... Peter Greenall, the chairman of the racecourse company, said that this year's race would not be re-run as trainers overwhelmingly felt it would not be practical from the horses' point of view.'

In the 'non-race', seven horses actually completed the 4 1/2-mile course, and there was genuine heartbreak when John White, who crossed the line first on Esha Ness, realized what had happened. He protested, 'I didn't see any flag the second time. When I reached the Chair, I saw some cones and thought that some of the protesters had got to the fence. I never heard anybody saying that it had been a false start and there were horses around me, so I assumed it was a race'. In fact, the starter had signalled a false start for the second time, but the recall flag was, in error, not shown. John Upson, trainer of the heavily backed Zeta's Lad, who completed one circuit of the course before pulling up, approached officials near the starting point to vent his anger. He later said, 'I've spent a year getting Zeta's Lad ready for this race. Now it has all come to nothing.' At a press conference, Peter Greenall said, 'Looking at the video, the recall flag wasn't up. The whole starting procedure will be reviewed'.

The fiasco, which was televized live to millions of viewers around the world, cost the betting industry and the Treasury millions of pounds. The Connell Report, published on 13 June, listed eight main conclusions, the principal ones being that human error and the 'Grey Gate' system of starting were to blame. After hearing evidence from 34 people and watching all the available films and videos, the committee reached the conclusion that Aintree recall man Ken Evans had indeed failed to wave his flag, but it did say, 'To imply that the failure of the advance flag man to act as he should have done was the sole cause of the ensuing problems would have been unfair and unrealistic'. As a result of the enquiry, a new starting gate and procedures were developed and rigorously tested in race conditions before the 1994 event.

The unfortunate competitors of the 1993 Grand National – the race was declared void.

Rugby

Murrayfield was the turning point for me as captain. I realized we had to be more ruthless and professional in our approach to these games. **Will Carling** in 1991, recalling how defeat led to the birth of the team which won back-to-back Grand Slams.

1905
Wales halt rampant All Blacks

WHEN THE NEW ZEALANDERS, making their first official visit to Britain, opened the tour against Devon in 1905, few in what they affectionately called 'the homeland' knew what to expect. They soon found out as the visitors won 55–4. While rugby had been played in England since 1823, the game did not start up in New Zealand until 1871. The New Zealanders proved to be fast learners. They were quickly christened the All Blacks, a nickname which arose from their sombre garb, although an alternative theory is that it was a corruption of the phrase All Backs, as their forwards proved just as mobile and skilful as their back division, revolutionizing the way the game was played.

The All Blacks proceeded to humble all the opposition England, Scotland and Ireland could muster. In their first-ever international, they beat Scotland 12–7. They beat Ireland 15–0 and triumphed over England by the same margin in a match watched by a then record crowd of 50,000 at Crystal Palace.

The tour raised interest in the game to new heights. When the All Blacks, led by Dave Gallaher, arrived in Cardiff to play Wales, they had won all their 27 games, scoring 801 points and conceding just 22. Gallaher was something of a rugby visionary and played in a unique position, standing off the scrum as the All Blacks packed down with just seven men instead of the usual eight. The tactic was described as unsporting and added to the controversy over the New Zealanders' jerseys, which had a special canvas collar sewn in. It was suggested that the eel-skin made them harder to tackle. Wales, always expected to be the toughest opposition for the All Blacks, were wise to their ploys and adopted the seven-man scrum themselves. The tourists, feeling the strain of playing two tough games a week for two months, were not at their best.

Even then, it took a controversial moment to send the All Blacks to defeat. Trailing to a try by Teddy Morgan, they launched a powerful attack, and centre Bob Deans reached the try line, only to be tackled by Morgan. Had he touched down? Opinion was divided, and the referee, who did not have a clear view, awarded a scrum instead of a try. Wales

hung on to win 3–0, inflicting the only defeat of a tour during which the All Blacks won 31 of their 32 matches, scoring 830 points and conceding just 39. Their perfect record was ruined by Wales, and debate still rages about the try that never was.

Overleaf: the England team celebrate their 24–0 win over Wales in the Five Nations, 1992 (see page 154).

Right: Bernard Partridge's illustration of New Zealand's victory, entitled 'the cub unlicked'. It appeared in Punch *in 1905.*

PUNCH, OR THE LONDON CHARIVARI.—OCTOBER 11, 1905.

THE UN-LICKED CUB.

[The New Zealanders have met several of our best Rugby teams, and easily defeated them.]

1927
The rise of the Tricolours

WHEN FRANCE reached the inaugural World Cup final in 1987, it was an historic day for the country. No French sports team had ever reached a world final before.

France's early internationals led invariably to heavy defeats. Dave Gallaher's 1905 New Zealand side played the first official game against France, winning 38–8 at Parc des Princes in Paris. The All Blacks captain said afterwards, 'At the present time the rugby football of France can hardly be said to have attained a very high level, but we were much surprised at it being anything as good as we found it to be'. He added, prophetically, 'Such enthusiasm as theirs must tell in the long run, even though it may be necessary for it to be bred through two or three generations'.

In the early days, enthusiasm wasn't enough. France lost their first international against England 35–8 in 1906, and in the next few years suffered some numbing defeats, including 36–4 to Wales and 27–0 to Scotland. France entered the Five Nations Championship in 1909–10, but between 1911 and 1920 lost 17 consecutive Five Nations games.

The French gradually became more competitive and started to evolve the free-flowing game for which they were later acclaimed – champagne rugby. The first overseas side to tour extensively helped to mould this style, with the New Zealand Maoris playing 15 matches throughout France in 1926. The Maoris' open, passing game was much admired and added to an upsurge in the sport's popularity. The standing of the game increased still further when the French had their finest moment so far in the following year. After 16 defeats spread over 21 years, the French finally beat England, winning 3–0 in a hard-fought match at the Colombes Stadium. It was a famous victory, especially as England won the Grand Slam the following year, and was the first of only four wins achieved against England between 1906 and 1950.

The development of French rugby was not without controversy. The French were often accused of rough play, and their domestic set-up had an element of professionalism about it that was frowned upon by the strictly amateur Home Unions. After repeated warnings, in 1931 the four Home Unions decided to expel France from the Five Nations because they were not satisfied with 'the control and conduct of the game' there. France's next appearance in the Five Nations was not until 1946–47, but during the years of exile they had built up a new, 15-man style which led to a golden age for the French game. In 1954, they shared the champion-ship for the first time and also beat the All Blacks. French rugby had arrived ... just as Gallaher had predicted it would.

France get the ball away from a scrum in the first French victory over England – Colombes Stadium, Paris.

1965

England v Scotland:
Hancock's great, mud-drenched try

THERE MAY HAVE been greater tries scored in the history of rugby, but few could equal the drama of Andy Hancock's solo run in the Calcutta Cup match between England and Scotland at Twickenham. With a couple of minutes to go in the match, he could hardly have thought that he was about to enter the sport's folklore. Scotland were on the verge of a famous victory, their first against England at headquarters for more than a quarter of a century.

Heavy rain during the day had turned Twickenham into a quagmire, and Scotland were dominant, with their powerful pack holding the upper hand in conditions not conducive to running rugby. The England fly half, Mike Weston, kicked everything that went his way, and Hancock was condemned to a miserable afternoon on the wing. Two passes came his way ... and he dropped them both.

With the final whistle imminent, Scotland were leading 3–0 thanks to a drop-goal from Chisholm, and they seemed in control, pinning England back deep inside their own territory. If anything, the Scots seemed likely to add to their winning margin as winger Whyte came in from the touchline, trying to run through the England defence. However, he was caught, and as a maul formed, the ball came out on England's side. Weston picked up and, harried close to his line, it seemed certain he would kick for safety. Instead, he gambled and decided to pass; looking up, he saw Hancock free, 13.5 m (15 yds) from his own line.

Hancock also looked up, and with opposite number Whyte having vacated the wing ahead of him, he spied a corridor of space and took off on what was to prove to be the longest run-in seen in international rugby. After picking up the pass, he still had 95 yds to go. It was a sprint to the line in the energy-sapping mud, with Hancock not daring to look behind him. He said afterwards that it was as if his 'feet were in glue, my calves ached and my lungs felt as though they were bursting'. He just managed to cross the line before he was tackled, and the unconverted try brought England a 3–3 draw.

England and Scotland players leap for a high ball in the 1965 Calcutta Cup match.

Hancock played just once more for England, winning three caps in all, but achieved a fame which players with ten times as many internationals would envy. However, he was never able to see his great moment captured on film, as all the press photographers, getting ready to take pictures of Scotland's celebrations, were encamped at the other end of the pitch!

1969
England's first closely guarded win over South Africa

FOR A LONG TIME, the 1969–70 South African tour was in danger of being called off, due to the strong anti-apartheid feeling in Britain. In 1968 the MCC had cancelled their cricket tour to South Africa when they had been told that they could not include Basil D'Oliveira, the Cape coloured all-rounder. When the Springboks finally arrived at Heathrow, they were greeted by groups of protesters, and from then on the tour was a cloak-and-dagger operation. The team's whereabouts were such a closely guarded secret that before games, the match-programme editors couldn't even get hold of them to find out team selections.

Their first match, against Oxford University, was switched for security reasons from Iffley Road to Twickenham, and the mood of the tour was set as a huge police presence was deployed. Specially erected fencing prevented a pitch invasion, but a few protesters did make it on to the pitch, with one making a short-lived attempt to climb the goalposts.

Surprisingly, the Springboks' biggest problems ended up coming from Oxford. The University side, captained by Chris Laidlaw, managed a shock 6–3 win – a remarkable display considering that the full England side had yet to record a win over South Africa. However, the tourists could be forgiven for not

having their minds fully on the game. Before the start, they were advised to have overcoats handy to cover up their Springbok gear, just in case they had to make a quick getaway.

England's first win against the Springboks was not long in coming. At the end of the first half, South Africa led 8–0. In the second half, a penalty and a conversion from captain Bob Hiller and a try from John Pullin put England 11–8 ahead, and they hung on to their lead until the end. This time the match was patrolled by a police contingent of 850.

The final match of the tour was the traditional finale against the Barbarians. The police attendance increased to 1,500, with the anti-apartheid protesters determined to succeed in stopping at least one of the games on the tour. Drawing pins and tacks were thrown on to the pitch and smoke bombs exploded, but the Springboks were not to be distracted and ended easy 21–12 victors to finish the tour on a winning note. However, the problems spelt the beginning of the end for South African tours abroad. For a one-off international against the USA in 1981, the venue was kept so secret that a crowd of just 25 turned up to watch the match. They were outnumbered by the 60 police providing security. South Africa had become exiled from the mainstream of world rugby.

Left: an anti-apartheid protester enters the pitch to argue with the South African players.

Right: the England and South African teams waiting to play their top-security match.

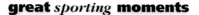

1971
The Lions roar on New Zealand tour

WHEN BRITISH LIONS manager Doug Smith predicted before the start of the 1971 tour to New Zealand that his side would win the series 2–1, with one match drawn, not many people took him seriously.

It was a fantastic suggestion. Ever since the all-conquering tours of 1905 and 1924, New Zealand rugby had dominated the Home Nations. The All Blacks' tradition of winning is such that their players state that they don't remember their victories – just their defeats. Furthermore, the British Lions had never before beaten New Zealand in a series on their home turf. In fact, the British Isles team had only ever won two internationals in New Zealand, and in their previous tour in 1966 they had suffered a 4–0 whitewash.

However, Doug Smith seemed to know something the Kiwis didn't – the quality of the Lions' back division. The men behind the scrum were one of the greatest sets of backs ever to have played together. They were led by Welshman Barry John, who earned such respect from the New Zealanders that they called him King John. Gareth Edwards, Mike Gibson, Gerald Davies, David Duckham and J. P. R. Williams added to a world-class back line. John had a remarkable tour, with his place-kicking eventually proving decisive in the Tests. He amassed 188 points in 17 games during the trip, beating the record for a British player on an overseas tour by over 100 points. Highlights of the matches were shown back in Britain, and John's performances made him one of the first superstars in the new world of televized rugby.

The Lions also had one of the best packs put together by any British side, including Irish legend Willie John McBride and Scottish prop Ian McLauchlan, nicknamed Mighty Mouse. The New Zealanders dubbed him Mickey Mouse, but not for long. The backs and forwards were bonded together by Carwyn James, Llanelli's master coach, and when they beat Wellington 47–9 Graham Williams, the All Black flanker and Wellington captain, called them 'the greatest team I have ever played against'.

Top: 1971 British Lions tour of New Zealand – victory was predicted by Lions manager Doug Smith.

Bottom: David Duckham escapes the defence and scores a try for the Lions.

The Lions reserved their flair for the regional matches. In the Tests, they played tight rugby, using John's brilliant tactical kicking. In the first Test at Dunedin, they won 9–3. New Zealand levelled matters with a 22–12 win in the second Test but the Lions won the third match 13–3, with John contributing a drop goal, two conversions and a try.

The final match at Eden Park was the most nerve-racking. The Lions turned an 8–0 deficit into an 11–8 lead, and the killer moment came when Williams, seemingly in a hopeless position, dropped a goal from 50 yards. The All Blacks levelled with six minutes to go, but the Lions finished on top, ensuring the 14–14 draw to clinch the series, with two wins, one defeat and a draw – just as Doug Smith had said.

Top: Gareth Edwards, British Lions' scrum half passes the ball from the midst of an All Black attack.

Bottom: *All Blacks and British Lions battle it out on the pitch at New Zealand's Eden Park, 1971.*

1973
Gareth Edwards' sensational try for the Barbarians

WHEN THE ALL BLACKS arrived for their seventh tour a year after their home defeat by the Lions, public interest was unparalleled. However, the young team failed to show the flair the growing rugby-viewing public wanted to see – it was left to the Barbarians to do that.

The workmanlike All Blacks beat England, Scotland and Wales and were held to a draw by Ireland. They relied on a safety-first, forward-dominated game, which was perhaps understandable as their usual air of invincibility was punctured when they were beaten by Llanelli, coached by their old tormentor, Carwyn James. They slipped still further when they were beaten by North West Counties, the first time they had lost to an English regional side.

However, the All Blacks were still unbeaten in internationals on tour, and they were in confident mood for their last game before moving on to France, the showpiece match against arch-entertainers the Barbarians in Cardiff.

The Barbarians are a unique club, made up chiefly of Five Nations players. A player is invited to join the club ... you cannot ask to join. The club holds no meetings, with all of its selections and organization done over the phone. Whoever did the phoning round for the match at Cardiff did a good job. The Barbarians included 12 of the 1971 Lions and were led by Lions captain John Dawes and guided by Lions coach Carwyn James.

The Barbarians had always had a reputation for playing enterprising rugby, but against the All Blacks they took the game to a new plane. In one of the most spectacular matches ever seen, their handling was superb. They threw the ball about with abandon, and by half-time they led 17–0, including one of the great tries of all time. The 90-m (98-yd) move was started by Phil Bennett and finished by Welsh team-mate Gareth Edwards. Picking the ball up under his own posts, Bennett effected three outrageous sidesteps to make a break, and the ball was moved upfield through seven pairs of hands, ending with Edwards sprinting in from about 40 m (43 yds). The roar from the capacity crowd of over 50,000 was so loud that it distorted forever the TV recordings of the great scrum-half diving over the line.

The All Blacks, average age 23, showed great spirit to fight back in the second half, led by abrasive back Grant Batty. Batty was booed by the Cardiff crowd whenever he got the ball. He responded by playing superbly, scoring two tremendous tries to reduce the deficit to 17–11. Williams, with another great Barbarians try, settled the affair, with Bennett converting from out wide to make it 23–11. It was one of the great British sporting performances and proved rugby's pulling power as a spectator sport.

Top: Fergus Slattery holds on to the ball for the British Lions, 1973 tour.

Bottom: Lions' Barry John moves forward with John Taylor in support, New Zealand, 1973.

1991
Rugby World Cup final:
Australia v England

THE 1991 RUGBY World Cup in Britain and France proved a grand affair, with the top 16 countries playing 32 matches in all, watched by a million spectators and two billion TV viewers in 70 countries worldwide. After a month of matches, the final pitted England against Australia. England, who had lost in the quarter-finals in a dismal game against Wales in the inaugural World Cup four years earlier, were a resurgent side under new captain Will Carling. Reigning Five Nations champions, they were in the middle of their back-to-back Grand Slams. To reach the finals, they had to pull off two tremendous wins on enemy territory, beating Scotland at Murrayfield and France at Parc des Princes. Australia, who had survived a scare against Ireland in the quarter-finals, had produced the display of the tournament to beat reigning world champions the All Blacks in their semi-final.

England's success had been based on their forward dominance and the tactical kicking of Rob Andrew, leaving little room for flair player Jeremy Guscott and prolific try-scorer Rory

England's Will Carling aiming to taking the ball past the Australian defence.

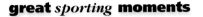

Top: *Michael Lynagh takes the penalty for Australia.*

Bottom: *Tony Daly of Australia scores the game's only try.*

Underwood to show their ability. Much of the build-up to the final centred on the style of play. Would 'boring' England take on the Aussies at their own game?

Everybody wanted an open game – even the groundsman had cut the grass at Twickenham to just one inch, its closest shave ever, to encourage running rugby. But whatever England's plans were, they needed a rethink as Australia built up a 9–0 lead by the break.

The second half was a tremendous affair. England fullback Jonathan Webb reduced the deficit with the first of his two penalties, but his side were denied a further score when Australian wing David Campese, making his 100th appearance for the Wallabies, deliberately punched the ball forward, thus preventing a try for Rory Underwood. Brian Moore, England's outspoken pack leader, felt it should have been a penalty try, saying after the match, 'David Campese showed today that he is not what he says, the saviour of rugby, but he's as cynical as the rest of us'. Just as controversial was England's apparent change of tactics. Instead of trying to grind down Australia with their outstanding forwards, they threw the ball wide, playing in frenetic fashion, only to be halted time and again by Australia's magnificent defence.

Australia ended 12–6 winners. Roger Uttley, the England coach, later recalled: 'As we approached the World Cup final, we agreed to play in the style that served us so well in Paris and Edinburgh. At some point, it was changed. Sitting in the stand, I couldn't believe what I saw when we started running from everywhere. I've never felt so sorry for a pack of forwards in my life. The World Cup was ours for the taking'.

Australia's Farr-Jones and Campese lift their team's hard won trophy, World Cup final 1991.

1991/92
Back-to-back Grand Slams for England

WILL CARLING made his England debut in January 1988 and within 10 months had been named as captain in a bold move by the English RFU (Rugby Football Union). Carling went on to captain England more times than any other player, taking them to the forefront of the game as the top northern-hemisphere side. In 1991 and 1992, his side won back-to-back Grand Slams for the first time since 1924, and sandwiched between the victories they reached the World Cup final.

The impetus for the two Grand Slams came from one of the country's most painful defeats in 1990, when they lost out in the Grand Slam decider against Scotland in Edinburgh. The home side withstood intense pressure to pull off a shock 13–7 win, and Carling admitted: 'Murrayfield was the big turning point for me as a captain. I realized we had to be more ruthless and professional in our approach to these games.'

The 1991 campaign started with a historic victory over Wales, England's first in Cardiff for 18 years, but the success was marred as Carling, manager Geoff Cooke and the England players refused to give interviews to the press after the match. The furore which followed was intense, but the team just became more closely knit. In their next match they got their revenge on Scotland, winning 21–12. Towering locks Paul Ackford and Wade Dooley cleaned up in

Top: Mickey Skinner drives forward helping England to a victory of 38–9.

Bottom: England's Richard Hill gets the ball from a scrum, leading England to a 21–12 victory.

the line-outs, while players like Peter Winterbottom, Dean Richards and Mike Teague added to a world-class back five. Among the backs, Rob Andrew's tactical kicking at fly-half and the place-kicking of Simon Hodgkinson and Jonathan Webb were used to turn pressure into points.

England took the Triple Crown, beating Ireland 16–7, and picked up more criticism for winning too efficiently! Scotland coach Ian McGeechan didn't subscribe to that view: 'That's as good an England team as I've seen. They have decided on a no-frills game because they don't want to let any other side into the game.'

Top: Dewi Morris celebrates his third try in three games, Five Nations 1992.

Bottom: Wade Dooley scores on his 50th cap, Mickey Skinner looks on.

Top: the England team celebrate their back-to-back Grand Slams.

Bottom: Dewi Morris encapsulates the exultant feelings of the England squad.

A narrow 21–19 win over France at Twickenham brought England their first Grand Slam since Bill Beaumont's 1990 success, and the team's second was not long in coming. After their performance in the 1991 World Cup final in November 1991, they were favourites when the Five Nations started in January 1992. If predictability was a feature of the side, there was an air of inevitability about the second Grand Slam campaign. England beat Scotland 25–7 at Murrayfield, won 31–13 at Parc des Princes against France, and beat Ireland 38–9 and Wales 24–0 to amass a championship record 118 points. With the northern hemisphere conquered, Cooke turned his attention to taking on the best in the world, Australia and New Zealand, admitting, 'I think we have closed the gap. But they are still running ahead of us, and we are running like hell to keep up with them'.

1995
Triumph of Nelson Mandela's rainbow nation

THE FIRST TWO World Cups had one notable absentee: South Africa, in exile due to its apartheid policy. But by 1991, the political situation had changed, and it was agreed that the Springboks would not only take part in the 1995 World Cup, but act as hosts.

Their return would also end, once and for all, questions about who was the best. During the 1991 World Cup, some South African fans had waved banners which read: 'You aren't the real world champs till you beat the Boks.'

South Africa's return from the rugby wilderness was celebrated by official tours from New Zealand and Australia in 1992. However, conditions were still volatile in the country, and Nick Farr-Jones, the Wallabies' captain, would have struck a chord with the 1969 Springbok tourists when he asked: 'What is the point of a rugby tour if we have to go everywhere with security men and guns?'

The tours proved one thing. The years of isolation had seen huge improvements elsewhere, and South Africa had a lot of ground to make up. After they were beaten by Australia, their coach admitted, 'We no longer play rugby like the rest of the world. They are playing a different game'. It was a desperate game of catch-up, but when the 1995 World Cup started, the South Africans gave evidence that they had bridged the gap, beating reigning champions Australia in the opening game.

Marshalled by half-backs Joost van Westhuizen and Joel Stransky, and with the inspired leadership of François Pienaar, the Springboks were driven on by the history of the occasion. From the moment when Nelson Mandela welcomed the world to his 'rainbow nation' at the opening ceremony, South Africa played with immense passion. They weren't the best side. That honour went to the All Blacks, by general consent, but they had an intensity which even the New Zealanders couldn't match.

England had knocked out Australia with a last-gasp Rob Andrew drop-goal in the quarter-finals, but the All Blacks, or more correctly giant wing Jonah Lomu, steamrollered past them 45–29 in the semi-finals. It was generally believed that the All Blacks would do the same to South Africa.

The match, though not a rugby classic, was the closest-fought World Cup final so far. Cheered on by the home crowd, which included the potent sight of new president Nelson Mandela resplendent in the green and gold of the Springbok kit, South Africa held the All Blacks. Extra-time loomed with the score at 12–12, but South Africa managed to win a scrum. The ball was worked back to Stransky, he kicked, and the dropped goal sealed a 15–12 win. The fanatics of 1991 had been right after all – you're not the champs until you beat the Boks.

Springbok François Pienaar receives the William Webb trophy from South African president Nelson Mandela.

Sailing

Am I bloody glad to see you buggers!
Round-the-world sailor **Tony Bullimore**, rescued by the Australian Navy after his yacht capsized in the Southern Ocean in 1997

1901
Sir Thomas Lipton and the America's Cup

URING THE 1890S, the America's Cup fascinated the upper echelons of British society. Even the future Edward VII, who had watched the first race back in 1851, became involved in the search for a successful British boat. The cost of putting together a racing team was phenomenal, since the yachts involved were far larger than the modern 12-m (40-ft) ones, many being over 22 m (72 ft) in length. One man rich enough to mount a challenge was Sir Thomas Lipton, who was convinced by the future king to enter his first yacht in the 1899 race. Lipton, a self-made millionaire, was already 51 years old and not much of a sailor, but he had the money and astute business acumen, spotting that the race was an ideal vehicle to advertise his now-famous teas.

Lipton's first yacht, the *Shamrock*, was soundly beaten by the American *Columbia* in the 1899 competition, but its performance whetted Lipton's appetite. In 1901, he was back with a new yacht, the imaginatively named *Shamrock II*. This vessel, whilst the work of the great boat designer George Watson (who later remodelled the King's own yacht *Britannia*) was not a particularly striking vessel. Sad to say, it was also an unlucky one and managed to lose its mast whilst tuning up in the Solent. By the time this damage had been repaired, there was precious little time to bring either the yacht or the crew up to racing trim.

The Americans had retained the *Columbia* to defend the title. This superb vessel had largely been financed by the magnificently wealthy financier J. Pierpont Morgan. Designed and built by the Herreshof company, no expense had been spared on the boat. It also had the advantage of being skippered by the hugely experienced Charles Barr, one of only two men to captain three consecutive Cup winners. Given all these factors, it is surprising that Lipton did so well. Despite losing all the races, his *Shamrock II* managed to perform far better than expected and reached 13 knots.

Whilst Lipton was destined to build no fewer than five *Shamrocks* and compete for the America's Cup right

up until 1930, he was never to win. He nonetheless always viewed his involvement in the race as a success. He gained huge amounts of publicity and his business boomed, due in no small part to the popularity he gained with the Americans. Lipton was 80 years old when he competed in his last race, a year before he died. After his final challenge had failed, he was presented with an enormous loving cup by the mayor of New York on behalf of the American people; a fitting testament to a sporting man.

Overleaf: the American entrant, Stars and Stripes, at the 1987 America's Cup (see page 168).

Right: The Columbia *and the* Constitution *battle it out in the first of the Final Races – America's Cup, 1901.*

1905
Across the Atlantic in 12 days

REGARDED BY MANY experts as the finest ocean racer of all time, the *Atlantic* was designed by William Gardner and built by Townsend & Downey of New York in 1904. Designed as an auxiliary three-masted schooner, it was to change hands no less than eight times during its 65-year career and to see many magnificent occasions. Without doubt, the finest of these was the transatlantic race for the German Emperor's Cup in 1905.

The race started at 12.15 p.m. on 17 May from the Sandy Hook Lightship in thick fog. The yawl *Aisla* was the first away, but because of the conditions it was difficult to tell who was in the lead. The yachts had a choice of two basic routes, the southern one favoured by the steam liners or a more northerly one. The northern choice, whilst being quicker, provided a very real hazard from icebergs.

Intent on setting a new speed record, Charles Barr, the captain of the *Atlantic*, chose the northerly route. The *Atlantic* caught up and passed the early leader, the *Hamburg*, on the afternoon of the second day and remained at the front of the race. The *Hamburg*, which was the Kaiser's own entry, came second. The competition was not really with the other yachts but with the sea itself.

Wilson Marshall, the owner of the *Atlantic*, was determined to set a new record for the passage to Europe, and Barr pushed the yacht mercilessly in order to achieve this. After a few days, Marshall, who was becoming alarmed at the pressure being put on his boat, begged Barr to reduce sail, but to no avail. The *Atlantic* sped on, setting an average speed of 14.2 knots by the end of the sixth day. Barr, a successful America's Cup skipper, continued on the northerly route and on one occasion passed close by an iceberg, an event which left many of his passengers terrified.

Blessed with a spell of almost-perfect weather, the *Atlantic* reached the Bishop's Rock, off the western tip of Britain, in just 11 days and 16 hours, and for a few glorious moments it looked as though the 12-day barrier would at last be broken. But it was not to be. Just 80 km (50 miles) off the Lizard, the wind died away to an almost flat calm, and it took the *Atlantic* an agonizing 12 hours to make it across the finishing line. The boat's final time for the crossing came to 12 days 4 hours 1 minute, easily a new record even if the 12-day target had eluded Barr. The *Hamburg*, the *Atlantic*'s closest rival, arrived over a day later, a massive margin of victory.

The record was to last into the 1980s, a brilliant achievement by the greatest ocean racer ever built.

Francis Chichester waves from the cockpit of Gipsy Moth IV *as he nears Plymouth, 29 May 1967.*

1967
Sir Francis Chichester
sails alone round the world

SAILING ROUND the world single-handed is a magnificent achievement when viewed in any light. When that voyage is undertaken by a man in his mid-60s suffering from cancer, it takes on an almost mythical quality. But that is just what Francis Chichester did.

This voyage was by no means Chichester's first great adventure. In 1930, he had been the first man to fly solo from England to Australia, and in 1964 he had set a solo record for crossing the Atlantic. This new voyage, however, was to be his greatest challenge. The vessel he chose to carry him around the globe was the 16.5-m (54-ft) *Gypsy Moth IV*, a purpose-built yacht constructed by Camper and Nicholson, which was launched in May 1966.

Chichester's great voyage commenced on 27 August of that same year, when he crossed the start line off Plymouth Hoe. From the beginning, *Gypsy Moth IV* proved to be a less than ideal craft for the job, being difficult to handle and having the ability to broach almost at will. When still 3,680 km (2,300 miles) from Sydney, the self-steering rig on the vessel failed, forcing Chichester to spend three gruelling days putting together an emergency replacement which fortunately held. He reached Sydney in 107 days at an average speed of 256 km (160 miles) per day.

Despite extensive modifications whilst in port, disaster befell *Gypsy Moth IV* within a day of leaving. In the middle of the night, the vessel was struck by a freak wave which capsized her. There was never any doubt that she would right herself, but the fact that Chichester survived with no more than a cut lip was a miracle. He proceeded across the Pacific to Cape Horn, the downfall of so many sailors. The conditions here were atrocious, with 16-m (50-ft) waves and winds of over 105 km/h (60 mph). Whilst traversing this frightening stretch of sea, Chichester passed close to the Antarctic Survey Vessel, HMS *Protector*, which sent back some remarkable photographs to an eager public.

7 July 1967: Queen Elizabeth II knights Francis Chichester – using the sword that Queen Elizabeth I gave to Sir Francis Drake in 1581.

Lone sailor, Francis Chichester, crosses the finishing line at Plymouth Harbour, after his epic round-the-world voyage.

Once around the Horn, Chichester was on the home run and reached Plymouth on 28 May 1967. His arrival home was greeted by hundreds of beacons lit along the coast and a huge flotilla of small craft that accompanied him into port. Ever a private man, Chichester was apparently not best pleased by all this attention.

Chichester was knighted at the Greenwich Meridian Line with the same sword used to bestow the honour on Sir Francis Drake. *Gypsy Moth IV* had covered 57,000 km (28,500 miles) by the time they reached home, yet Chichester felt no love for the vessel, describing her as 'cantankerous and difficult to handle'. Sir Francis Chichester, who had started out as a shepherd in New Zealand earning 10 shillings a week, had certainly come a long way.

1969
One-and-a-half times
round the world – non-stop

WHILST THE VOYAGES of Sir Francis Chichester are well known, those of Bernard Moitessier remain largely unheard of outside sailing circles.

All his adult life, Moitessier had been fascinated by the exploits of Joshua Slocum, a nineteenth-century American sailor. Slocum had built his yacht the *Spray* himself, modelling it on an oyster boat. Setting off from Boston in 1895, he sailed around the world, the first man to do so. He was 54 years old, and the voyage took him over three years.

It is not surprising that such a story should provide inspiration for another sailor. Moitessier's yacht, the steel-hulled Bermuda ketch *Joshua*, was named in honour of Slocum and custom-built to compete for the first-ever *Sunday Times* Golden Globe Trophy.

The *Joshua* started off well, sailing down through the Atlantic towards the Cape of Good Hope. Rounding the Cape, Moitessier, unlike Slocum, sailed eastwards, aided by the strong winds of the Roaring Forties. The *Joshua* was in the leading group of the race, and by the time Moitessier sped off to the south of Australia and New Zealand, things seemed to be going very well indeed.

With the Forties in his sails, Moitessier set course straight across the Southern Pacific, rounding the Horn on 5 February. It was at about that point that the ever-enigmatic sailor did something no one could have predicted, perhaps not even himself. With victory almost in sight, he dropped out of the race. A message catapulted to a nearby ship read: 'I am continuing non-stop towards the Pacific Islands because I am happy at sea and perhaps could also save my soul.' With all thoughts of winning the race now gone, Moitessier could sail on as he pleased, which is what he did, finally alighting at Tahiti in French Polynesia. He had spent a total of 301 days at sea without ever coming ashore. Eight months were spent in the Roaring Forties, an area which requires the utmost skill to navigate. Moitessier had passed Australia twice and circumnavigated the globe one-and-a-half times non-stop – without doubt one of the greatest feats of endurance sailing ever accomplished.

There is no doubt that this achievement is every bit as marvellous as Sir Francis Chichester's 1967 voyage, yet it remains relatively unknown. This is perhaps due to Moitessier's intensely private personality. In one of his few interviews, he was asked why he abandoned such a good race position. He answered, 'I enjoy the solitude of the sea and to race for such records is simply an insult to her'. – a fittingly enigmatic answer from one of this century's most remarkable mariners.

1983
Australia II wins the America's Cup

WHEN THE POTENTIAL challengers for the 25th defence of the America's Cup began arriving in Rhode Island in the early summer of 1983, few expected anything out of the ordinary. After all, the Americans had won the last 24. However, this time things were going to be different.

The Americans, in the guise of the New York Yacht Club, tended to follow a rather rigid procedure when it came to organizing their defences of the Cup, with each new boat being very much a development of the last. No one ever criticized this hidebound way of doing things since the Americans always won.

Despite entries from France, Italy and Great Britain, it was the Australians who were going to provide the real competition. Alan Bond and his team manager, Ben Lexcen, had recognized that they needed a radically different yacht to beat the Americans. That is just what they had acquired in the shape of *Australia II*. As well as being considerably lighter than the average 12-m (40-ft) vessel, *Australia II* had a radical hull design which made it far more manoeuvrable and responsive than conventional designs.

Left: Liberty *and* Australia II *competing for the 1983 America's Cup.*

Right: Australia II *out of the water. The craft is considerably lighter than the average 12-m (40-ft) vessel.*

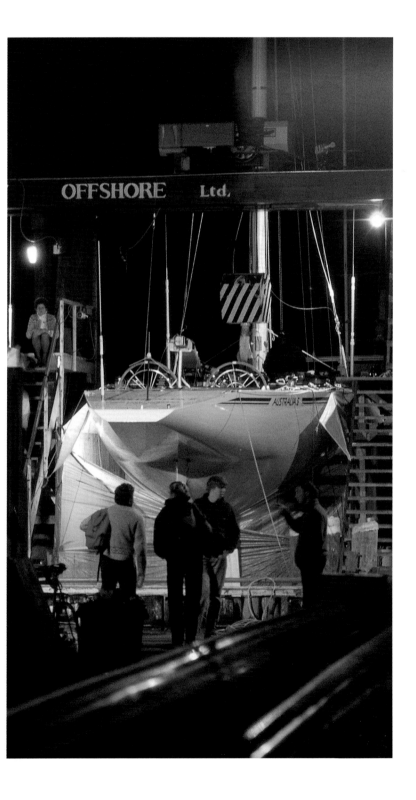

From the moment they arrived, the Australians did their best to keep this keel secret, concealing it behind a plastic curtain every time the vessel was lifted from the water. The Americans, now more than a little concerned at the ease with which *Australia II* had swept away the opposition in the heats, began to voice objections. Despite the fact that the hull had been cleared by the race inspectors, they made several unsuccessful attempts to have the Australian vessel banned, going through the rule book with a fine-toothed comb. In the end, all this served to do was to make the NYYC very unpopular, even amongst the Americans themselves.

The first race of the final took place on 14 September, and against all expectations the Americans won by a comfortable 1 minute 33 seconds. The following day they won again, and suddenly it began to look like business as usual. The next day's race was called off, but on the 18th the Australians romped home by a staggering 3 minutes 14 seconds. Things were looking interesting again. Although the Americans won the next race by 44 seconds, against all the odds the Australians won the last three races and the 'Auld Mug' – the first time that it had left America in 132 years.

Left: *the spectacular sight of* Australia II *in action, as seen from the air.*

Right: *the sun shines on Australia's ecstatic Alan Bond, raising the 1983 America's Cup trophy.*

1987
Dennis Conner has his day

ALAN BOND'S forcible removal of the 'Auld Mug' from the New York Yacht Club served to increase interest in the America's Cup race by several orders of magnitude. The revolutionary hull design of *Australia II* was now public knowledge. Bond, in a post-race bout of elation, had revealed all to the world, so the technological edge which had allowed the Australians to win was now available to all. Events were to make Bond rue the day he had given away his secret.

There were no fewer than 13 different syndicates vying to challenge the Australians, and even the defenders were putting forward four more to decide who should have the honour of defending *Australia II's* crown. Much to Bond's chagrin, it was a rival boat which finally won the right, leaving him to look on in frustrated rage when the final arrived. The vessel chosen was the *Kookaburra*. Despite being a magnificent yacht, it lacked the edge which only experience can provide.

The Americans were represented by Dennis Conner and his *Stars and Stripes*. Conner, whose magnificent skill had prevented a far worse defeat for the Americans in 1983, was back with an independent syndicate, the traditional NYYC entry having floundered at the organizational stage. Conner's yacht, as was the norm with American entries, was not particularly radical in design, but was nevertheless perfectly built to race in the conditions expected in Fremantle. The *Stars and Stripes'* main competition in the elimination rounds came in the shape of New Zealand's *KZ-7*, the first-ever 12-m (40-ft) yacht to be built entirely from fibreglass. In view of its less than inspiring name, *KZ-7* was almost immediately dubbed the 'Plastic Fantastic', and the name stuck. There was some controversy surrounding this entry, there being a suggestion that the new material did not fall within the rules of the Cup. Despite sweeping all before them in the eliminators, however, the 'Plastic Fantastic' was put firmly in its place by Conner and his veterans, with the New Zealanders winning only one race.

When it came to the race proper, it was to be won by experience. With the American and Australian yachts far closer in ability than they had been in 1983, Conner's superb racing skills were allowed to shine, and the *Stars and Stripes* romped home to a 4–0 victory. The America's Cup was back where it belonged, and Dennis Conner entered the record books as the first skipper to lose and win it.

Left: a superb bird's-eye view of America's Stars and Stripes. *America's Cup, 1987.*

Right: American Dennis Conner wins back the America's Cup from the Australians.

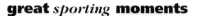

1997
Mayday! Tony Bullimore and Thierry Dubois rescued

THE VENDEE GLOBE is probably the toughest challenge a sailor will ever face: racing non-stop and single-handed around the world. It takes a very special kind of sailor to take part in this sort of activity, and whilst no one can deny the excitement and fulfilment to be gained, there is no getting away from the fact that it is also extremely dangerous.

Despite the best-laid plans, things will inevitably go wrong, and just two days after Christmas 1996, the Italian Raphael Dinelli had to be rescued by fellow competitor Peter Goss, at no small risk to himself. This selfless act received considerable coverage in the media. Just as it was dying down, another two racers, France's Thierry Dubois and the Englishman Tony Bullimore, activated their Argos distress beacons within 16 km (10 miles) of each other, around 2240 km (1400 miles) south-west of Perth, Australia. The weather conditions at the time were horrendous, but at least the Argos system ensured that the locations of the yachts were pinpointed.

The Australian Navy and Air Force immediately commenced a search-and-rescue operation. Dubois was found fairly quickly, and an RAAF Orion aircraft managed to drop him another life raft and emergency supplies so that he could await the arrival of a Navy ship. This should have taken only a couple of days to arrive, but due to the weather it was not until the early hours of 8 January that he was finally picked up. Despite his ordeal, he was in surprisingly good health.

The plight of Tony Bullimore was worse. His yacht had been located at around the same time as that of Dubois, but it was upturned with no sign of life. As the days passed, the chances of finding him alive dwindled, and despite everyone's hopes and prayers Bullimore was more or less written off as dead. But single-handed sailors are made of sterner stuff! When the Australian frigate *Adelaide* finally approached the upturned yacht, Bullimore bobbed up in the water beside it and with true English reserve announced to the stunned Australians, 'Am I bloody glad to see you buggers!'. Bullimore, who was 54 years old, had survived for over four days in a tiny air-pocket in the upturned hull of his 18-m (60-ft) yacht *Global Challenger*.

Despite having rigged a hammock for himself, he was still partially submerged in the freezing water with only a chocolate bar to eat.

Apart from some frostbite to his fingers, Bullimore made a full recovery, and – despite the protestations of his wife on prime-time television – is organizing his next challenge for the Vendee Globe. Dubois, at 29 considerably younger, has also shrugged off his experiences and continues to sail.

Sailing is often seen as a glamorous, relaxing pastime, but there is no denying its extremely dangerous side.

Tennis

10

She really believes it's her court and no one can take it away from her. **Zina Garrison** after losing the 1990 Wimbledon final to Martina Navratilova, who won her record ninth singles title.

1969
Gonzales v Pasarell: The marathon match

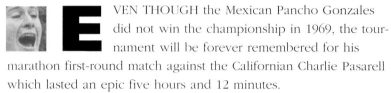

EVEN THOUGH the Mexican Pancho Gonzales did not win the championship in 1969, the tournament will be forever remembered for his marathon first-round match against the Californian Charlie Pasarell which lasted an epic five hours and 12 minutes.

It was common belief that Gonzales, known for his fiery temperament on court, was past it. Proving his critics wrong, he provided the Wimbledon crowd with one last great match. His opponent, the stylish Charlie Pasarell, was 16 years younger. The fact that Gonzales was able to come back to win 22–24, 1–6, 16–14, 6–3, 11–9 was a great testimony to his fitness and determination at 41 years of age.

In his late teens, Gonzales had turned up at his first serious tournament in scuffed tennis shoes. Close to 1.83 m (6 ft), he possessed a great all-round game, including a huge serve that was to destroy opponents all over the world during his glamorous playing days. At 33 he retired, claiming that he was sick of all the travelling involved in being a tennis player. However, Gonzales made numerous comebacks, defeating everybody in sight. Ken Rosewall once said that Gonzales was 'hell on two feet to play'.

Nobody would have argued with Rosewall's assessment as people watched the Wimbledon drama. It began on a Tuesday evening and finished deep into Wednesday afternoon.

Throughout, Gonzales smiled when he was winning and scowled when he was fighting for his tennis life. When the scowl was revealed, his opponent sensed danger and the crowd anticipated excitement.

Gonzales went into the match with a new media-inspired nickname, 'The Old Fox'. He left the court on the Tuesday evening amidst a torrent of jeering when he claimed that it was too dark to see the ball. When play resumed the following day, 14,000 fans waited in anticipation. They were not disappointed. Gonzales eventually triumphed after he and Pasarell got through an incredible 112 games and 13 sets of balls. The match is the longest in the history of the championships, and is likely to remain so since the tie-break system now in force limits the length of all but the last set. It was truly remarkable that both Gonzales and his opponent were able to sustain the quality of their play over such a long period of time. At the end, an exhausted Gonzales said, as phlegmatically as ever, 'Towards the end I was getting cramp on the inside of my thigh. Suddenly Pasarell seemed to be nervous and tense, while I felt all right. It was my greatest comeback ever'.

Overleaf: one of tennis's most famous faces – Bjorn Borg of Sweden (see page 175).

Right: two images of 12th-seeded Richard 'Pancho' Gonzales, in action during his victorious first round of the Men's singles at Wimbledon, 25 June 1969.

1977
Virginia Wade wins Wimbledon

THE CENTENARY championships and the Queen's Silver Jubilee year provided the perfect background for Virginia Wade to win Wimbledon's women's singles crown in the presence of Her Majesty.

On the momentous Friday of the final, Wade woke feeling stiff after a gruelling semi-final victory over Chris Evert. She also carried a huge burden of expectation upon her shoulders, as every sports fan in the UK was willing her to win the championship. Wade took nothing for granted, however. She put a pillow over the telephone and listened to Rachmaninov's second symphony with the volume turned up. Just before the match commenced, she went out on to the centre court in an attempt to absorb the unique atmosphere.

Throughout the championships, Betty Stove had proved to be a very effective, aggressive player, and she continued in this vein in the final, using her imposing physique to claim the opening set 6–4. Although Wade was not playing that badly, she was clearly under immense pressure. This changed dramatically in the second set, when she held her serve to lead 4–3. This game was crucial as it could have gone either way. Wade gained a huge boost from it, following up by winning seven consecutive games. Her increasing intensity during this spell was evident in her sudden private gestures of self-encouragement.

Wade dominated the third set. Her spell of consecutive games was finally broken by Stove in the fifth game of the final set. But this was just a minor setback for Wade, who went on to take the set 6–1. She had finally won her national championship at the 16th attempt. There was a huge roar as she raised her arms to her adoring fans. Flags waved everywhere, and the crowd broke into a spontaneous chorus of 'For She's a Jolly Good Fellow'. Stove modestly drifted into the background, and said later that she enjoyed the celebrations.

Britain's Virginia Wade wins the 1977 women's singles titles at Wimbledon.

*A triumphant Virginia Wade
holds her winner's shield high,
Wimbledon 1977.*

After the victory Wade bubbled over, saying, 'It was so wonderful with the Queen there, the crowd cheering for her and cheering for me, the Duchess of Kent waving, all the singing. It was so friendly. Just like a fairytale'. After becoming the champion in a pulsating 98 minutes, Wade was asked to describe her performance. She spoke of herself as being on a roll after she had lost the first set: 'I don't know how, but the ball seemed to get bigger and bigger. I felt that I could not miss it.' Wimbledon had seldom experienced anything like it. The Queen's presence added to the magnitude of the occasion. The emotion surrounding the victory was engendered in part by patriotism but also by the public's recognition of a player who, at the age of 31 and after many years of trying, had finally won through, when her chances of ever doing so had been totally disregarded.

 *John McEnroe*

1981
McEnroe ends Borg's reign

JOHN McENROE'S victory over Bjorn Borg in 1981 was a momentous one, as it ended Borg's undisputed five-year reign as Wimbledon men's singles champion. Many felt that the volatile American's victory was poetic justice after the Swede had beaten him in the 1980 final. In 1981, the New Yorker McEnroe, nicknamed 'Superbrat', defeated the Swedish master in a riveting match, winning 4–6, 7–6, 7–6, 6–4 in three hours and 22 minutes.

Throughout the tournament, McEnroe was living on a sword's edge with the constant threat of disqualification hanging over his head. A fine of £5,000 was recommended for his conduct during his semi-final match. A fine of £750 was imposed for his 'unsportsmanlike behaviour' in his first-round match against Tom Gullikson. The petulant American was fined a further £375 for incidents in the men's doubles. In the final, both players got off to a flying start, but Borg's superior ground strokes won him the first set. McEnroe, increasing in confidence, became an imposing figure at the net during the second set, volleying superbly and making it difficult for Borg to pass him.

Left: *the USA's John McEnroe on his way to winning his first Wimbledon title.*

Right: *a worried Bjorn Borg, about to hand over his five-year title to 'Superbrat' John McEnroe.*

The first two sets had been shared, and the standard of tennis was exceptional. Borg had a real opportunity to take command of the match in the third set when he had four set points on the McEnroe serve. On each occasion, an inspired McEnroe produced an accurate serve and highly effective volleys to deny Borg. This lost opportunity proved to be decisive as McEnroe went on to take the tie-break with a confident forehand volley.

By the fourth set, McEnroe appeared to be gathering confidence by the second. He was serving with power and looked increasingly at ease with Borg's serve. His ploy of slicing his returns to keep the ball low was causing Borg all sorts of trouble. The battling Swede some-how managed to hold on to his serve four times in the final set, but the inevitable happened in the final game of the match. The American star came out of Borg's shadow to seal victory with another crisp forehand volley to break the Swede's serve.

An ecstatic McEnroe said, 'You've got to give everything in a match to beat him', whereas an understandably more sombre Borg compli-mented his American counterpart: 'On the really important points he hit his first serve almost every time.' It had take McEnroe 12 gruelling months to shed a stone (14 lb) in weight and immeasurable application to strengthen the few small technical faults in his game to overcome the might of Borg.

It is common belief that genius is 10 per cent inspiration and 90 per cent perspiration. The 1981 final seemed to endorse this theory, and although it would be true to say that McEnroe's behaviour was unacceptable, perhaps, in the context of his achievement, it becomes a little more understandable.

A jubilant John McEnroe after beating hot favourite Bjorn Borg for the Men's singles title at Wimbledon, 1981.

1983
Noah wins the French Open

AFTER 37 YEARS of frustration, the French finally produced a player with the ability to win their own championship on the red clay of Roland Garros. The tournament was greatly affected by temperamental weather conditions, but the fascinating tennis on display emphasized a shift in hegemony from America to Europe. This coupled with the scintillating play of a Frenchman by the name of Yannick Noah attracted record crowds totalling 250,000 for the two weeks.

Noah had been discovered in the Federal Republic of Cameroon by Arthur Ashe in 1970. Ashe must have been impressed by his own scouting abilities as Noah outran everyone in Paris before defeating defending Swedish champion Mats Wilander in the final. Noah's path to the final included some notable scalps, the most impressive of which was the defeat of the world number one Ivan Lendl in the first round. Lendl had been left shell-shocked as the sheer aggression of Noah's play destroyed the Czech's faith in his usually dependable technique.

Noah expressed immense joy following this first-round triumph, and his infectious happiness, a feature of the championship, alleviated the general gloominess caused by the adverse weather. Perhaps the most amazing aspect of Noah's victory was the way in which he continued to persist with his aggressive serve-and-volley game. He

confounded critics who stoically believed that the serve-and-volley game could not succeed on slow European clay as he beat Wilander, one of the best baseliners in the world, in straight sets.

The final itself was a fascinating duel between two players with completely opposite styles and skills amidst incredible scenes of emotional fervour and unashamed nationalism. The French idol served better and volleyed extraordinarily well on the sluggish court, regularly taking the attack away from the Swede despite obvious signs of nervousness. Not only did Noah win; he won in grand style. He obviously loved to win. The match was played in an atmosphere of harmony and devotion to skill with Wilander putting up a determined and solid performance to keep his grasp on the crown. The crowd were completely transfixed and seemed to hold their breath until the last point was won before finally dissolving into a frenzy of Gallic delight.

Rarely had the Roland Garros Stadium seen such spectacular scenes. Noah's father literally fell on to the court in his eagerness to embrace his 23-year-old son. There was scarcely a dry eye in the house as France's newest favourite son accepted the trophy from Marcel Bernard, the last winner of the French championship way back in 1946. Noah was both mentally and physically drained, but his attacking policy had paid off. Wilander, generous in defeat, admitted, 'He was too good for me.' Having served and volleyed fantastically to take the French title, Noah incredibly refused to cross the Channel to Wimbledon that year, as he felt that he did not have the game to win there.

Left: *Yannick Noah after beating Mats Wilander of Sweden at the 1983 French Open.*

Right: *the face of joy – France's Yannick Noah after winning the title on home soil.*

1985
Becker wins Wimbledon for the first time

WHEN A 16-YEAR-OLD German by the name of Boris Becker entered the 1984 Wimbledon championships, he ended up leaving the tournament in a wheelchair nursing torn ankle ligaments.

At the 1985 Stella Artois Championships at Queen's Club in London, the dress rehearsal for Wimbledon, Becker emphatically defeated Johan Kriek to take the title. Despite Kriek's prediction that Becker could repeat this performance at Wimbledon two weeks' later and win the tournament, no one believed it.

Germany's 17-year-old star:
left: *Boris Becker during his match against Kevin Curren;* ***right***: *a victorious Becker, Wimbledon's new male champion.*

Becker's victory in the Wimbledon final over South African Kevin Curren – 6–3, 6–7 (4–7), 7–6 (7–3), 6–4 – meant that the record books had to be rewritten. At the age of 17 years and 227 days, he had become the tournament's youngest winner. In addition to this, the strapping young Becker became the first unseeded winner and first West German champion.

It would be fair to say that Wimbledon has witnessed better finals, as Curren's constant unforced errors never caused the match to boil over. However, rarely has the All England Club seen a performance of such astonishing quality from a player with such limited experience.

During the early exchanges in the final, Becker did not have everything his own way, as the first two sets were shared. In the third set, Curren was a break-up serving at 4–3. It was this game which both players agreed was crucial to the outcome of the match. Curren had been causing Becker considerable trouble by consistently playing to the German's backhand, continuing this policy in the eighth game of the third set. It soon became apparent that the practice Becker was gaining on his backhand had resulted in a gradual improvement, and Curren was left in complete shock as Becker unleashed some formidable backhand returns to take the game. The precocious West German realized that the title was within his grasp. He took the third set with a combination of powerful precision on the serve and headlong dives to make seemingly impossible volleys. These made it increasingly difficult for Curren to get back into the match.

Becker's dominance was emphasized on match point, when he produced an explosive serve which caught the edge of Curren's racket before flying into the crowd. Becker's parents looked on proudly, and a handful of West German spectators waved the red, black and yellow of their national flag over the centre court. A disconsolate Curren said that Becker could be number one in the world one day. 'He is only 17 and has got a lot of time for improvement.' When Becker entered the post-match press conference, the reporters broke into spontaneous applause. When told that he had won £130,000, he replied 'That's a lot'.

Wimbledon's 17-year-old star holds his trophy high in front of a mesmerized crowd.

1989
Sanchez-Vicario defeats
Graf to win the French Open

FOR A LONG TIME, Spain was starved of top female tennis players. During the French Open championship at Roland Garros in 1989, it appeared that the Spanish at last had been blessed with a formidable tennis talent. Teenaged prodigy Arantxa Sanchez exuded a tremendous amount of energy both on and off the tennis court. She was a complete revelation; her work rate was phenomenal and her self-belief completely unshakeable. This was especially evident in the final of the French Open, when she defeated world number one Steffi Graf in three exciting sets and in doing so sent shock waves throughout the world of tennis.

Sanchez's success stemmed from a background rich in tennis. Her parents lived in Barcelona and belonged to a local club. They had fallen in love with the sport and encouraged their four children to take it up. As a result, three of the four had become players on the professional circuit.

During the championships, Sanchez performed to a level which did not befit her age, proving that age was no barrier to success. Theoretically, she should have been challenging for the junior title and easing herself into the senior circuit. Instead, she became the youngest winner of the championship as she battled past the red-hot favourites for the trophy. During the tournament, much of the attention had focused upon the other teenaged sensations, Monica Seles and Jennifer Capriati. However, Sanchez crept through on the blind side to oust the seemingly unbeatable Graf in a titanic two hours and 57 minutes, becoming the lowest seed to win one of the major tournaments since 1962.

The match was a closely fought battle which could have gone either way. Sanchez narrowly won the first set 7–6, but lost the second 3–6. During the third set, she revealed an incredible amount of energy for a 17-year-old as she scampered all over the court. The Spanish starlet eventually broke Graf in the 11th game and went on to win the match. With tears streaming down her face she received a standing ovation. In the post-match celebrations and reviews, everyone seemed to be delighted by Sanchez's achievement. This was especially the case amongst her fellow female competitors, who enjoyed her laid-back attitude and sense of humour.

Sanchez-Vicario proves the worth of Spain's female tennis players, beating Steffi Graf to take the French Open title.

Perhaps the key to Sanchez's victory was her total love for the game. 'Money has never really meant very much to me.... The most important part of my career, I believe, is that I am enjoying myself.' Graf, gracious in defeat, emphasized her opponent's love for the game: 'Arantxa played awfully well. She hit some unbelievable shots. She's one of the ones who really enjoys playing and she's a nice person. I feel good for her.' Sanchez's victory was an amazing upset when one considers that the Argentinian Gabriela Sabatini had been the only player previously to have beaten Steffi Graf.

1990
Navratilova wins her record ninth Wimbledon singles title in style

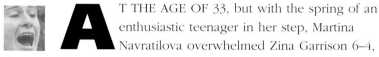

AT THE AGE OF 33, but with the spring of an enthusiastic teenager in her step, Martina Navratilova overwhelmed Zina Garrison 6–4, 6–1 to realize her dream of a record ninth Wimbledon singles title.

The final was hardly a great one. Garrison took the first game to love, but never really came to terms with what was required to defeat Navratilova as the veteran's style and class took control of the match. As Garrison's last despairing lob flew out, Navratilova turned to her invited friends with her arms outstretched in a victory salute. In a frenzy of emotion, she went over to her chair and briefly kneeled down on the hallowed turf. To many, it seemed as if she was going to kiss the ground, or maybe pluck a few blades of grass, to accompany the piece of the All England rockery she carries around the world in her kit bag for good luck. Garrison described Martina's achievement as 'unreal' and talked of not being able to comprehend it.

Navratilova rushed to embrace each of her entourage in turn. Some observed this with irony, saying that it was perhaps the toughest test her suspect left knee had been put through. Early on in the Wimbledon fortnight, the Queen of Wimbledon had complained about some wayward synovial tissue in her knee. This seemed to be the only thing creaking in Martina's game. In all other aspects, it ran as smoothly as it ever had done.

Navratilova has surely faced more difficult opponents than Garrison on finals day. Garrison, who often made the wrong choice of shots, pointed out why it was so difficult to compete with Navratilova in the final: 'She really believes it is her court and no one can take it away from her.' A delighted Navratilova had no trouble expressing her feelings: 'This tops it all. I've worked so long and so hard for it. They say good things are worth waiting for.' The record-breaking American was pleased that she won the tournament by playing the style of tennis for which she had been renowned throughout her career. However, she did not care if she had to 'scratch and crawl out there. It didn't have to be a thing of beauty by any means. They don't put an asterisk saying, "She won the record but she really didn't play well." It's just nice to win in style as well'.

The dynamic Martina Navratilova winning her record ninth Wimbledon singles title.

A beaming Navratilova holding up the women's singles title shield. 1990.

Navratilova's record ninth title is unlikely to be broken in an age when tennis careers are much shorter than her 18-year reign. At least Helen Wills Moody, who had shared the record of eight victories with Navratilova, had some consolation in reflecting that her victories came from only nine visits.

Pete Sampras

1990
Sampras powers his way to his first US Open

THE AMERICAN PETE SAMPRAS was only 28 days past his 19th birthday when he was able to produce and sustain a display of classic elegance and power to become the youngest winner of the US Open in New York and, with a ranking of 12, the lowest seed to win the championships since 1966. Sampras had spent numerous hours of his life watching tapes of his tennis idols, Rod Laver and Ken Rosewall. His ambition was to be recognized as a right-handed Rod Laver.

The stroke play and power game of Sampras made the 1990 event a memorable one. His formula for success included a remarkable ability to remain cool in the heat of battle and to maintain relentless pressure, often beginning with 190 km/h (120 mph) serves followed by either fluent ground strokes or crisp volleying. Sampras blasted his way through the draw, sweeping aside former champions in the process. Ivan Lendl must have wished that he had not given Sampras advice earlier as the Californian steamrollered past him. John McEnroe described Sampras as being 'as cool as a cucumber' after he was brushed aside by his American apprentice. The serve was the key to the Sampras performance. 'I've been serving so well that it puts a little seed of doubt in the mind of my opponents,' he said. 'They know that if they have one bad game the set can be over'.

As the tournament progressed, Sampras showed increasing maturity as his count of service aces moved towards the 100 mark. In the final, he faced the other American tennis sensation and his great rival, André Agassi. Agassi's volatility and swash-buckling tennis had taken some of the shine off Sampras's displays, but the final revealed the better player as Sampras destroyed his opponent 6–4, 6–3, 6–2 with an awesome display. The tall Californian played textbook tennis as Agassi was completely overwhelmed in a mere hour and 42 minutes. He was only able to salvage eight points on the Sampras serve in the first two sets. A bemused Agassi described the defeat as 'an old-fashioned street mugging. I had my backside kicked. Everything he touched turned to gold. The way he played he should come back to Vegas with me and play the casinos'. Like Agassi, Sampras was completely awestruck by his own performance.

'This is ultimate tennis. Whatever I do in the rest of my career I will always be the US Open champion,' he said.

Sampras had prepared extensively for the tournament. He spent a lot of time on the courts as well as running and lifting weights. He also stated that he owed a great deal to both his family and his coach Joe Brandi. 'I worked really hard at the Nick Bolleteri tennis academy,' he declared. 'So there is no question that hard work pays off'.

19-year-old Pete Sampras playing against compatriot André Agassi at the 1990 US Open.

Winter Sports

... it couldn't get any better than that.
Christopher Dean (of Torvill and Dean) on the pair's 'perfect sixes' score in the 1984 Sarajevo Winter Olympics.

1969
The Czech ice-hockey team defeats the USSR – twice

 QUESTION: when has a game of ice hockey between two countries ended up in the leader of the victorious country being deposed? Answer: In March 1969.

If you get bored with people who say politics have nothing to do with sport, just refer them to the small matter of two ice-hockey internationals between Czechoslovakia and the Soviet Union in March 1969. The games had little to do with sport and everything to do with politics.

In the record books, the matches, played on 21 March and 28 March are listed as two victories for the Czech side over the mighty USSR. But what the record books do not tell the reader are the circumstances in which both matches took place.

For that you have to delve into the history books. In January 1968, Alexander Dubcek had become the leader of the Czechoslovakian Communist Party and effectively ruler of the country. He initiated a programme of political reform which was to become known as the 'Prague Spring'. In Moscow, Brezhnev and his cronies were determined to crush these reforms. In August 1968, the USSR invaded Czechoslovakia and imposed its own stricter brand of communism. Dubcek was allowed to remain in power, but there was no doubt who was in control.

Just two months later, the countries faced each other on the ice-hockey rink. In the 38 years since the World Championships had begun, the competition had never thrown up such drama. The two matches were switched to Stockholm rather than played in Prague because of fears over security. The Soviets skated on to the rink as world champions, having won the title every year since 1961. In total, they were to win the championships 24 times before the USSR ceased to exist in 1991. Its domination of the event is demonstrated by the fact that the country with the second highest number of wins – Canada – triumphed only 11 times. Czechoslovakia was to win the title six times.

But the form book was out of the window in March 1969. In a tense and low-scoring first game, the Czechs won sensationally 2–0. A week later in a pulsating match, they scraped home 4–3. The victories sparked off huge celebrations back home

Overleaf: Mark Johnson scores for the US in the 1980 Olympics (see page 188).

Right: the USSR being roundly defeated in sport by the Czechs; though politically it was another matter all together.

which took the form of reprisals on Russian soldiers and Russian-owned properties. Moscow was incensed. Within weeks, Dubcek was replaced. More than 20 years of suppression were to follow.

The Soviets went on to win the world championship in 1969 and for another two years after that. The Czechs lost two games to Sweden, and any chance of overall victory had gone. But they could claim a moral victory for certain.

1976
Downhill all the way
for Franz Klammer

NEXT TO FRANCE'S Jean-Claude Killy, Franz Klammer is the most famous skier the world has ever seen. He is certainly the most exciting. His uninhibited, courageous and risk-taking style endeared him to fans worldwide and made him a legend in his native Austria.

Klammer's flamboyance was never in greater evidence than in his breathtaking victory in the Winter Olympics at Innsbruck in 1976. The Olympic title went alongside four World Cup downhill titles and a gold medal in the combined event in the 1974 world championships. In total, he won 26 World Cup events.

Born in 1953 in the Austrian town of Mooswald, Klammer entered the Winter Olympics with the full weight of the Austrian nation expecting nothing less than gold from their hero. In 1975, he had secured his first-ever World Cup downhill title by showing incredible form. That season, he won eight out of the nine down-hills. In one race at Wengen, Switzerland, he destroyed his fellow racers, winning by a massive margin of 3.54 seconds. He missed out on the overall title, which takes into account the slalom event as well, only by losing in the final race.

The men's downhill event – the Blue-Riband event of the Winter Olympics – was the very first medal contested in 1976. On the technically demanding Patscherkofel course, Klammer was

drawn to go 15th – the last of the recognized skiers and the least-favoured position. In the lead was Switzerland's Bernhard Russi, a second-and-a-half ahead of his nearest rival, Italy's Herbert Plank. For a Swiss to win the gold medal in an Austrian-held Olympics would have been very hard for many Austrians to stomach. But at the top of the course, Klammer caught an edge in a rut, throwing him yards off-line and losing him vital seconds. Incredibly, Klammer, with legs and arms flailing, made up the lost time and was ahead at the vital checkpoints. The memory of the Austrian charging down the mountain in his yellow suit looking for all the world as if he would lose it at every corner will linger for a long time. He crossed the line in 1 minute 45.73 seconds, and a nation went crazy.

Klammer had achieved sporting immortality, and Austria had its Gold Medal. Austria was to win just one more gold medal at the 1976 Olympics, but small matter. They had won the most important event.

Left: Franz Klammer photographed in 1976, the year of his Olympic victory in Innsbruck.

Right: Austrian hero Franz Klammer in breathtaking action, 1 February 1976

1980
US ice-hockey team triumphs over USSR

AT THE 1980 Lake Placid Winter Olympics, the 'Big Red Machine' – the Soviet Union's formidable ice hockey team – rolled into town hot favourites to win the gold medal. The Soviets had won five gold medals and one bronze out of the six previous Olympic ice-hockey competitions. They were the first seeds and the favourites despite the competition being held in the USA. But the USSR fell victim to the unfancied US team on the night of 22 February and lost the gold in one of the greatest upsets ice hockey had ever seen. The match was to become known as 'The Miracle on Main Street' after the name of the street on which the Olympic ice rink was situated.

Both teams went to Lake Placid undefeated after five games. But the Americans were still given little chance of upsetting the USSR. Just a few days before the Olympics, the two teams had met and the USSR had won 10–3. A similar result was expected that night. But somehow, the US team pulled off a remarkable result, winning 4–3.

At first, everything appeared to be going to plan with the USSR leading the USA by 3–2 at the end of the second period. The score was not a fair reflection of the game as American goal-tender Jim Craig had made save after save just to give the Americans the chance of pulling off the great shock. Incredibly, the US team pulled level with over half of the final period remaining. A little over a minute later, Captain Mike Eruzione hit an un-stoppable shot from about 9 m (30 ft) to give the US team the lead. The Soviets were forced on to the attack,

Top: the triumphant US team during a Cold War ice-hockey match.

Bottom: America's Mark Johnson scores a goal past the waiting USSR goalkeeper.

but some desperate defending and more heroics from Craig kept them out. The last few seconds were counted down and the buzzer appeared to be the signal for the whole of America to celebrate. The stunned Soviets suddenly found themselves un-willing guests at one of the largest-ever Olympic-inspired parties.

The drama was heightened by the international situation at the time of the match. In 1980, the Cold War had again worsened, with the Soviet invasion of Afghanistan and stalling arms talks being the signal for yet another freeze in USA–USSR relations. Jimmy Carter, anxious to please the public in a presidential election year, would later show his hawkish side by leading the boycott of the Summer Olympics held in Moscow. He even telephoned the American coach Herb Brooks after the game to congratulate the team. For an extra touch of symbolism, the match took place on George Washington's birthday.

Two days later, the Americans played Finland to secure the gold medal. Despite being 2–1 down as they entered the third period, they recovered to win 4–2. This was only the second time the USA had won the ice-hockey gold.

Celebrations at the 1980 Winter Olympics, Lake Placid.

1984

Torvill and Dean – perfection

PERFECTION OCCURS RARELY IN SPORT. But on 14 February 1984, at the Sarajevo Winter Olympics, it did. That was the night Jayne Torvill and Christopher Dean – Britain's legendary ice-dancing pair – scored perfect marks for their performance, an interpretation of Ravel's *Bolero*. Nine judges all gave the British pair the maximum six mark for artistic impression. It was such a landmark performance and score – the first time nine perfect sixes had been awarded – that many believe no other ice-dance pair will ever again reach such incredible heights.

Success launched the pair – who became famous enough to be known just by their surnames – into a different sphere from any other former ice-skating champions. They turned professional and toured the world with their ice-dance show. But they will always be best remembered for their performance that February night in what was then Yugoslavia.

Torvill, who worked in an insurance office, and Dean, who was a constable in the Nottinghamshire police force, had first competed in the Olympics in the 1980 Lake Placid games where they had finished fifth. In the years between the 1980 and 1984 Olympics, they began to dominate the ice-dancing competition. By the time of the next Olympics, they had won three world

Perhaps the most recognizable opening scene ever: Torvill and Dean's Bolero *at the 1984 Winter Olympics in Sarajevo.*

A superb example of Torvill and Dean's ice-dancing skill, Sarajevo, 1984.

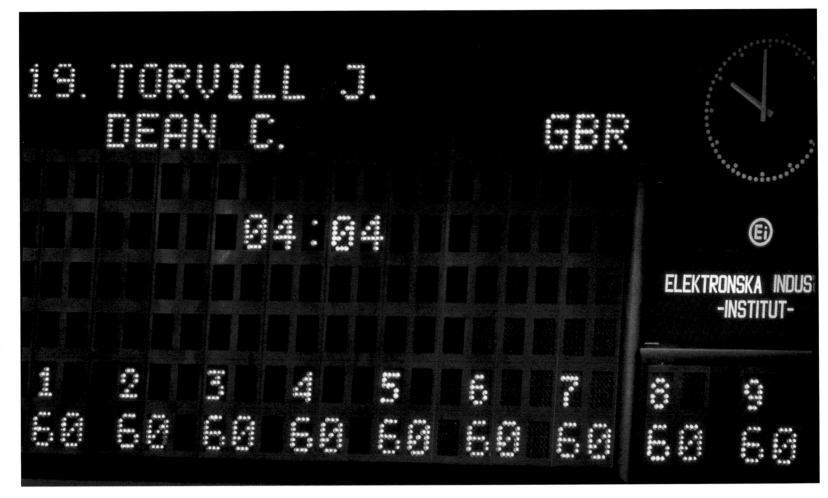

Top: that row of perfect sixes for artistic impression – the maximum score possible.

Bottom: the most famous ice dancing duo of all time, Torvill and Dean prepare to begin their Bolero routine.

championships. At the 1983 World Championships in Helsinki, they confirmed their status as the premier ice-dance couple. Despite being hampered by injuries – Torvill with a bad back and shoulder, Dean with fluid on the knee – the pair skated to victory. As a result they were firm favourites to win in Sarajevo.

By the end of the compulsory dance section and the original set-pattern dance, the gold medal was virtually assured despite 50 per cent of the marks still being up for grabs. All that remained was the free dance. Torvill and Dean were simply in a different class from the others that evening. With Princess Anne in the audience, they held the crowd spellbound for four minutes with a flawless display. The dramatic ending was followed by massive applause; hundreds of flowers showered on to the rink. The dance sequence was to be replayed over and over again on television.

Afterwards, Dean said that the two had not suffered from nerves on the night. He admitted that 'it couldn't get any better than that', but his main worry was that now they had achieved the perfect score, he had no idea what they would do next. Torvill described the night as 'like being in a dream'. After the pair had returned to the Olympic Village, they broke the alcohol ban by celebrating with champagne at a reception organized by Princess Anne.

Britain's gold-medal heroes:
Torvill and Dean after their
perfect routine.

Bibliography

American Football, Baseball & Basketball

Aaseng, Nathan, *Sports Great Michael Jordan*, Hillside, 1992

Angell, Roger, *Five Seasons: A Baseball Companion*, London, 1977

Bjarkman, Peter, C., *Encyclopedia of Major League Baseball*, Westport, 1995

Clary, Jack, *30 Years of Pro Football's Greatest Moments*, Nashville, 1976

Ecker, Tom and Don King (eds), *Athletic Journal's Encyclopedia of Basketball*, West Nyack, 1983

Green, Jerry, *Super Bowl Chronicles, A Sportswriter Reflects on the First 30 Years of America's Game*, Indianapolis, 1995

Jares, Joe, *Basketball: The American Game*, Chicago, 1971

Kahn, Roger, *Joe and Marilyn: A Memory of Love*, New York, 1986

Malone, Jerry, *American Football*, Loughborough, 1988

Reichler, Joseph, *The Great All-Time Baseball Record Book*, London, 1981

Rowe, Peter, *Guinness American Football: The Records*, London, 1987

Taragano, Martin, *Basketball Biographies: 434 US Players, Coaches and Contributors to the Game 1891–1990*, London, 1991

Vancil, Mark, *NBA Basketball Basics*, New York, 1995

Athletics, Gymnastics & Swimming

British Amateur Gymnastics Association, *Know the Game: Gymnastics*, London, 1994

Cross, Christine and Peggy Wellington, *Nutrition for Swimming – Your Personal Guide*, Leeds, 1992

The Dorling Kindersley Chronicle of the Olympics, London, 1998

Harrison, Ted, *Kris Akabusi On Track: the Extraordinary Story of a Great Athlete*, Oxford, 1991

McLoughlin, Maria, *Gymnastics*, Tiptree, 1988

McManners, Hugh, *Water Sports: Outdoor Adventure Handbook*, London, 1997

Pearson, David, *Play the Game: Gymnastics*, London, 1991

Wallenchinsky, David, *The Complete Book of the Olympics*, London, 1996

Welch, David (ed.), *The Daily Telegraph Sport Yearbook and Diary 1998*, London, 1997

Zeitvogel, Karin and Sarah Springman, *Triathlon: the Complete Guide to Multi-sport Success*, Huddersfield, 1994

Boxing

Golesworthy, Maurice, *Encyclopaedia of Boxing*, London, 1988

Cooper, Henry, *Henry Cooper's Most Memorable Fights*, Norwich, 1985

Garber III, Angus G., *Boxing Legends*, Newton Abbot, 1985

Heller, Peter, *Tyson, In and Out of the Ring*, London, 1996

Schulman, Arlene, *The Prizefighters, An Intimate Look at Champions and Contenders*, London 1994

Cricket

Atherton, Mike, *A Test of Cricket: Know the Game*, London, 1996

Barrett, Norman (ed.), *Daily Telegraph Chronicle of Cricket*, Enfield, 1994

Bradman, Sir Donald, *The Art of Cricket*, Lane Cove, 1984

Botham, Ian, *Don't Tell Kath*, London, 1994

Khan, Imran, *All Round View*, London, 1988

Football

Collett, Mike, *Guinness Record of FA Cup*, Enfield, 1993

Glanville, Brian, *Champions of Europe*, Enfield, 1991

Kelly, Stephen E., *Back Page Football*, Harpenden, 1988

Miller, David, *Cup Magic*, London, 1981

Motson, John, *Second to None*, Harmondsworth, 1972

Pelé with Robert Fish, *Pelé: My Life and the Beautiful Game*, New York, 1977

Revie, Alistair, *All Roads Lead to Wembley*, Harmondsworth, 1971

Golf

Alliss, Peter, *The Lazy Golfer's Companion*, London, 1995

Rosaforte, Tim, *Tiger Woods – The Makings of a Champion*, New York, 1997

Sommers, Robert, *US Open – Golf's Ultimate Challenge*, Oxford, 1996

Stanley, Louis T., *A History of Golf*, London, 1991

Updike, John, *Golf Dreams: Writings on Golf*, London, 1996

Horse Racing

Bedford, Julian (comp.), *The Racing Man's Bedside Book*, Cambridge, 1997

Booth, Bill, *A Day at the Races – a Guide to Horse Racing*, Harrogate, 1994

Francis, Dick, *The Sport of Queens*, London, 1986

Green, Reg, *National Heroes, The Aintree Legend*, Edinburgh, 1997

McIlvanney, Hugh, *McIlvanney on Horse Racing*, Edinburgh, 1997

West, Julian and Barry Roxburgh (eds), *The Spirit of Racing*, Northumberland, 1997

Rugby

Bath, Richard (ed.), *The Ultimate Encyclopedia of Rugby*, London, 1997

Jones, Stephen, *Endless Winter*, Edinburgh, 1993

Miles, Keith, *The Handbook of Rugby*, London, 1995

Reyburn, Wallace, *Twickenham, The Story of a Rugby Ground*, London, 1976

Starmer-Smith, Nigel (ed.), *Rugby World 98*, Harpenden, 1997

Sailing

Cook, Peter and Barbara Webb, *The Complete Book of Sailing*, London, 1977

Faith, Nicholas, *Classic Ships, Romance and Reality*, London, 1995

Hornsby, D. T., *Ocean Ships*, Shepperton, 1996

Raban, Jonathan, *Coasting*, London, 1989

Rayner, Ranulf, *The Paintings of the Americas Cup*, Newton Abbot, 1986

Rayner, Ranulf, *The Story of Yachting*, Newton Abbot, 1989

Tennis

Digby, Edward, *Sporting Gentlemen, Men's Tennis From the Age of Honour to the Cult of the Superstar*, New York and London, 1995

Douglas, Paul, *The Handbook of Tennis*, London, 1995

Dunstan, Keith, *Tennis, a Dictionary*, Newton Abbot, 1984

Evans, Richard, *Open Tennis, 25 years of seriously defiant success on and off the court*, London, 1993

Sanchez-Vicario, Arantxa, *The Young Tennis Player*, London, 1996

Snyder, John S., *Tennis: great moments and dubious achievements in tennis history*, San Francisco, 1993

Winter Sports

Brace, Ian, *Play the Game: Ice Hockey*, London, 1990

Gamma, Karl, *The Handbook of Skiing*, London, 1992

Matthews, Peter, *Guinness Encyclopedia of International Sports Records and Results*, Enfield, 1993

Torville, Jayne, and Christopher Dean, *Facing the Music*, London, 1995

GLOSSARY

Ashes
The trophy for which England and Australia play Test matches.

BBC Sports Personality of the Year
A prestigious annual award in which the general public vote for their choice of sporting hero.

Becher's Brook
The biggest fence in the Grand National.

Bodyline
In cricket, fast bowling aimed at the batsman's body; also known as leg theory, bowling short, bowling bouncers, intimidatory bowling. The term bodyline is now almost exclusively used to describe the 1932–33 England tour of Australia, when the England bowlers developed the technique to combat Don Bradman's batting prowess.

boundary
In cricket, the outer limit of the field. A ball crossing the boundary on the ground counts as four runs; a ball crossing the boundary without having touched the ground counts as six runs.

Calcutta Cup
In rugby, the trophy for which England and Scotland play annually in the Five Nations championship.

Commonwealth Games
A championship athletics meeting for track and field events in which the Commonwealth's member countries participate every four years.

crease
In cricket, generally used to mean the line in front of the stumps from where the batsman plays. The bowling crease is the line beyond which the bowler may not go when delivering the ball.

European Cup
Football's, or soccer's, major European club trophy; now superseded by the European Champions' League.

Five Nations
In rugby, an annual competition between England, Wales, Scotland, Ireland and France.

FA (Football Association) Cup
In football, an annual competition for which most clubs enter, even those from the lower leagues.

Football Association
The governing body of English football. The Premier League is part of the FA which also controls England teams at all levels.

Football League
The organization which controls the First, Second and Third Divisions of English football.

Grand National
Annual horse race held over jumps at Aintree in Liverpool, England. Renowned for the size of the fences and the endurance required of horse and jockey to race twice round the course.

Grand Slam
Term used to cover the major annual tournaments within a sport. In rugby, achieved if one country wins all their matches against the other four in the Five Nations championship.

Home Unions
The governing bodies of a sport in England, Scotland, Wales and Ireland.

innings
In cricket, a division of the match. Each member of the team takes a turn to bat until they are all out or until the team declares. In games other than one-day games, each team is required to bat twice.

Irish Sweeps Derby
A top horse race in Ireland.

Jockey Club
Governing body of horse racing in England.

leg before wicket (leg before, lbw)
In cricket, if a batsman's leg prevents the ball from hitting the stumps, the batsman is out.

long-off/long-on
In cricket, fielding positions.

National Football League
The governing body of American Football. In 1970 the NFL was restructured into two conferences, the American Football Conference (AFC) and the National Football Conference (NFC).

National Hunt
Horse racing over fences, rather than on the flat.

not out
In cricket, a batsman who leaves the field without being adjudged out by the umpires.

over
In cricket, six balls bowled successively from one end of the wicket.

pitcher
In baseball, the player who delivers the ball to the hitter.

RFU (Rugby Football Union)
The governing body of rugby in England.

run out
In cricket, when the fielding side knocks the bails off the stumps before the batsman has reached the crease.

scrum
In rugby, a way of restarting play after an infringement. The forwards pack down and push in formation.

spinner/off-spinner
In cricket, a bowler who uses the technique of spin or off-spin to deliver the ball.

Super Bowl
In American Football, trophy played for each year by the winners of the AFC and NFC.

Tattenham Corner
A famous point in the Derby, a horse race run on the flat every year at Epsom, England.

Test match
In cricket, the name given to an international match; usually played in series.

Triple Crown
In rugby, not an actual trophy but an honour accorded to one of the home countries (i.e. England, Ireland, Scotland or Wales) during the Five Nations championship, if they win all their games against the other three.

wicket
In cricket, the stumps and bails; the area between the two wickets.

Wisden
In cricket, a prestigious annual publication summarizing the previous season and detailing results.

World Series
Annual baseball competition in US.

PICTURE CREDITS

Allsport: Al Bello 12–13, Al Bello 14, Al Bello 20 (l), Otto Greule 20 (r), Otto Greule 22 (l), Mike Powell 22 (r), Al Bello 23 (l), Otto Greule 23 (r), 27 (t), Tony Duffy 33, 34 (l), Tony Duffy 35 (l), Tony Duffy 36, Tony Duffy 39, Tony Duffy 40, Tony Duffy 41 (t), David Cannon 41 (b), Mike Hewitt 42 (l), Nathan Bilow 42 (r), Mike Hewitt 43, Gray Mortimore 44, 45, Mark Thompson 46, Shaun Botterill 47, Gary M. Prior 48–49, Adrian Murrell 68–69, 77, Adrian Murrell 78 (all), 79 (all), 80 (all), Ben Radford 81 (all), 109 (all), 110 (r), David Cannon 112–13, Steve Powell 118 (all), David Cannon 120 (all), David Cannon 121, David Cannon 122 (all), Rogers 123, Rogers 124 (t), David Cannon (124), Stephen Munday 125 (l), David Cannon 125 (r), David Cannon 126 (all), Stephen Munday 127, Simon Bruty 128–29, Gary M. Prior 135 (t), 135 (b), Dave Sanderson 137, 138 (l), Steve Powell 138 (r), Howard Boylan (l), Simon Bruty 139 (r), 140, 141, David Cannon 142–43, 145, 146, 147, 148 (all), 149, 150 (all), Simon Bruty 151, Billy Stickland 152 (b), Shaun Botterill 152 (t), Russell Cheyne 153, Gray Mortimore 154 (t), Russell Cheyne 154 (b), Billy Stickland 155 (t), David Cannon 155 (b), David Cannon 156 (t), Billy Stickland 156 (b), David Rogers 157, 170–71, Tony Duffy 173, Tony Duffy 174, Steve Powell 175 (l), 175 (r), Tony Duffy 176, 178 (all), 179, Simon Bruty 180, 181, 182, 183, Steve Powell 191, Tony Duffy 192 (b). **Allsport/Hulton Getty:** 15 (all), 16–17 (all), 24–25, 26 (all), 31 (all), 53, 75 (l), 82–83, 84, 85, 94, 95, 96–97, 98, 100, 101, 103, 104 (l), 105, 132 (all), 133 (all), 134, 136. **Associated Sports Photography:** 38. **Colorsport:** 106, 184–85, 188 (all), 190, 193. **Empics:** Sven Simon 104 (r), 110 (l), 111. **Hobbs Golf Collection:** 114, 116, 117, 119, **Mary Evans Picture Library:** 130, 144. **Popperfoto:** 18, 19, 28 (all), 60–61, 86, 107, 108, 192 (t). **PPL Ltd:** Nick Rains 158–59, 166 (l), Barry Pickthall 166 (r), Nick Rains 167 (l), Bob Fisher (r), Nick Rains 168 (all). **Topham Picturepoint:** 27 (b), 29 (all), 30, 32 (all), 34 (r), 35 (r), 37, 50–51, 52, 54, 55, 56, 57, 58 (all), 59 (all), 62, 63, 64, 65, 66, 67, 70 (all), 71 (all), 72, 73, 74, 75 (r), 76, 87, 88, 89, 90, 91, 92, 93, 99, 102, 115 (all), 131 (all), 160–61, 162, 163, 164, 169, 172 (all), 177 (l), 187 (all).

AUTHOR BIOGRAPHIES

Ian Cole: Introduction

Ian Cole started as a reporter with the *Ilford Recorder* after leaving school. He entered Fleet Street aged 24, working at the London *Evening News* from 1972 to the paper's closure in 1980, at which time he was Sports News Editor. From 1982, he was at the *Daily Express* for 15 years, apart from a year spent with the ill-fated *London Daily News*. He is Chairman of the Sports Writers' Association of Great Britain, a member of Essex County Cricket Club and a proud holder of a season ticket at West Ham.

Chris Ewers: Rugby

Chris Ewers is a professional journalist, who lives and works in both Berkshire and London. He specializes in writing on cricket and rugby.

David Harding: Athletics; Cricket; Golf; Winter Sports

David Harding is a sports-mad journalist who has worked on newspapers, magazines and television. He rarely breaks a hundred on the golf course, finished last in his school's 1500 m race, bowled two overs for 36 last summer and cannot ice-skate. He is therefore uniquely skilled to write on any of these sports.

Nigel Gross: American Football, Baseball & Basketball; Boxing; Cricket; Sailing

Nigel Gross has been an author for some 15 years and is also a keen collector of trivia. He has written over 30 books and contributed to numerous television shows and magazines. He now lives in Kent where he continues to write across a broad spectrum.

Karen Hurrell: Horse Racing

Karen Hurrell is a well-known author of many books, and writes widely for magazines both in the UK and in Ireland. She lives in London with her two sons.

Dylan Lobo: Tennis

Dylan Lobo is an avid sports fan and researcher with a degree from Staffordshire University. His specialist subjects are tennis and football, though he researches or writes about, all aspects of sport.

Jason Tomas: Football

After spending 10 years on the staff of the *Sunday Times*, Jason Tomas switched to writing for the *Observer*. He is the author of nine books on football, including *Soccer Czars* and a profile of Alan Shearer.

Subject Index

Index of Names

great *sporting* **moments**